THE HANDBOOK OF INFLATION HEDGING INVESTMENTS

THE HANDBOOK OF INFLATION HEDGING INVESTMENTS

Enhance Performance and Protect
Your Portfolio from Inflation Risk

ROBERT J. GREER

Editor

McGraw-Hill

New York Chicago San Francisco
Lisbon London Madrid Mexico City
Milan New Delhi San Juan Seoul
Singapore Sydney Toronto

The McGraw·Hill Companies

2 3 4 5 6 7 8 9 0   DOC/DOC   0 9 8 7 6

ISBN 0-07-146038-1

This publication is designed to provide accurate and authoritative information in regard to the subject matter covered. It is sold with the understanding that neither the author nor the publisher is engaged in rendering legal, accounting, futures/securities trading, or other professional service. If legal advice or other expert assistance is required, the services of a competent professional person should be sought.

—From a Declaration of Principles jointly adopted by a Committee of the American Bar Association and a Committee of Publishers

McGraw-Hill books are available at special quantity discounts to use as premiums and sales promotions, or for use in corporate training programs. For more information, please write to the Director of Special Sales, Professional Publishing, McGraw-Hill, Two Penn Plaza, New York, NY 10121-2298. Or contact your local bookstore.

 This book is printed on recycled, acid-free paper containing a minimum of 50% recycled, de-inked fiber.

Library of Congress Cataloging-in-Publication Data

Greer, Robert J.
  The handbook of inflation hedging investments : enhance performance and protect your portfolio from inflation risk / by Robert J. Greer.
    p. cm.
  Includes bibliographical references and index.
  ISBN 0-07-146038-1 (hardcover : alk. paper)
  1. Portfolio management. 2. Investments. 3. Hedging (Finance) 4. Inflation (Finance)
I. Title.
  HG4529.5.G738 2005

  332.67'8—dc22   2005018203

CONTENTS

PREFACE

⑥

This *Handbook of Inflation Hedging Investments* has been written by investment practitioners for serious investors. It is designed to meet the needs of those investors who are concerned about preserving and enhancing the purchasing power of their portfolios, which is a matter of increasing concern. We are finding that even mild inflation, over enough years, can seriously impact the real value of assets.

Another feature of this book, as shown by a quick review of the chapter titles, is that it is not a book about traditional stocks and nominal bonds. Many of the strategies described might be considered "alternative," which conveys an additional feature—diversification. That is a second major benefit of investment strategies which provide inflation protection.

Because there is a wide range of inflation hedging strategies, I have been joined by experts in each of these various specialized markets. These writers are full-time participants in the investment industry, which should give their contributions additional relevance. My thanks to all of them for sharing their ideas. And my wish for you, the reader, is that their ideas will enable you to enjoy better *real* returns for your portfolio.

Robert J. Greer
November 2005

CONTRIBUTORS

Mike Amey
PIMCO

Robert D. Arnott
Research Affiliates, LLC

Mary Ellen Aronow
Hancock Timber Resource Group

Clark S. Binkley
Hancock Timber Resource Group

John Brynjolfsson
PIMCO

James E. Burton
World Gold Council

Richard Co
Chicago Mercantile Exchange

Joseph Eagleeye
Premia Capital Management, LLC

Merrie S. Frankel
Moody's Investors Service

Robert J. Greer
PIMCO

Margaret Harbaugh
Property & Portfolio Research, Inc.

Susan Hudson-Wilson
Property & Portfolio Research, Inc.

Alan James
Barclays Capital

Jill Leyland
World Gold Council

John Lippmann
Eurohypo AG

Dan Nash
Morgan Stanley Commodities

Sam Oh
Morgan Stanley Commodities

Michael Pond
Barclays Capital

Katharine Pulvermacher
World Gold Council

Ivan Skobtsov
PIMCO

Sayee Srinivasan
Chicago Mercantile Exchange

Hilary Till
Premia Capital Management, LLC

Courtland Washburn
Hancock Timber Resource Group

Mihir Worah
PIMCO

Don Yocham
PIMCO

CHAPTER 1

WHY WORRY ABOUT INFLATION?

Robert J. Greer
PIMCO

For generations of investors the phenomenon of inflation has proven to be both important and unpredictable. Whether it is sovereigns debasing their currencies to improve trade, gold rushes that suddenly raise the money supply, inventions such as railroads or the intranet that significantly boost productivity, or guns *and* butter policies of governments, the future path of the price of goods and services is dependent on too many unknowns to predict with any acceptable degree of certainty. Yet the path that inflation takes undoubtedly affects the returns that investors receive. It also affects how well they can ultimately meet their liabilities. With most investors' investment horizons extending over decades rather than a few years, planning for inflation is crucial, however difficult it may at first seem to be. The tools and concepts described in this Handbook will help investors to realize that inflation-hedging assets help to reduce their uncertainty. These assets are also referred to as *real return assets*, because the only real return is an increase in purchasing power over and above inflation.

The majority of the investing careers of most readers of this Handbook have been in a period of declining inflation, as shown by Exhibit 1–1. In fact, as recently as 2003, there was more concern in the US about potential *de*flation—a phenomenon that has troubled an economy as large as Japan's for several years. But there are signs that the long-term disflation that we have experienced may have come to an end. And that is not just because, in Exhibit 1–1, we see recent inflation rates to be above the long-term downward trend.

Readers with longer memories, or who have read their history books, will know that inflation can seriously impact the economy and investment returns. They will know that inflation has sometimes come as a surprise. By looking at Exhibit 1–2, which shows inflation over the last 100 years, we can see that it has not just been in the 1970s that inflation became a problem, and that it has been a problem in Europe as well as in the US.

Sanguine investors say that the experience of the last 100 years, with inflation surprises, will not happen again. We have more sophisticated monetary and fiscal management. We have a global excess of both labor and manufacturing capacity relative to demand. But it does not require a 1970s style inflation to

EXHIBIT 1-1

Government Spending and Inflation

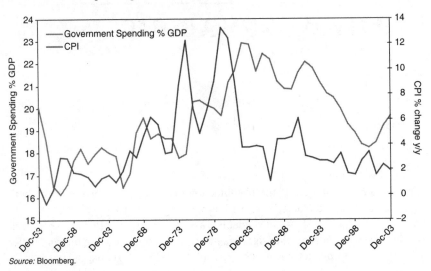

Source: Bloomberg.

EXHIBIT 1-2

Inflation History

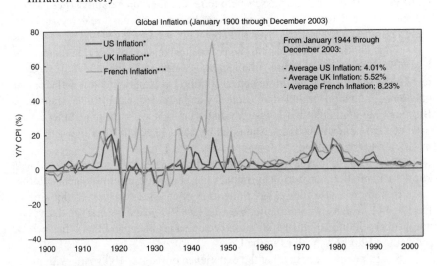

[1]Average Global Inflation from January 1944 through December 2003.
Source: US Bureau of Labor Statistics.
* USA BLS Consumer Price Index
** UK Retail Price Index
*** France Consumer Price Index

create problems for investors. Milder and sustained inflation can affect investor returns and also affect the liabilities with which those investors are trying to deal.

LIABILITIES ARE AFFECTED BY INFLATION

Many different kinds of investors are affected by inflation as they attempt to manage their assets in a way that will meet their eventual obligations. Consider the following:

- *Defined benefit plans* certainly have sensitivity to inflation. Put simply, the higher that inflation runs in the long term, the higher will be the total benefits paid out to beneficiaries. Some defined benefit investment officers argue that inflation does not matter that much, because higher inflation leads to higher interest rates, which gives them a higher discount rate with which to calculate the present value of their liabilities. Recent experience has contradicted that thinking. Moreover, that thinking is valid only in the rare case where a defined benefit plan actually locks in predetermined benefits upon hire that do not adjust with rising inflation. In this unusual case, investment officers of defined benefit plans might actually prefer higher inflation! This is because they will ultimately be paying fixed dollars at some future date while in the interim they are investing at interest rates that rise as inflation rises. However, most plans have benefits that rise with inflation and hold a mix of assets that, for the most part, neither provide protection against inflation nor rise or fall in value in a way that is related to the present value of liabilities. Finally, if the pension plan also has COLA provisions, their liabilities are even more closely tied to inflation.

- *Endowments* also have liabilities tied to inflation. Universities look to their endowments to help pay for a variety of operations, plant maintenance, salaries, etc. All of these costs go up with inflation. Endowments also can benefit especially from the diversification aspects of real return assets. Because they do not control the flow of new contributions to the fund, they must be cautious about maintaining a steady value for the fund, because they typically pay out a set percentage of assets. Any diversifying asset will help a portfolio achieve lower volatility for the same level of return.

- *Foundations* are similar to endowments, though they do have more flexibility in their funding commitments. Foundations typically have little new money coming in, so their need for steady portfolio values is similar to endowments. Also, foundations would like to maintain the same level of grant-giving every year in real terms, in order to provide a constant level of societal benefit. But, as one CIO of a foundation put it, "Most of our grants are fairly short term in nature. Though we would not like to, we could reduce the number of grants we give in a year where investment returns are poor."

- *Insurance companies* have varying levels of need for inflation assets. Life companies typically have little need, because their liabilities, as determined by their actuaries, are usually in nominal terms. Property and casualty companies, on the other hand, have a little more exposure to inflation, because some of their liabilities are impacted by price increases. Unlike the institution mentioned above, though, P&C liabilities are generally fairly short term, as those companies can adjust somewhat to higher expected costs by adjusting their premium charges when policies are renewed.

- *Individual investors* have the greatest need for inflation hedges, because they save for retirement, whether in an IRA or as part of their employer's defined contribution plan. Those investors are not looking for absolute funds when they retire; they are looking for purchasing power. They cannot consume dollars. They will, however, need to consume groceries, health care, gasoline, and a host of other living expenses. And those expenses surely will go up as inflation goes up. The individual is not like a corporate pension plan that can look to its sponsor for additional funding if needed. The individual is not like a college that does have other resources (including a drive for alumni contributions) if the endowment falters. The individual is not like a foundation that can cut back on its funding of grants. That individual investor—and those who are responsible for the investments of that individual—have the greatest exposure to inflation and hence the greatest need for real return assets.

INFLATION OUTLOOK

As we look at the causes of longer term inflation, and also the causes of the disinflation of the last 20 years, it is not simply a matter of saying that inflation is caused by "too many dollars chasing too few goods." First, it is not just goods, but also services that are part of our general inflation. Second, it is not just dollars, but yen, pounds, euros, and other currencies that create global demand for these goods and services. Consideration must also be given to the cost of producing those goods and services, which means that productivity—of labor and capital—plays a part in determining changing price levels.

One important indicator of the potential for inflation is the role that the government plays in the overall economy. Much of what the government spends our money on does not directly contribute to the productivity of the economy or to the supply of goods and services that we buy. Also, after a long-term trend downward in the government's role in the economy, the trend is reversing. Exhibit 1–3 shows that government expenditure as a percent of GNP in the US is now increasing after a long decline. It is not a coincidence that the previous decline in the role of the government in the economy coincided with declining US inflation. With the expected increase in expenditures for Social Security and Medicare, few observers expect that government expenditures will grow at a rate slower than the overall economy for some time to come. Moreover, the government now has the sanction of the voters to get more involved in the economy. After a period of declining involvement, regulations have increased. Since September 11, 2001, the government has the sanction to be more involved with security. Also, since the "deflation scare" of 2003, the government has more economic excuses to spend in order to keep us away from that deflationary abyss—and as a result makes it more likely that we will be driven into a period of rising inflation.

E X H I B I T   1-3

Year on Year Core CPI

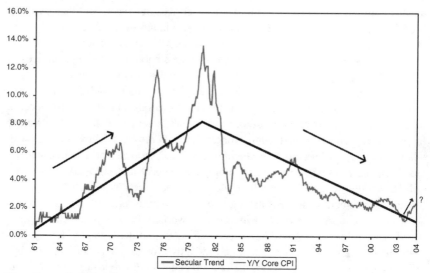

Source: Bureau of Labor Statistics.

In the US, there is another driver of an increase in secular inflation. Not only is the government spending more than it takes in as revenue, leading to continual fiscal deficits, but the entire US economy is spending more than it generates, leading to continual trade deficits. So far those deficits have been accommodated by other countries (most notably China and Japan) who want to keep their own workforce employed, and therefore support the dollar so that US citizens can continue to buy goods made abroad. But at some point this may not continue. And the resulting weaker dollar can lead to higher inflation.

Some commentators legitimately ask why we do not already have higher inflation, because we are running both fiscal and trade deficits, and the Federal Reserve is still fairly accommodative, keeping fed funds below the inflation rate as measured by the CPI. The answer is that there is still an excess of labor and manufacturing capacity on a global basis. However, that generalized condition may not hold forever. Meanwhile, shortages of goods and services in particular parts of the economy could appear, including parts of the economy that are affected by commodity prices, because there is not particularly an excess of commodity production capacity on a global basis.

DEMOGRAPHICS

There is at least one more reason to expect that inflation might be more endemic in the next 20 years than it was in the last twenty. We can expect the value of goods and services to go up relative to the value of a dollar because we are going to have more people trying to make that trade of paying financial assets in return for receiving real assets. It is a simple matter of demographics. The US baby boom is moving toward retirement, and they will be cashing in their stocks and bonds to buy the groceries, gas, and medical services they need. But there will not be enough productive workers (age 20–65) to provide those goods and services. In 2005, in the US, there are about 4.9 active workers for every person over 65. This means that a worker in the economy must produce enough goods and services to satisfy his own requirements, and enough goods and services also to sell to others. He shares that requirement of producing beyond his own needs with 3.9 other workers in order to insure that the economy has enough goods and services to meet the needs of one person over 65. But more people will be retiring than will be entering the workforce. By 2035, that single worker will only have 1.7 fellow workers with whom to share the burden of producing goods and services for a retired person. Goods and services will be in shorter supply compared with the dollars that retirees will be wanting to spend to purchase the things they need. Note that this is not a "financial" problem of retirees having enough money to retire. It is a "goods and services" problem of there not being enough workers to provide all the requirements needed by the population. To accommodate this demographic reality, it is likely that workers will have to remain productive for longer periods before they retire, that they will have to reduce their expectations for lifestyle during retirement, and that the value of the goods and services they need will escalate relative to the value of the financial assets (i.e., dollars) that they want to trade for those goods. In other words, there is a demographic driver to potential future inflation.

INVESTOR RESPONSE

If indeed inflation is likely to increase, investors need to be wary. Traditional stocks and bonds have not performed particularly well in periods of rising inflation. For bonds the reason is obvious. Rising inflation leads to rising interest rates, which causes bond prices to decline. Only when a bond matures and can be reinvested at those higher rates will the investor benefit. For equities, also, history shows that rising inflation has not boded well for stock prices. Some investors seek that "safest of all" investment, T-Bills. Economic theory tells us that T-Bills should provide a real return in excess of the rate of inflation, with no credit risk and no interest rate risk. But even T-Bills, during some periods of rapidly rising inflation in the 1970s did not provide a positive real yield. And at other times of more stable inflation, the real yield on T-Bills was insufficient to satisfy most investors' needs.

These periods of rising inflation are just the time when investors need higher returns to meet their liabilities, as already outlined. This shows the need for new investment products or new approaches to traditional investment products. That is what this Handbook is about. We cannot be certain that we will have higher inflation. But we can be certain that if inflation rises, our liabilities (and thus our need for returns) will rise with it. So inflation hedges should be part of the portfolios for most classes of investors.

These inflation hedges often have another attractive feature as well. Because they respond to changing inflation in a way that is different from plain vanilla stocks and bonds, they provide diversification to a portfolio. As we have all learned, adding diversification will enable us to achieve higher expected returns for the same level of risk, regardless of the level of inflation.

This Handbook is organized to serve serious investors who are seeking real returns. "Real," as in inflation-adjusted. "Real" rather than illusory. "Real" in that it maintains purchasing power for the goods and services we need. We cover various strategies and assets in a way that provides meaningful knowledge of what works, how it works, and how it can be implemented. We then conclude with a discussion of how to incorporate real return assets into an overall portfolio.

CHAPTER 2

INFLATION-LINKED BONDS

Alan James and Michael Pond
Barclays Capital

INTRODUCTION

If investors are seeking an inflation hedge, they can directly achieve that specific objective by owning inflation-linked bonds. If held to maturity, these bonds, when issued by a sovereign state, provide a government-guaranteed return in excess of a stated measure of inflation.

In the following, we begin with a brief history of inflation-linked bonds and their general structure. We then discuss the benefits these securities can provide for both issuers and investors. Next we provide detail on the individual sovereign markets and major investor classes as well as an overview of the growing corporate inflation-linked bond market. Finally, we present an introduction to the expanding inflation derivatives market.

HISTORY OF INFLATION-LINKED BONDS

The history of inflation-linked bonds stretches back over 200 years. The first widely issued notes linked to the price index of a basket of goods were by the Commonwealth of Massachusetts in 1780. These "depreciation notes" were interest-bearing bonds with terms of up to 8 years issued to soldiers during a period of rapid price rises resulting from the Revolutionary Wars. The price index, for a basket of beef, corn, wool, and leather, had risen by 32 times in the 3 years prior to the initial creation of the debt. These notes did not have a lasting impact, however, being converted into nominal notes once peace returned and the galloping inflation subsided.

The issuance of bonds linked to price levels was barely seen again until after the Second World War, even though it was a topic raised by a number of notable economists of the late 19th and early 20th centuries. John Maynard Keynes lobbied the British Government to issue inflation-linked gilts in 1924, though his arguments fell on deaf ears, coming soon after one of the most extreme periods of deflation that the UK has ever seen. The most vociferous academic voice behind both the theory and practical aspects of inflation-linked bonds though was proto-monetarist Irving Fisher of Yale University. From 1911 onwards, he wrote in depth about indexation in general and linking bonds to price indices in particular. However, he was not solely a theoretician. He convinced the Rand-Kardex Company, which he had cofounded, to issue 30-year bonds indexed to wholesale prices in 1925. In practice this innovation was not a great success.

The structure was not copied and the bonds were subsequently converted into gold-linked notes.

Fisher developed a theoretical framework breaking down nominal yields of bonds with the same credit risk into three components—inflationary expectations, a real yield that investors demand over and above those inflationary expectations, and a "risk premium." The risk premium reflects the assumption that investors want additional compensation for accepting undesirable inflation risk when holding nominal bonds. This equation then links a nominal yield with that of a real yield from an inflation-indexed bond. These components are multiplicative, i.e.:

$$(1 + n) = (1 + r)\,(1 + f)\,(1 + p)$$

where n = yield on nominal bond; r = real yield on index-linked bond; f = inflationary expectations; and p = risk premium.

As long as inflation and interest rates are relatively low then this can be approximated with an additive form:

$$n = r + f + p$$

In practice it is extremely difficult to break down the differential between nominal and real rates into inflationary expectations and risk premia. Even if this could be done, the risk premium would also have to be separated from a liquidity premium, which is currently negative, given the size of inflation-linked markets relative to nominals. The market has taken to combining these two components as "break-even inflation," often referred to just as "break-even" or "bei." This should represent the rate of inflation at which returns are equalized on the nominal and inflation-indexed bonds. Most commonly this is a simple spread to a "comparator" nominal bond issue of similar maturity, but break-evens vs. interpolated curves are also used, particularly for relative value measurements. Historically "Fisher break-evens" have been quoted using more correct multiplicative calculations, e.g., for an annual bond:

$$(1 + \text{bei}) = \frac{(1 + n)}{(1 + r)}$$

Simple break-even spreads are followed much more than Fisher break-evens nowadays, but the difference between the two is very limited in a low inflation and low interest rate world. For instance for an annual bond with a real yield at 2% and a nominal yield at 4% the distortion is only 4 bp.

General Structure

While there are many structures of bonds with cash flows linked to inflation, bonds whose underlying value increases with the level of a price index are both the most common and the most important. Most government bonds linked to inflation have this capital-indexed structure. The value of the bond principal increases at the same rate as the underlying price index, albeit subject to a slight time-lag as price levels are not known instantaneously. Coupons are paid as a fixed percentage of this principal, thus increasing in size as the level of the price index rises. As long as the linking price index is representative of the consumption basket, the purchasing power of each payment from this kind of bond is not impacted by inflation. These bonds thus provide known cashflows in real terms, and known real returns if held to maturity. Bonds that are linked to inflation rates rather than price levels or have leverage in their link to a price index do not possess this certainty of real value that makes inflation indexed bonds the ideal real asset.

Issuance

Why Are Inflation-Linked Bonds Issued?

By far the largest issuers of inflation linked bonds in general, and especially inflation indexed bonds where the security's principal amount grows over time according to a specified index, are governments. There are both supply and demand reasons why this is the case. These factors have varied over time and among countries but they are likely to continue to mean a greater proportion of the inflation-linked supply will come from governments than from other institutions. The early issuers of inflation-linked bonds following the Second World War were often doing it out of necessity to raise money in environments of a very high level of inflation and high uncertainty, but it is not coincidental that the market for global linkers in developed markets has undergone its fastest development in a phase of almost unprecedented low and stable inflation.

When the UK started the first substantial issuance programme of inflation-linked debt among developed countries in 1981, the official reasons the Treasury gave were threefold. First was to highlight the commitment of the government to an anti-inflationary policy following high inflation in the previous decade, peaking at over 27% in 1975 and again exceeding 20% in 1980. Second was to achieve cheaper funding by saving the inflation-risk premium, which was again high due to the volatility of previous years. Third was to increase the flexibility of monetary control by introducing a new source of funding, reducing the reliance on money market instruments for funding when the stated aim of the Treasury was to control the money supply.

While the initial reasons for UK issuance may now appear somewhat anachronistic, to some extent they still apply to countries considering issuing inflation-linked bonds for the first time, particularly developing countries who have had a similar high inflationary backdrop in recent years. For most post-industrial nations the anti-inflationary credibility argument has been greatly reduced, though not removed, by the transfer of responsibility for monetary policy to independent central banks. Saving the inflation-risk premium is less of a certainty in practice than in theory, especially in a low-inflation economy, as witnessed by the US, where for several years break-evens were notably below both actual and expected inflation. It depends on a combination of the degree of inflation uncertainty within the economy and market-specific supply and demand factors, but in the long-term there remains a legitimate expectation, particularly in countries with aging populations where the demand for protection of future purchasing power is high. Achieving flexibility from the addition of a new source of funding remains a significant argument, but without the monetarist overtone that accompanied the original UK decision. Now it is more about achieving cost-efficient funding through maximization of the investor base.

An additional long standing argument that has become more important with independent monetary policy-making is that a well-defined real yield curve offers a social benefit of clearly observable market break-even levels for policy makers. Alan Greenspan argued as much in his testimony to the House of Representatives in 1992, 4.5 years before the first US Treasury issuance. All the major global central banks now make reference to break-even levels in assessing inflation expectations, though with varying degrees of caution attached. The FOMC pays particular attention to forward break-evens, especially the 5-year-forward break-even,[1] which they argue strips out short-term seasonal and transitory factors. In theory, break-evens should be particularly important for central banks with inflation targets as they offer an indication of the credibility of this policy, albeit in practice changing market dynamics may distort meanings significantly.

More recently, increasing emphasis has been placed on the beneficial risk characteristics to governments of issuing inflation-indexed bonds. With tax revenues essentially growing in real terms it makes sense for a significant proportion of a government's revenue to be linked to inflation. The counter-argument is that this only holds if there is a tendency for tax revenue to rise faster than expenditure as prices rise. This is likely to be the case if a country is running a significant primary surplus but may not be so for a country with large budget deficits or an increasing debt burden, due perhaps to an aging population to whom the government has a significant real liability from state pensions.

A potential long-term benefit to a government issuing a large percentage of its debt in inflation-linked bonds is cyclical. Provided inflation and growth are related across the economic cycle, inflation-linked debt should tend to be a fiscal stabiliser compared with nominal debt. The fiscal impact of a deflationary downturn on a country with a significant stock of inflation-linked bonds ought to be less severe than a country with only nominal rate debt. Other than a stagflation scenario, the main risk to this hypothesis is late in the economic cycle, when after a strong growth period inflationary pressures may continue to grow even as output is already falling away. Equally, issuing at the start of an economic upswing may well be optimum timing as it is likely that during such a phase inflation risk premia are likely to be high until policy acts to contain inflationary pressure. This normally coincides with a period of high funding needs but low rates when extending the average life of the debt portfolio is advantageous. 2003 and 2004 fit this scenario ideally for the global economy so the upswing in government supply then should have come as no surprise.

One persistent criticism of governments issuing inflation-linked bonds is that any form of inflation indexation is insidious and pernicious, potentially causing any external inflation shock to have a magnified effect on domestic prices.

---

1. The 5-year-forward break-even is the 5 year break-even inflation rate 5 years from now, which is implied by the spot 5- and 10-year break-even rates.

In Finland, the first government issuer of inflation-linked debt in 1945, where it became the main source of funding, indexation was outlawed in 1968 because of fears that a currency depreciation the previous year could trigger an inflationary spiral. Chile and Israel are examples of countries where extensive indexation has historically made tackling very high inflation more difficult but both continue to rely heavily on inflation-linked debt. It has now been broadly accepted that it is only economy-wide indexation that is liable to cause contagion, not linkage of bonds alone. The country where the resistance to indexation had been most extreme was Germany, as a result of previous experience with hyperinflation, especially from 1922 to 1923. Indexation was outlawed in the post-war constitution until 2003, albeit technically this ceased to be valid with the formation of the Euro area. Now even Germany has accepted the theoretical argument in favour of inflation-linked issuance.

The remaining arguments for governments to issue inflation-linked bonds apply just as much to corporates. There are diversification benefits to including inflation-linked bonds as a source of funding alongside nominal debt. The strongest stems from portfolio risk reduction, as the cost of inflation-linked debt is not tightly correlated to either short- or long-term nominal rates. A balance of fixed, floating, and inflation-linked debt thus reduces the volatility for an issuer just as much as it does for investors. An additional benefit is the back-dated cash-flows for a capital-indexed bond compared to a similar maturity nominal bond. Assuming positive inflation expectations the real yield and real coupon of a linker will be lower than for an equivalent nominal bond and hence initial coupons will be smaller; albeit this is offset by the expected larger size of the uplifted principal for the capital-indexed bond. This may be more important for corporate borrowers than a government given the higher discount factors and lending costs that they face.

While there are portfolio-based arguments why most large corporates should consider issuing inflation-linked bonds alongside other forms of debt, it does depend on the nature of a firm's revenues and expenditures. Many firms are reluctant to consider issuing inflation-linked paper because they see themselves exposed to costs that rise with the level of consumer prices, in particular labour costs. This fear leads to demand to buy inflation-linked rather than issue bonds, but is only strongly valid if wage growth for the company is itself indexed due to convention or wage-bargaining pressures. Ultimately the corporates with the strongest incentive to issue inflation-linked bonds have inflation-linked revenues. Sometimes these may be explicit, for instance, an infrastructure firm whose revenues are contractually linked to inflation, as is often seen in UK private finance initiatives for building of hospitals. Other important inflation linkages that produce inflation-linked supply are regulatory in nature, e.g., price caps for utilities that increase with inflation, or for agencies with tax-linked revenues. Other firms may have a balance of their exposure to inflation encouraging some issuance without explicit exposures, for instance supermarket chains who may have limited pricing power relative to the consumer price index but sell most of the basket of goods that make up the index.

Why Invest in Inflation-Linked Bonds?

Capital-indexed bonds, where the principal is indexed to a specific inflation index, are the ideal format for an investor looking for a financial asset that retains its purchasing power. Other structures, such as those where only the coupon payments are linked to inflation, may not provide this same protection. Government inflation-linked bonds define the almost risk-free real yield by which all other real return assets should be judged. Who, though, should buy them? There is a clear demand from institutions with explicit inflation-linked liabilities. More subtly there is a case for those entrusted with savings for individuals to consider, since the reason for this saving is ultimately deferred consumption. For an individual, for whom a consumer price basket is likely to be the most representative approximation of their own cost of living, inflation-indexed bonds provide the closest match to liabilities that will need to be met in the future. However, as will be discussed below, there are strong reasons why inflation-linked bonds should be included in almost any broadly-based portfolio.

THE ROLE OF REAL-RATE INSTRUMENTS IN PORTFOLIOS

Inflation-indexed bonds have a position in almost any total-return portfolio, not just those focussed on real returns. Both theoretically and in practice they have a lower volatility than similar maturity nominal bonds while average returns are not dissimilar in the medium to long run. Considering the simplified Fisher equation, the volatility of real yield is lower than that of the nominal yield provided the covariance between the real yield and break-even is not significantly negative

if $n = r + \text{bei}$,

then $\text{var}(n) = \text{var}(r) + \text{var}(\text{bei}) + 2 \{\text{covariance}(r, \text{bei})\}$

While real yields are usually less volatile than similar maturity nominal yields, except in extreme cases such as large asset reallocation phases, where there is temporary dislocation, the back-dated nature of linker cash flows means that the sensitivity of inflation-linked bonds to changes in real yields is greater than the sensitivity of nominal bonds for the same change in nominal yields, tending to offset the benefit. This can be a particularly important factor at the long end of the curve. For example, a 30-year real bond can have a real duration of 24 years, which may be 50% more than an equivalent 30-year nominal bond, which might have a nominal duration of 16. The method that is most commonly used to try combining real and nominal bond durations within a single portfolio is to use a beta approach, i.e., estimating the sensitivity of changes in real bonds to changes in nominal bonds and then multiplying the real duration by the beta to create an equivalent nominal duration. However, an approach based on historic betas is far from perfect, and it is not always obvious what type of beta to use. In fact, choosing a beta is an art as much as a science. Using historicals as a guide, one should also consider various scenarios that might push rates higher or lower and how real rates are likely to react relative to nominals in each, then one might develop an appropriate beta from that analysis (Exhibits 2–1 to 2–3).

EXHIBIT 2-1

Major Market Attributes

	Number of Bonds	Market Value ($bln as of 3/31/05)	Linking Index	Lag (Months)	Coupon Frequency	Deflation Floor
Australia	3	$ 6.7	Australian CPI	6	Quarterly	Yes
Canada	4	$ 25.4	Canadian NSA CPI	3	Semi-Annually	No
France	8	$ 112.4	French national CPI ex-tobacco, Euro HICP ex-tobacco	3	Annual	Yes
Greece	1	$ 5.4	Euro HICP ex tobacco	3	Annual	Yes
Italy	4	$ 50.4	Euro HICP ex tobacco	3	Semi-Annually	Yes
Japan	3	$ 8.7	Japan CPI ex-fresh food	3	Semi-Annually	No
Sweden	5	$ 32.1	Swedish NSA CPI	3	Annual	Some
UK	9	$ 184.1	RPI	8	Semi-Annually	No
US	16	$ 299.3	US NSA CPI	3	Semi-Annually	Yes
South Africa	4	$ 8.4	SA NSA CPI	4	Semi-Annually	Yes

Source: Barclays Capital.

EXHIBIT 2-2

Growth of the Inflation-Linked Bond Market

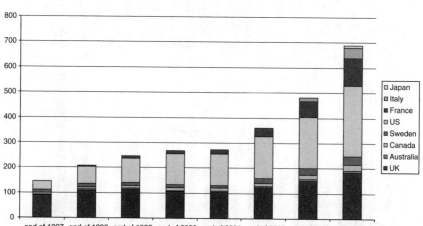

Source: Barclays Capital.

15

Yield betas are most commonly estimated between real and nominal bonds because they are the most easily observable. Nevertheless, there are two types of yield betas, those based on yield levels, and those based on yield changes. Yield betas tend to stay relatively stable for several months but can then change sharply. This is largely because market participants get comfortable with market interaction

E X H I B I T   2–3

BTP€i08 and Nominal Comparator Illustrative Cashflows

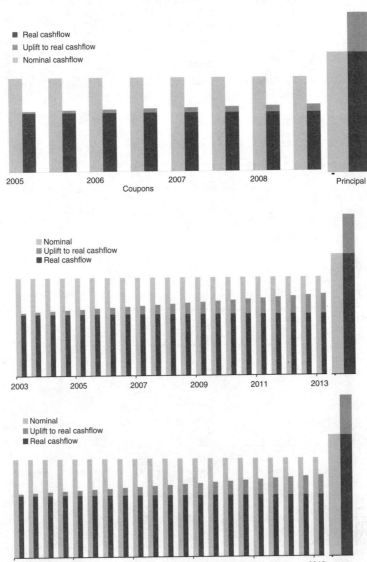

E X H I B I T   2–3

Continued

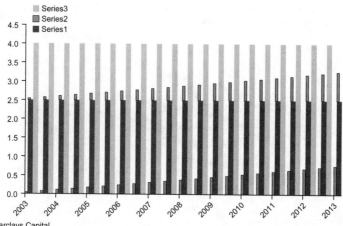

Source: Barclays Capital.

between the nominal and yield markets and it becomes self-reinforcing until a shock changes this dynamic. This shock could be fundamental, as in the case of a change in monetary policy perception, e.g., if a central bank takes a much more hawkish line towards fighting inflation, tending to push the beta higher particularly for the longer end of the curve as increased central bank credibility may keep forward inflation expectations in a rather tight range. Although it might just as easily be triggered by market flow or technical events such as supply or seasonal carry.

As Exhibit 2–4 shows, in practice inflation bonds have tended to trend within relatively tight yield beta regimes vs. nominal bonds. These regimes have extended from several months to as long as 2 years and have tended to occur quickly, with a transition period of no more than a month. This period has then been followed by a new regime in which the beta is quite different from that of the previous regime. Since September 2003, both the European and US markets appear to have moved into a different phase, with no equilibrium beta regime establishing itself. This may be a sign of uncertainty in the market during a phase of portfolio reallocation. However, we see a significant chance that there. has been a more fundamental shift as liquidity in the market has improved. Instead of inflation-linked bonds being traded as a spread product to nominal bonds they now appear to behave more like an independent asset class. While fundamental longer-term beta relationships are likely to hold, it may just be that medium-term trading regimes are a thing of the past.

Another form of beta between nominal and real bonds is total-returns beta, which again can be assessed on a level or change basis. This format is particularly applicable if inflation volatility is high or the analysis is over a long period because inflation carry becomes an important element that yield comparisons do not capture. The disadvantage is that it is less readily observable and hence less

E X H I B I T   2–4

Yield-Level Beta Regimes since 2002 (TII Jul '12s)

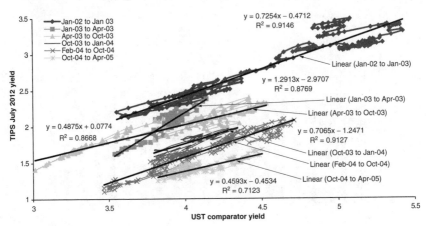

Source: Barclays Capital.

widely used by market makers, losing the self-reinforcing element that tends to keep yield betas more stable (Exhibit 2–5).

Real and nominal bond durations cannot accurately be combined using a beta approach; if they could then they would not be truly distinct asset classes. In practice, it is useful to consider a likely beta as a starting point for risk

E X H I B I T   2–5

TIPS Return Volatility Relative to Nominal Comparator

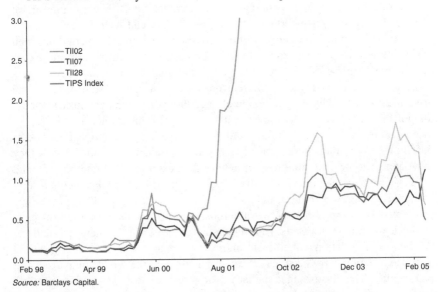

Source: Barclays Capital.

assessment and for use in broad portfolio allocation. An appropriate beta to use depends on the nature of the holdings. For a market maker facing constant mark-to-market it makes sense to look at rolling yield change betas with relatively short time frames, e.g., 1-month and 3-month. For a tactical real money investor, where little or no leverage is used in contrast to hedge fund investors, looking to follow market trends and less constrained by daily volatility, a rolling 3-month yield level beta may be appropriate. For a long-term investor it may be more appropriate to consider a very long-term returns beta relationship and only consider whether to reestimate this on an infrequent basis, e.g., annually.

The annual total return for the TIPS market index between 1997 and 2004 was 0.5% higher than that of a Treasury index of maturity-matched securities, while the monthly returns volatility was only 55% as high. However this volatility benefit varied both over time and across the curve. Up until 2001 real returns volatility was extremely low, less than 30% of equivalent of the volatility of a maturity-matched nominal index, but between 2002 and 2004 it was 75%. The volatility of the TII 2028 returns between 2002 and 2004 was equal to that of the nearest nominal due to the duration differential offsetting the lower yield volatility. As they shorten down the curve, nominal returns volatility of TIPS fall much less quickly compared to those of nominal bonds, so very short TIPS only have significant volatility benefits over nominals for real return funds, which are typically benchmarked to a basket of inflation-linked bonds or other real assets. For total return funds and nominal bond funds the greatest diversification benefits of holding TIPS thus usually come in the belly of the curve.

The problem with inflation-linked bonds for a bond fund that is benchmarked to a nominal bond index is that adding linkers increases tracking-error risk vs. the benchmark, even if absolute returns volatility is reduced. It is thus difficult for a fund with a broadly index-tracking remit to hold inflation-linked bonds except on a tactical basis. However an unrestricted active fund is likely to gain on average from a long-term holding of linkers in the belly of the curve as well as tactical positioning. The risk reduction from the lower volatility of linkers should enable more risk to be taken elsewhere and hence potential yield to be earned. Bond funds restricted from earning the full benefits of portfolio diversification open to funds with broader total return goals arguably have relatively more benefit from diversifying into an asset class they are allowed to buy.

For total return funds, arguably there ought to be little role for nominal bonds unless there is a large premium attached to inflation-linked bonds for their lower volatility. In historical total-returns portfolio analysis for both the US and France, inflation-linked bonds dominate nominal issues except at the short end, and absolutely when maximizing real total returns. However, for a large part of the early period of both markets, there was a negative premium for linkers vs. nominals because of limited investors and perceived illiquidity. Now that there appears to be a risk premium in both markets there is clear room for a combination of nominal and real bonds for a total return fund unless it is focussed purely on real returns. By contrast, looking at the longer history of the UK market from the 1980s, high inflation uncertainty meant a very significant risk premium and limited room for linkers within portfolios that did not have inflation liabilities. Now that the risk premium is significantly lower there is more value for other investors to be involved, especially at shorter maturities, where pension and insurance demand is lighter.

THE INFLATION-LINKED BOND MARKETS
US

TIPS History

While officially called Treasury Inflation-Indexed Securities (TIIS), they are more commonly known as Treasury Inflation Protected Securities (TIPS) and we will use the latter as it is market convention. The US Treasury first issued inflation-protected securities in 1997 in order to broaden its investor base, diversify their debt service costs and create liabilities that were more closely aligned with the government's main asset—tax revenues. Initial issuance was in 5-, 10-, and 30-year securities. TIPS are structured such that they pay a fixed coupon on a principal amount which is adjusted for inflation. The inflation index used is the not-seasonally adjusted headline CPI. There is a par floor on the principal at maturity so the investor is protected from deflation from issue date to maturity, but not between.

There was limited initial support as investors used them primarily as a tactical trading vehicle. The small number of participants resulted in both low trading volume and a low beta to nominal yields. Break-evens were generally the main catalyst for investment decisions. In 2000, the iSTIPS market was launched when the Treasury began allowing dealers to strip TIPS and trade the coupon and principal components separately, where the principal component carries the floor, although to date there has been only scarce interest in iSTRIPS. Most trades have been in lieu of structured products or derivatives. While iSTRIPS have not yet been a huge success, it was important as a sign of the Treasury's commitment to the TIPS program when many market observers were questioning its durability. Despite this commitment, the Treasury reduced TIPS issuance commensurate with reductions in the nominal calendar until only an annual 10-year note, with just one reopening auction, existed in 2001.

With 5 years of history and the 5-year TIP issued in 1997 having matured in 2002, the TIPS market finally started to gain broader acceptance. Consultants begin recommending TIPS in earnest and due diligence and approval processes were begun. There was also increased interest in mutual funds and other funds tied to the TIPS index as investors begin to make diversification allocations into TIPS as a new "asset class."

Increasing demand led to significant growth in 2004 as the Treasury issued nearly as many TIPS that year as it did in the previous three. They also announced a major expansion of the program to include two 5-year auctions and two 20-year auctions per year, in addition to the existing quarterly 10-year note auction cycle. Alongside growth in the cash market was a developing inflation derivatives market. CPI futures began trading at the CME in early 2004 and volume in the CPI swaps market increased significantly along with issuance in inflation-linked corporate notes.

TIPS Issuance Summary

Exhibit 2–6 shows annual TIPS issuance since 1997. While issuance in the first 3 years of the program was just above $30 billion, it declined to only $16 billion in 2000 and 2001. The reduction, however, was not a reflection on the TIPS program but rather the impact of budget surpluses where all Treasury issuance was being reduced. With the return to deficits in 2002, issuance began to grow and the $63 billion issued in 2004 was as great as all TIPS issuance in the prior three years. We expect increased growth to continue in 2005 and are expecting $70 to $80 billion in issuance, bringing the size of the Barclays Capital US Inflation-Linked Bond Index to over $350 billion by the end of 2005 (Exhibits 2–7 and 2–8).

Increased issuance has driven an improvement in liquidity as well. Trading volumes have tended to spike around auction weeks as they are seen as liquidity events in an otherwise low-volume product. However, it appears that this pattern has begun to change. Average daily trading volume in 2004 was $5.8 billion per day but is running at a $9.5 billion pace in 2005, so nonauction liquidity periods are clearly moving up with the growth in both the size of the market and the number of participants.

The Inflation Index—CPI-U

The inflation index used for TIPS is the not-seasonally adjusted US City Average All Items Consumer Price Index for all Urban Consumers (CPI-U). The CPI-U measures price changes for urban consumers of a fixed basket of goods and services of constant quality and quantity. The index was first introduced in 1978 and currently reflects the buying behavior of 80% of the US population.

E X H I B I T   2–6

Annual TIPS Issuance

Annual TIPS Issuance $ Billions, 1997 - 2004, estimated 2005

Source: Barclays Capital.

E X H I B I T   2–7

TIPS Issuance as a Percentage of All Treasury Note and Bond Issuance

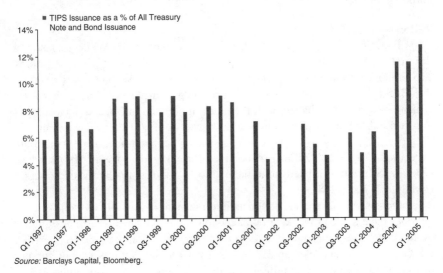

Source: Barclays Capital, Bloomberg.

E X H I B I T   2–8

TIPS Market Value and Average Daily Volume

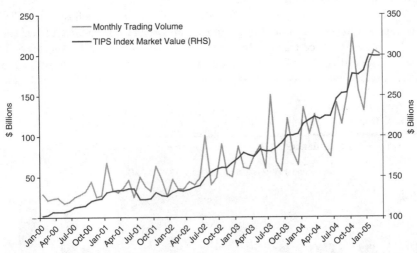

Source: Barclays Capital, Bloomberg, Federal Reserve.

Prices are collected from 85 urban areas, which include 21,000 retail and service establishments. Rents data are gathered from 40,000 landlords and tenants as well as 20,000 homeowner occupants. Prices are collected for over 200 categories, which are classified under eight major groups.

Breakdown of CPI-U Components   The basket of goods and services and the item weights are determined from the Consumer Expenditure Survey (CEX). Since the CPI is a fixed-weight index, the implicit weights remain the same from month to month. A related concept is the relative importance of an item. Relative importance in essence means that if the price of a particular item rises more than the average price increase of items in the basket then the relative importance of that item increases. To illustrate, the price of crude oil, as measured by WTI, had risen from around $20 per barrel in January 2002 to near $45 per barrel in December 2004. A result of that increase is that the relative importance of energy has risen from 6.2% to 7.99% during the same time period. Exhibits 2–9 and 2–10 highlight the change in the relative importance of the eight major categories from 1997 to current weights set in 2004.

Seasonals   As TIPS are linked to the not-seasonally adjusted index, seasonal patterns of inflation have played a significant role in the US market. Exhibit 2–11 presents estimated seasonal adjustment factors per month. The tendency that can easily be seen here is the positive pattern at the beginning of the year vs. the negative bias going into year end.

In theory, since seasonal factors are reasonably known, an efficient market should not react to seasonal patterns, but this has certainly not been the case. The seasonal pattern in inflation has historically resulted in a similar pattern in break-even rates. Exhibit 2–12 shows that breakevens have typically risen into the "good" seasonal period and fallen in the second half of the year. As discussed below, TIPS reference the CPI-U index with a 3-month lag. For example, December's negative seasonal bias impacts TIPS carry in February. Hence, the reaction in breakevens has typically been with a lag as well. As the market

E X H I B I T   2–9

1997 CPI-U Weights

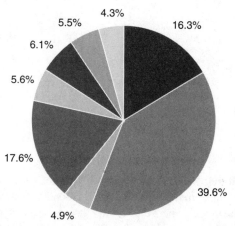

Source: Barclays Capital, Haver Analytics.

EXHIBIT 2–10

Current CPI-U Weights

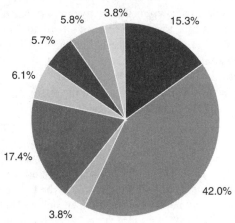

Source: Barclays Capital, Haver Analytics.

EXHIBIT 2–11

CPI Seasonal Adjustment Factors

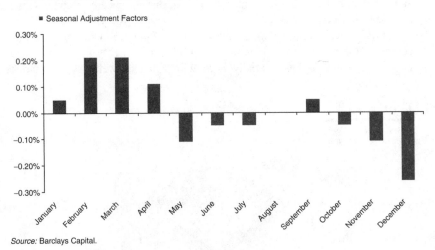

Source: Barclays Capital.

becomes more efficient, we would expect that this season bias in breakevens will begin to weaken (Exhibit 2–13).

The Canadian Model: Basic Structure and Math of Reference Index

TIPS, along with most major inflation-linked bond markets outside the UK, follow the Canadian model, where the security pays a fixed coupon on the inflation-adjusted principal. The principal is adjusted on a daily basis using an index ratio

EXHIBIT 2-12

Historical Seasonals of the 10-Year Break-Even Inflation Rate

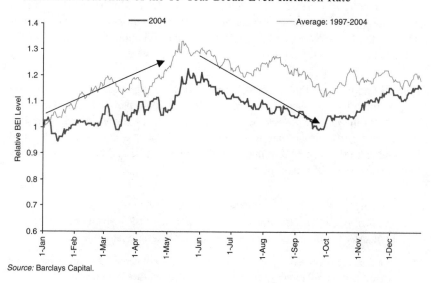

Source: Barclays Capital.

EXHIBIT 2-13

Zero-Coupon Inflation Swap Cashflows

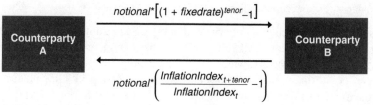

Source: Barclays Capital.

which quantifies the rate of growth in inflation or deflation between the issue date and settlement date. The index is lagged 3 months from the settlement date; for example, for April 1, 2005, the CPI-U for February 2005 applies. We compute the index ratio as follows:

Index ratio = Reference index/Base CPI index

where the base CPI index is the reference index at issue date and,

$$\text{Reference index} = CPI_{m-3} + (t-1)/D_m(CPI_{m-2} - CPI_{m-3})$$

where

CPI_{m-2} = is the price index for month $m-2$

CPI_{m-3} = is the price index for month $m-3$

D_m = is the number of days in month m

m = is the month in which settlement takes place

t = is the day of the month on which settlement takes place

For settlement amounts, real accrued interest is calculated as for ordinary Treasuries. Clean price, which is the trading price and does not include either the inflation or coupon accrual, and is multiplied by the Index Ratio to arrive at a cash settlement amount. For coupons paid, the (real) semi-annual coupon rate is multiplied by the Index Ratio, and likewise for the par redemption amount (with the cash value subject to the par floor).

Floor   In addition to the above structure, TIPS are embedded with a deflation floor. At maturity, an investor will not receive less than par. The floor would be applicable if the index ratio was less than 1, which would only occur if there had been deflation from issue date to maturity. The floor is a European option and only applies to the principal at maturity. Coupons can be and have been paid off a principal amount less than the par amount.

Tax   On August 25, 1999, the Internal Revenue Service published "final regulations" covering the tax treatment of inflation-indexed instruments. Investors should consider the entire document, but a key paragraph is detailed below:

> The final regulations provide rules for the treatment of certain debt instruments that are indexed for inflation and deflation, including Treasury Inflation-Indexed Securities. The final regulations generally require holders and issuers of inflation-indexed debt instruments to account for interest and original issue discount (OID) using constant yield principles. In addition, the final regulations generally require holders and issuers of inflation-indexed debt instruments to account for inflation and deflation by making current adjustments to their OID accruals.

Thus, the inflation escalation of principal in the US is taxable as income annually, even though the Treasury will be making inflation payment at maturity. This creates a phantom inflation tax, which for nontax-exempt investors such as insurance companies and individual investors may make ownership in TIPS unattractive. To ameliorate this problem, in 1998 the Treasury issued a Series I Savings Bond program targeted at individual investors. These bonds are tax exempt for 30 years.

Rules and regulations governing the tax treatment of TIPS can be found at the following link: ftp://ftp.publicdebt.treas.gov/gsrintax.pdf.

France started issuing inflation-linked bonds in September 1998 with a similar format to TIPS, except paying coupons annually. The OATi 3% July 2009 was linked to the French CPI excluding tobacco (as the legal basis for all indexation in France excludes tobacco). The link to domestic inflation meant that initial interest was largely from French investors. The OATi 3.4% 2029 followed a year later. The first two bonds were launched via syndication but more recent new bonds have been launched via multiple-price auctions, while all reopenings are also via auctions. The market for French CPI-linked bonds has continued to grow despite France starting to issue Euro HICP-linked (excluding tobacco) bonds as well in 2001. Indeed the existence of two parallel markets has actually encouraged more liquidity by offering trading opportunities between the inflation bases.

France launched the OAT€i 3% 2012 by syndication in October 2001 with the same format as OATi bonds but a different linking index, the Euro HICP (harmonized index of consumer prices) excluding tobacco. The original decision to link bonds to French CPI just before the launch of the Euro area was taken because the Euro inflation index was barely tested and subject to revision. The clamor from international investors to have exposure to Euro inflation grew steadily though, and France was keen to maintain its leadership in the asset class within the Euro area to maximize its investor base. Switch terms were offered out of the old 10-year French CPI bond at the launch to encourage development of a sufficiently large and liquid issue. The same happened a year later when the 2032 €i was issued with switching out of the OATi29 offered, but the two inflation-linked markets have proved remarkably complementary and grown together. France auctions linkers monthly, often with a combination of OAT€i and OATi bonds offered.

The development of the market for €i bonds in Europe cannot be separated from the parallel development of the inflation swaps market in Euro HICP ex-tobacco, which quickly became the most developed in the world. The maturity of the market was enhanced when Greece became the second government issuer of €i bonds in March 2003, with its GGB€i 2025 exactly mimicking the structure of French bonds right down to the July 25 coupon date. Despite this, the early part of 2003 saw notably more issuance of structured notes linked to inflation in nonaccreting structures than government supply. This supply was mainly retail issuance to individuals in Italy, who commonly invest in structured products and remember very high inflation much more recently than in other developed markets. The supply was all hedged by issuers using mainly inflation swaps, with the result being that both bond and swap break-evens were driven considerably richer, encouraging the Italian government to act.

Italy syndicated the BTP€i 1.65% 2008 in September 2003, the 5-year maturity most closing matching that of the structured corporate issuance. BTP€is have the same format as French OAT€is, i.e., a Canadian capital-indexed structure with a deflation floor and indexed to Euro HICP ex-tobacco. The only significant difference is semi-annual coupons, albeit as with nominal BTPs the convention is for yields to be quoted annually. While the initial bond was unusually short for a new market, subsequently the BTP€i curve has been extended to 30 years, and Italy has overtaken France as the largest issuer of €i bonds. New bonds have been launched via syndication and this method was also used for reopenings, but Italy has moved towards single price auctions for monthly reopenings, with the exception of the long end of the curve. While the success of the Italian programme has tempted other Euro countries to consider issue too, in practice there was no new issuer in 2004, though Germany indicated that it would issue in 2005.

The format of the UK linkers is notably different from the other major markets, though the bonds are still a capital-indexed structure. There is no floor to the principal repayment, in contrast to most other markets. They are linked to the retail price index, the RPI, which when UK linkers were first issued in 1981 was the universally-followed measure of consumer inflation in the UK, although by no means the only candidate considered. Many pension funds wanted wage-indexation to be used instead, as most defined benefit liabilities at the time were linked either to firm specific salaries or the average earnings series. Arguments were also made for the GDP deflator, as the broadest measure of inflation and that to which tax revenue was most closely tied. In practice the RPI was a clear choice as it was more timely, widely followed and not prone to revision. Despite the change of the monetary policy target in 2003 to CPI from the previous RPI except mortgage interest costs, there is no risk of a change to the basis of UK linkers as almost all defined benefit pension fund liabilities now are at least partially linked to the RPI. CPI is based on Eurostat HICP principles and produces a consistently lower estimate of inflation due to a geometric index weighting rather than the arithmetic weighting used for the RPI. On average the measurement and coverage gap from the inclusion of a broader range of housing cost components mean RPI is around 0.7% to 0.8% higher than CPI, but this spread has been as high as 2.1% and as low as −0.4% in recent years.

When UK linkers were proposed in 1980 the existing tax law meant that the next coupon payment had to be known, though this is no longer the case. With coupons paid semi-annually this meant a lag of 8 months was adopted. Having a known nominal value for the next coupon means that neither the true real value of this payment nor the bond overall can be calculated. In the absence of a better alternative at the time the UK chose to quote all bond prices in nominal terms and then use an assumption about future inflation to calculate a real yield. Despite having no clear consensus from previous consultations about changing the format of UK linkers, the Debt Management Office announced that new issues from 2005 would be of a Canadian format instead. Existing bonds of the old format using nominal pricing are still issued, however. Issuance methods for gilt linkers have varied, but currently auctions are at the same price for all successful bidders, in contrast to nominal gilts, where auctions are variable price.

Market convention for the assumption necessary to calculate traditional UK linker real yields is 3%, but prior to 1998 other assumptions were used, with the Bank of England also quoting real yields using 5% and 10%. The sensitivity to this assumption is very large at short maturities, but becomes increasingly small the longer the duration of the bond as the value of the initial cash flow becomes less important and later cashflow valuations converge towards a true real yield. Each time an RPI number is released UK linker real yields mechanically adjust as this number replaces the previously assumed increase ($1.03^{(1/12)}$ or 1.00247). A higher number than the assumption mechanically increases the real yield of all linkers, though impacting the front end much more than longer bonds, while a month-on-month change below the 0.247% number mechanically reduces real yields. While this produces discontinuities in yield series, this method means that all known inflation information is included in the yield as soon as it is known, rather than after a lag as in the Canadian model.

Canadian real return bonds account for only a small proportion of the government inflation-indexed bond universe but the Canadian format has undoubtedly been successful, now being followed to a greater or lesser extent by all major issuers. The first RRB was launched in 1991, a 2021 issue. All subsequent issuers have had maturities close to 30 years, focusing on the pension sector despite demands from elsewhere for issuance at shorter maturities too. The linking index is the not-seasonally adjusted, all-items CPI. Issuance has consistently been via relatively small quarterly auctions.

Sweden issued its first inflation linked bond in 1994, a zero-coupon 2014 issue. Swedish linker prices, when quoted, include accreted inflation but the market generally quotes solely on real yields following the Canadian format, albeit with annual coupons. Early bonds had no deflation floor, but they have been included in new issues since 1999 following unease over a brief deflationary period and the popularity of such floors for TIPS and OATis. In order to maintain liquidity in the relatively small market, the Swedish National Debt Office conducts small, fortnightly, multiple-price auctions across the curve. The Debt Office can also buy and sell bonds to market makers in the secondary market only slightly away from market levels, so when there are heavy or unbalanced flows the size of issues can change.

Japan issued its first JGBi in March 2004 following the Canadian format. The only difference was that the inflation reference is based on the 10th of the month rather than the 1st due to the relatively late release date for Japanese CPI that could otherwise create problems. Japan chose not to include a deflation floor partly due to the difficulty in pricing the embedded option given the much greater chance of exercise than in other economies. In addition, both the Ministry of Finance and the Bank of Japan were keen to be able to interpret the break-even spread as a measure of inflation expectations, which would have been difficult if the real yield contained a significant embedded-option value. Initially holdings were restricted to domestics and central banks, but these restrictions were relaxed in April 2005, following clarification of the tax status of the bonds. While issuance began slowly, with only a 10-year supply in limited size for the two fiscal years following the launch, the potential for the market to develop is substantial given the funding needs of the Japanese government and the high degree of inflation linkages for pension liabilities in Japan.

Other Inflation-Linked Bond Markets

Aside from the major developed inflation linked markets described above there are inflation-indexed bonds in a number of other developed countries. Australia was a frequent issuer of inflation-linked bonds between 1984 and 2003, and may resume issuance if the budget surplus ever turns into deficit. The structure of the issues differs notably from both the Canadian and UK models, in large part due to the fact that Australian inflation is only produced as a quarterly series. New Zealand's only existing inflation-linked bond, issued between 1995 and 1999, follows a similar structure. Iceland has no domestic nominal government debt but does have a small amount of linkers. More importantly the Icelandic mortgage market is also linked to CPI, with the majority now in a format akin to TIPS.

Denmark has no government linkers, but a significant subsector of its large callable mortgage market was inflation-linked until 1999, when tax changes meant an end to further issuance.

Of emerging markets with inflation-linked debt the four most active are South Africa, Israel, Brazil, and Mexico, all of which hold frequent auctions. South Africa has the most similar structure to the major markets; its Canadian-format bonds have a deflation floor but a 4-month lag. There is also corporate inflation-linked supply and even a small inflation-swaps market. Israel has relied on inflation funding since it was formed, and is notable for galloping inflation developing in the early 1980s, partly as a result of economy-wide indexation. The format of linkers has varied over time but modern Galils are relatively standard capital-indexed bonds. Even so, they do not follow the conventions of other markets, e.g., with base inflation point the last known value at issue and the inflation ratio updating when data are released. This has discouraged international investment in Galils, even though they made up a majority of Israel's debt until 2003 and there have been international buyers of nominal debt in recent years.

Mexican inflation-linked bonds, Udibonos, all pay out cashflows based on the increase in the CPI index since 1995. Initially these were relative short-maturity issues, but since 2001 only 10-year bonds have been auctioned. Mexico has also seen relatively significant corporate supply. Brazil is notable for having two separate types of inflation-linked bonds that are linked to different price indices with regular supply and full yield curves in both. NTN-Bs are linked to CPI but NTN-Cs are linked to an index of general market prices, the IGP-M. This price series comprises 30% CPI, 60% wholesale prices, and 10% construction costs. While South America has a long and occasionally chequered history of inflation-linked markets in Asia, there has been a notable lack of issuers before 2005, when several of the large economies announced they were considering issuing. Another notable addition to the global linker market has been Poland, which launched its first Canadian-format linker in 2004.

Corporate supply in inflation-linked bonds has been significantly less important relative to government issuance than in nominals. Apart from French agency supply the only substantial issuance of capital-indexed bonds has been in the UK, but in both markets it is now often more cost-efficient for natural issuers to pay inflation via swaps and fund with nominal bonds instead. UK nongilt linkers make up less than 10% of the total accreting market by value, including some swapped supply. Most corporate issuance of bonds with inflation linkages involves structured notes, with the issuers hedging out their inflation exposure in the inflation swaps market, as discussed in the inflation derivatives section later in this chapter.

Major Holders of Inflation-Linked Bonds

Before the start of the TIPS market in 1997, most countries that issued inflation-linked bonds were either emerging markets with inflation problems or countries with large private pension funds who experienced significant demand for inflation-linked exposure. In the UK the majority of bonds are still owned by pension funds, 56% by market value in 2004, while 28% of the remainder are held by insurers. Only 7.5% of UK pension fund assets are held in linkers, so, as the accounting pressure to match liabilities and reduce volatility grows, their holdings may become even larger. By contrast, life insurers generally have a tighter liability match already and as sales of inflation-linked products are now rare they are likely to become a smaller percentage of the total market. In Canada and Australia there is an even greater bias towards pension funds. In Sweden, while pension funds are the largest holders of linkers, insurers are not far behind, holding 42% of the market by value as of the end of 2004. Swedish life insurers may increase their holdings from the current 34% of the market as regulation moves more towards the UK line on liability matching.

A broader range of investors have been involved in the TIPS market compared to the older markets above. The majority of TIPS holders continue to own them as diversification from core positions, though this is slowly changing. Mutual funds were the heaviest early buyers of TIPS and remain the largest managers of the asset class, albeit with an increasing amount directly mandated from pension funds and endowments. Total return funds and bond funds now commonly hold TIPS within their portfolios while there are an increasing number of real return funds for whom TIPS are the core asset. Endowments and lottery funds have also proved natural buyers of TIPS. The insurance sector is notably less important than in Europe, mainly because inflation-linked life policies are much rarer. One of the main reasons the Treasury reintroduced 5-year TIPS issuance in 2004 was to encourage central bank buying. Foreign official institutions have become an increasingly important feature of the market, but remain relative small in TIPS compared to their nominal treasury holdings.

Pension reform may encourage more buying of TIPS by private defined-benefit pension schemes, but as of 2004 their exposure to all Treasuries was modest at only 3% of total allocations. The absolute scale of private defined-benefit assets is 20% smaller than the $2 trillion state and local government sector. More importantly, state and local government pension scheme liabilities have relatively more explicit price indexation rather than wage indexation, and also much more frequently have indexation commitments beyond the period when a member of the pension scheme is an active contributor. State and local government schemes are already the largest pension fund buyers of TIPS and their liabilities mean the potential for increased buying is substantial. On the other hand, federal pension reform is unlikely to impact the state sector significantly, so their relative importance of the private sector defined benefit sector may increase. As in other countries, to date few TIPS have been bought for defined contribution pension schemes, which remain skewed heavily towards equities.

Demand for French CPI bonds grew significantly in 2002 when accounting changes made structural holdings by French life insurers easier. Life insurers' CPI liabilities are mainly long dated, but the strongest demand for shorter French CPI exposure has developed due to the linking of "Livret" deposit accounts, which are interest-bearing savings accounts, to inflation. While in theory the official Livret A-rate was supposed to be set with reference to inflation before the OATi market was launched, in practice the level was politically determined until mid-2004, when a formula linking it to an average of French CPI and 3-month money plus 25 bp came into effect. This effectively created over €100 billion of French CPI liabilities. The liabilities are partially offset by some of the interest rates charged for social lending, mainly housing projects, also being based on the same formula. In addition to the government bond curve there are several French agency capital-indexed issues. Most importantly the social security agency CADES has been issuing French CPI-linked bonds since March 1999. As of the end of 2004 its four benchmarks had a market value of over €10 billion and help to better define the French CPI real yield curve. CADES sees itself as a natural issuer of French CPI-indexed bonds due to its income being tax linked, but it also uses inflation swaps to further increase its exposure when demand to receive inflation leaves this as a more attractive funding route than issuing bonds.

While there is clear overlap between the demand base for Euro HICP bonds and OATis, there are significantly more inflation liabilities explicitly linked to French CPI. Euro inflation is a proxy for a wide range of other liabilities, leading to a broader range of investors. Those needing to match country-specific inflation liabilities more tightly must rely on the derivatives market, with inflation swaps markets of varying depth in most Euro-area country CPIs. As in the US, most investors in €is hold them for diversification within their portfolios. There is notably less potential for pension fund buying than in the US absent major pension reform transferring liabilities from the state sector. Few Euro-area countries have large pension markets with the exception of the Netherlands, where regulation has encouraged most pension funds to remove the soft wage indexation previously embedded within their liabilities, removing structural inflation exposure. Life insurance demand varies between countries depending on whether there have been policies with inflation linkages. Several countries have demand profiles similar to France, but notably in the largest single market, Germany, there are no inflation liabilities. A final major type of holder of the €is are covered bond banks and others holding in asset swap form, at times over 20% of the market. This is discussed in more detail in the inflation derivatives section later in this chapter.

Inflation Derivatives   Inflation derivatives have been around since the early 1990s, but it is only in recent years that they have developed from being an exotic offshoot of government inflation-linked bond markets. Inflation swaps in parti-cular are now an integral part of the armoury for addressing inflation-linked liabilities. Inflation swaps in the UK are now commonly used by pension funds, but it is in the Euro area where the growth of the market has been most spectacular, complementing the growth of liquidity in the bond market. Asset-swap trading is the main mechanism integrating the world of inflation swaps and bonds, and in Europe many market makers now run their inflation swap and bond positions alongside each other in the same way as occurs in the nominal market.

In contrast to inflation-linked bonds, inflation swaps are usually not real-yield instruments, with their value dependent purely on inflation. Combining inflation and nominal swaps can straightforwardly create real-yield exposures, but most trade is done on break-evens. Inflation derivatives are traded on an over-the-counter basis that allows extreme flexibility. This makes them the ideal instruments to create structures to offset inflation liabilities, or to create structures that are attractive to particular investors. Zero-inflation swaps form the building blocks of most inflation-related swap structures. Zero-swap break-even quotes enable an inter-dealer market, allowing inflation swap houses to trade their relative exposures on a consistent basis whatever complex structures are created for end-users.

A zero-coupon inflation swap is a pure exposure to the final level of the price index. One counterparty agrees to pay the cumulative percentage increase in the price index over the tenor of the swap while the other pays fixed. There are no cashflows involved until the final level of the index is known or the position is unwound (though long tenor zero-coupon swaps sometimes have market-to-market reset agreements embedded in them).

The inflation base of a zero-coupon swap is subject to a lag, as are inflation-linked bonds, and the lags used vary between markets. In US CPI and French CPIx swaps the standard lag is the same daily-interpolated 3-month lag as in TIPS and OATis respectively. In the most liquid market for Euro HICPx swaps, the lag is not interpolated, rather being based on the actual inflation release for a given month. The standard trading period here is a 3-month lag. For instance, throughout April most trades involve calculation from the January HICPx, but it is possible to trade with shorter and longer lags on agreement and brokers increasingly show alternatives. In UK RPI swaps, base months are also used, but with a 2- rather than a 3-month lag. Interpolated references have the advantage of consistency for comparison with underlying Canadian-style bond markets, but not for traditional UK linkers. The Euro market adopted the monthly convention from the UK, as swaps traded before the first €i bond was launched, but the format can encourage short-term two-way trading, the screen value being valid for the whole month rather than changing daily. Thus while it has the disadvantage of producing a discontinuity in the market each month as the base changes, there have been attempts to change the convention in both the French and US markets.

Apart from zero-coupon swaps there are two other common formats of inflation swaps. The first is year-on-year swaps, where one counterparty receives the annual rate of inflation and the other receives fixed. This mimics the coupon format of many structured notes. In the US payments are most commonly monthly, and in Europe yearly, while six-monthly and quarterly payments are also known. While almost all the risk from such bond positions can be offset with zero-coupon positions, there is a path dependency that cannot be entirely neutralized: effectively each coupon is a reset so perfect replication with zeros involves chained forwards. The other common format is an accreting bond mimicking cash flow, most commonly transacted on asset swap trades.

As with nominal bonds, an inflation-linked asset swap converts exposure from a bond format into a LIBOR-based one. By no means all trading between inflation bonds and swaps is conducted as true asset swaps, any more than is the case for trading between nominal bond markets and swaps. Tactical positions are often taken between the two markets using zero swaps as the most liquid instrument, but for long-term positions asset swaps are used. The complexities of an asset swap for an inflation-linked bond are somewhat trickier than for a nominal bond but the principal is the same, matching the characteristics of the bond and derivative cash flow to leave a floating cash-flow stream that can be measured against LIBOR. In the absence of substantial payers of inflation outside of governments, inflation asset swaps provide the mechanism to create payers of inflation. In theory, governments could pay inflation directly. At least one small Euro country has done so, but in practice it is unlikely for large sovereigns.

Long-term investors wanting exposure to government bonds in asset-swap form often find that it is cheaper to buy inflation-linked bonds than nominals due to the lack of payers of inflation in the face of ongoing demand. In Europe there is a wide range of banks that need exposure to suitably-rated collateral, especially covered bond issuers who need to hold very large amounts of government bonds in asset-swap form until maturity. When Italy launched the BTP€i08, the bond effectively traded at a LIBOR-plus level, almost 10 bp cheaper than corresponding maturity nominal bonds. This spread was sufficiently wide to encourage covered bond banks to set up systems to hold inflation-linked rather than nominal bonds as collateral. Once the systems were in place the potential for buying bonds and paying inflation was substantial. The BTP€i08 has at various times been held mostly in asset-swap positions, occasionally leading to a squeeze in the cash bond until it is rich enough to force long-term holders to lighten their positions. Knowing that there are ultimate buyers in the market encourages range trading by tactical investors on the basis of relative asset-swap levels, especially, but not exclusively, for Italian bonds.

Asset swapping is a much less prominent feature of the US markets than in the Euro area, mainly due to the lack of natural asset swap buyers of nominal treasury bonds. US TIPS asset swaps have traded as much as 30 bp cheap to those of nominal Treasuries, as there are very few payers of inflation, but a demand for inflation swaps to hedge structured issuance. For shorter TIPS there are investors willing to trade the relative spread, knowing ultimately they can hold as an arbitrage to maturity if the spread does not narrow, but this is less so longer on the curve. Structured notes thus consistently offer worse value than TIPS, and in order to achieve true yield pick-up substantial credit deterioration is needed. There is a demand for structured corporate paper with inflation-linked coupons mainly as they provide a more tax-friendly structure than TIPS, for which tax is payable on the accrued principal as well as the coupons paid. This idea of paying tax on the "phantom" accrued inflation was addressed in more detail within the TIPS section. Also in an attempt to address the need for tax-advantage inflation-linked bonds, there is a small but growing inflation-linked municipal bond market where interest in mutual funds is developing. Some of these various credit structures can also offer leveraged exposure to inflation that is not possible with accreting bonds, though it should be noted that standard year-on-year coupon bonds actually have less inflation exposure than similar maturity government bonds, particularly at longer maturities.

Asset swapping has been a less prominent feature of the UK inflation derivatives market than elsewhere. This is mainly due to the market developing along very different lines from the US and Europe, where the primary driver has been structured note-issuance hedging. There have been periods where there has been significant issuance by supranationals and others who have swapped their exposure back into nominal form, but generally this was in a standard bond format. The UK market has seen inflation swap flows for much longer than elsewhere, but until 2004 it was rare for there to be any inter-dealer repositioning. Previously the market was sufficiently lumpy that when an investment bank had an inflation payer lined up it was in their interest to find a pension fund with the appropriate demand and pass through almost directly rather than highlighting the flow.

In recent years a sharply higher percentage of UK pension funds have given themselves the ability to take inflation swap positions as their actuaries, consultants and advisers have all highlighted the benefits of using them for efficient liability management. The majority of funds by value can now use them, though that is not to say they currently do. There are now sufficiently numerous suppliers of inflation and pension and life insurance funds looking to receive inflation that the two-way broker market has flourished. The growing depth of the market encouraged investment banks to show live reference prices, which has enabled significantly more entities to get involved. While most turnover is still in RPI swaps, there is a significant minority of demand and supply that is limited price indexation (LPI), i.e., accreting RPI exposure, but with an annual cap and floor. The LPI business has grown substantially but remains a more face-to-face market akin to the RPI swaps business in years gone by. While demand is mainly for 0% to 5% LPI, the standard inflation liability that pension funds accrued from 1997 to 2005, there are a range of other LPI exposures from before this date that are only now being addressed. Supply comes mainly from contractual payment flows from project finance and property-related deals that have other caps and floors in them, though when LPI trades significantly richer than RPI investment banks are often willing to take the basis risk.

The main benefit of using inflation derivatives rather than bonds for an organization with inflation-linked exposures is flexibility. This can be split into two main advantages. First, the inflation swaps can be tailored much more tightly than bonds to match liabilities if those liabilities are clearly defined. Second, while most inflation-linked pension exposures are real-yield exposures, using inflation swaps gives a fund the ability to separate their nominal duration decisions from addressing their inflation exposures. For instance, in late 2004 and early 2005 several UK pension funds faced with new accounting regulations that encourage liability matching chose to address their RPI exposure by using inflation swaps, but not to lock in real rates at historically low levels below 1.50%. This drove long-linker asset swap levels very cheap, encouraging both tactical investors to buy long linkers on asset swap and corporates to pay inflation.

Both inflation and interest rate swaps can potentially offer opportunities for funds to leverage their cash while actually reducing risk. For example, if a pension fund has to address a liability mismatch by buying bonds, they have to sell other assets with higher expected returns such as equities. If instead they use swaps then they only need to commit a small cash exposure against their long-dated swaps but still have a lower risk vs. liabilities than a traditional pension fund asset mix. An additional form of derivative that enables a similar leveraging advantage, but is more applicable for funds with goals based on an index, is total-return swaps. These can be used to match the performance of either a bond or index, less some prearranged cost of carry, while only committing a fraction of the capital. For instance, a medium-sized real return fund can choose to take index exposure via total-return swaps and use the remaining capital to try to outperform their index.

CONCLUSIONS

While the history of inflation-linked bonds dates back more than a hundred years, the markets for them have only become developed over the past few years. However, the recent expansion has been dramatic and is expected to continue. As much as the natural starting point was sovereign issuance, which itself will continue to grow both in size and number of issuers, the next phase of development will likely come in the increased importance of the derivatives and credit markets.

Investors in inflation-linked bonds continue to expand in number and sophistication. Information content embedded in inflation-linked bonds is forcing investors to recognise their exposure to erosion of purchasing power and think more in real return space when considering liabilities and this is further expanding demand which appears to growing at roughly with the pace of supply.

As much as inflation-linked bonds should be considered a separate asset class from the rest of the fixed-income world, they are also part of a broader class of real-return instruments discussed in this book. Government inflation-linked bonds are the closest thing to a risk-free asset in a real-return framework, and as such should form the core of any low-risk portfolio. In addition to inflation-linked bonds, a true diversified real-return portfolio might include commodities and real estate, and even less-liquid markets such as timber, art and wine. We believe the increasing focus on the need for real returns will move this asset class from an "alternative-investments" category to something much more in the mainstream.

HISTORICAL RETURNS

Annual Returns by Country since 1997—Local and Hedged into $s

	Australia	Canada	France	Italy	Sweden	UK	US
Local returns							
1997	7.93%	4.65%			8.42%	13.91%	
1998	12.83%	5.89%			3.87%	19.93%	4.02%
1999	1.59%	7.82%	0.12%		0.64%	4.35%	2.24%
2000	12.94%	16.80%	5.63%		11.46%	4.24%	13.19%
2001	6.00%	0.08%	5.18%		4.98%	−0.88%	7.98%
2002	9.98%	15.69%	13.11%		14.62%	8.38%	16.98%
2003	3.47%	13.09%	8.30%		6.42%	6.80%	8.19%
2004	12.47%	17.66%	11.21%	9.37%	11.17%	8.27%	8.66%
Hedged returns							
1997	7.80%	7.13%			9.92%	13.10%	
1998	13.39%	6.72%			5.15%	17.72%	4.02%
1999	1.93%	8.39%	2.39%		2.57%	3.85%	2.24%
2000	13.49%	17.77%	8.09%		14.53%	4.68%	13.19%
2001	5.11%	−0.10%	4.85%		4.88%	−1.93%	7.98%
2002	6.85%	14.87%	11.78%		12.15%	6.16%	16.98%
2003	0.13%	11.54%	7.43%		4.75%	4.43%	8.19%
2004	8.23%	16.61%	10.65%	8.79%	10.38%	5.10%	8.66%

Source: Barclays Capital.

Five-Year Returns and Sharpe Ratios across Asset Classes, as of January 2005

	High Yield Market Index	European World Government Bond Index	Corporate Index	S&P 500	Treasury Index	Global IL Index (Hedged)	TIPS Index	GSCI	Mortgage
Average monthly returns									
1 year	0.6	0.55	0.34	0.42	0.18	0.85	0.49	1.6	0.28
3 years	0.9	0.48	0.55	0.25	0.37	1.22	0.79	1.85	0.33
5 years	0.42	0.37	0.52	-0.25	0.41	0.69	0.66	0.72	0.39
Standard deviation of returns									
1 year	1.14	0.71	1.43	2.28	1.38	2.13	1.95	5.55	0.86
3 years	2.82	0.97	1.67	4.37	1.68	2.29	2.12	5.23	0.8
5 years	2.88	0.93	1.45	4.71	1.49	2.11	1.77	5.12	0.76
Sharpe ratio									
5 years	0.15	0.39	0.36	-0.05	0.27	0.33	0.37	0.14	0.52

Source: Barclays Capital, Bloomberg, The Yieldbook.

Correlation Grid with Other Assets and Inflation, February 1997 to January 2005

	High Yield Market Index	World Government Bond Index	Corporate Index	Treasury Index	Mortgages	GSCI	S&P 500	Russell 2000	Global Linker	REIT
High yield market index	1.00									
World government bond index	−0.01	1.00								
Corporate index	0.39	0.79	1.00							
Treasury index	−0.07	0.91	0.83	1.00						
Mortgages	0.04	0.76	0.78	0.83	1.00					
GSCI	−0.06	−0.05	−0.05	−0.02	−0.04	1.00				
S&P 500	0.49	−0.19	0.08	−0.23	−0.08	−0.09	1.00			
Russell 2000	0.52	−0.20	0.08	−0.23	−0.09	−0.06	0.99	1.00		
Global linker	0.07	0.59	0.62	0.64	0.47	0.14	−0.09	−0.08	1.00	
REIT	0.30	0.08	0.23	0.02	0.02	0.07	0.29	0.32	0.20	1.00

Source: Barclays Capital, Bloomberg, The Yieldbook.

CHAPTER 3

INFLATION-LINKED BONDS: PORTFOLIO CONSTRUCTION AND OPPORTUNITIES FOR ACTIVE MANAGEMENT

Mike Amey, John Brynjolfsson, Ivan Skobtsov, and Mihir Worah
PIMCO

Previous chapters motivated the need for real returns, and described how inflation-linked bonds work. In this chapter we jump in feet-first to address how fiduciaries go about creating and optimizing portfolios of inflation-linked bonds.

Rather than starting with the abstract, we begin with the concrete. After making the distinction between a strategic and a tactical allocation to ILBs, we go on to provide an overview of benchmark selection in the case of a strategic allocation. After all, before a portfolio manager can use the tools to add value he/she, needs a benchmark against which skill may be measured. What are some common benchmarks, and how would one choose between them?

Next, we discuss portfolio construction. We begin by briefly discussing structuring a portfolio to passively replicate a benchmark. The focus however is on structuring actively managed portfolios. For actively managed portfolios, one needs to "right-size" active management positions that represent a divergence from the benchmarks, and therefore represent active risk.

Third, in the meat of this chapter, we discuss specific tools portfolio managers use to add value in ILB portfolios. We explore concepts including real portfolio duration management, break-even inflation trading, global sector rotation and corporate ILB replication. In addition, we contemplate arrangements in which a portfolio manager can utilize out-of-benchmark bonds in order to outperform an inflation-linked bond benchmark.

In the last section, we cover the remaining questions that clients, consultants and other fiduciaries might have: How large an allocation, active or passive, global or domestic, external management or internal staff management. Hopefully, the reader will have determined by the time they get to that section that they need real returns (Chapter 1), a little bit about how inflation-linked bonds work (Chapter 2), and learned in this chapter something about tools for adding value, the types of benchmarks available, and how portfolios are structured. With this chapter as a roadmap, a fiduciary can move forward with implementing an allocation to inflation-linked bonds.

STRATEGIC VS. TACTICAL

Throughout investment management there are strategic allocations and tactical allocations. A simple distinction between the two is that strategic allocations are determined externally, by a client, board, or policy and incorporated into a portfolio manager's benchmark. Tactical decisions, on the other hand, are deviations from benchmarks. Tactical decisions are employed at the discretion of a portfolio manager in an attempt to outperform a client's benchmark and thereby achieve a client's alpha target.[1]

ILBs are generally well suited for strategic allocations since they can easily be thought of as a separate and distinct asset class. ILBs are not equities; they are not cash. Though legally speaking they are bonds, from an asset class perspective they are distinct in that they protect against inflation, the bane of traditional bonds. Most of this chapter discusses inflation-linked bonds in this context of a deliberate strategic allocation to the asset class.

Recall that strategic allocations incorporate the top-level strategic needs of an organization. These strategic allocations are based upon abstract goals of an organization's investment effort (high return, low risk, preservation of purchasing power), as well as the more concrete aspects of an organization's liabilities, top-level mean-variance optimization, and other asset allocation techniques. Strategic allocations are sized based upon a top-down macroassessment of the asset allocation implications.

Such strategic allocations could involve hiring an external specialty manager, utilizing an internal manager, or perhaps simply modifying the benchmark of an existing manager to include inflation-linked bonds. The defining aspect of a strategic allocation is that a target exposure is determined at a top level (Trustee, Board, CIO, Principal, or Staff).

Early in the development of the US ILB market most allocations were tactical in nature. Existing fixed income managers purchased ILBs within existing assignments. They were implementing a view, the manager's view, that ILBs would outperform their benchmark (or more specifically, would outperform that portion of their benchmark for which the ILBs were substituting). Many managers and clients celebrated this approach.

Over time, the industry has moved toward strategic allocations. The rationale for this is multifold. There is certain logic to focusing the bulk of ILB holdings in the hands of ILB specialists whom the client has evaluated and designated. There is a more fundamental perspective on this decision as well. It is unlikely that tactical allocation will, by happenstance, result in the optimal long-term allocation from the perspective of a client's liabilities, diversification, and needed returns. In particular, a tactical allocation, based on a core bond portfolio manager's optimization of alpha and information ratio,[2] is likely to be much smaller than that which clients would optimally have.

---

1. "Alpha" is a term commonly used by clients, consultants, and investment managers to describe a portfolio's performance in excess of a benchmark.
2. Information ratio is defined as the ratio of alpha to the standard deviation of alpha, and is a measure of risk adjusted return.

SELECTING A BENCHMARK

Investors choose to invest in ILB portfolios for a number of reasons. Common reasons are explicit matching of inflation-linked liabilities, diversification of returns across asset classes, and as an absolute return strategy. An understanding of the reasons behind the choice of an inflation-linked bond portfolio is key to defining a benchmark. Here, we discuss the motivation behind, and characteristics of, different benchmark choices.

Liabilities Linked to Domestic Inflation

Consider, as an illustrative example, the case of an investor with liabilities linked to domestic inflation. This could be a pension fund, where future payouts to retirees are indexed to inflation. Alternately, this could be an endowment that is used to pay for goods and services (salaries, maintenance of physical structures, etc.) that escalate with inflation.

We highlight below some choices of benchmark for such investors.

The simplest case would be defining a benchmark consisting of domestic ILBs where the duration of the benchmark closely matches that of the liabilities. Consider the case of a typical pension plan where the average duration of the liabilities might be 15 years. This is longer than the typical duration of a benchmark consisting of all ILBs issued by a country (Table 3–1).

In such a case, the investor could restrict the benchmark to consist only of longer-maturity ILBs. For example, the real duration of the US ILB index restricted to maturities greater than 10 years is 16.9 years (Table 3–2). Similarly the UK 10+ years ILB index has a duration of 14.6 years.

Depending on the investor's views on volatility and returns of shorter-maturity ILBs vs. the longer-maturity ILBs, he/she could obtain the same duration

T A B L E   3–1

Composition with Country Breakdown of the Barclays Global ILB Index

Country	Number of Bonds	Market Value (USD)	Duration	Duration Contribution
AU	3	6,699.90	8.96	0.08
CA	4	25,221.80	16.20	0.54
FR	8	113,822.70	9.39	1.42
GB	9	190,923.10	11.01	2.79
IT	4	53,083.70	8.14	0.57
JP	3	8,686.90	8.98	0.10
SE	5	32,455.70	10.82	0.47
US	16	322,441.10	8.82	3.78
Grand Total	52	753,334.90		9.75

Source: Barclays Capital. As of 06/30/2005.

T A B L E   3–2

Composition with Country Breakdown of the Barclays Global 10+ Years ILB Index

Country	Number of Bonds	Market Value (USD)	Duration	Duration Contribution
AU	2	5,081.60	10.29	0.17
CA	4	25,221.80	16.20	1.31
FR	4	41,365.60	15.50	2.06
GB	5	116,264.10	14.62	5.45
IT	1	7,840.50	22.29	0.56
SE	3	24,926.20	12.56	1.00
US	4	91,342.90	16.88	4.94
Grand Total	23	312,042.70	15.48	15.48

Source: Barclays Capital.

exposure by using a benchmark with a 9-year duration levered 1.6 times. This would match the interest rate and inflation sensitivity of the liabilities, but not the convexity profile. As a reference the duration of the US ILB index is 8.8 years (Table 3–1).

Recognizing the fact that inflation rates in the industrialized countries are correlated over long time frames (especially in economically linked regions) (Exhibit 3–1), the investor may choose a benchmark of global inflation-linked bonds. This buys the investor diversification while still maintaining, to a large degree, domestic inflation exposure. Note, choosing a global ILB benchmark conveys an inherently different message to an investment manager than choosing a domestic ILB benchmark with the discretion to invest globally: returning one to the strategic vs. tactical allocation issue discussed earlier. Choosing a global ILB benchmark is a strategic decision that imposes diversification amongst ILB markets on the portfolio manager. Having a domestic ILB benchmark with global discretion allows the portfolio manager to tactically invest in foreign markets when the opportunity for outperformance exists.

Investors with inflation-linked liabilities in countries without well-developed ILB markets could use the correlation between inflation rates to choose a benchmark of global ILBs, or ILBs of a specific foreign country or region whose inflation rate most closely matches that of the investor. For example, Sweden has a well-developed ILB market, while Norway does not. An investor could use the known correlation (0.60) between inflation rates in the two countries to hedge Norwegian inflation exposure with Swedish ILBs. Similarly, one can use the fact that Germany is 30% of the EMU, and German inflation has a 55% correlation to EMU inflation to hedge German inflation with ILBs indexed to EMU inflation.

EXHIBIT 3–1

Correlations to Industrialized Countries Inflation Based on Annual Inflation
Rates as Published by the IMF 1969 to 2003

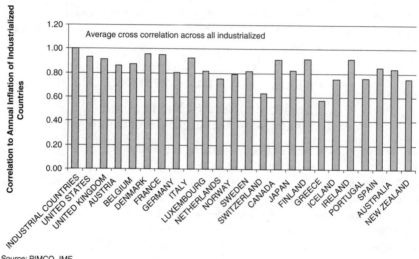

Source: PIMCO, IMF
See appendix for disclosure regarding German CPI

Finally, investors who want to maximize returns and have a tolerance for
volatility could choose a benchmark of ILBs that was aggressively levered, say
10- or 20-fold. Such an approach is more often used as an absolute return strategy
rather than as an explicit hedge against inflation-linked liabilities.

A final decision to be made if one decides to choose a benchmark of global
ILBs is whether the currency exposure should be hedged, or left unhedged.
Opinions regarding whether to go with a currency-hedged benchmark or with a
currency-unhedged benchmark vary. It is our position that the currency and bond
decision can be separated. The distribution of global currency exposure for a
given client can be determined based on top-level currency-related factors. These
might include the distribution of liabilities, distribution of income, relative
deposit rates, and prospects for exchange-rate appreciation. Such a framework
could involve frequent or occasional adjustments based upon views of a currency
expert, overlay manager or the like. It might even, at the periphery, incorporate
some aspects of inflation risk management as discussed previously.

On the one hand, the ILB allocation can be best understood, managed, and
monitored if it is done on in the context of a currency-hedged benchmark. ILBs
being relatively low-risk instruments are not that volatile. On the other hand,
given that allocations to ILBs are often relatively large, and represent a low-risk
portion of a client's asset allocation, and that value added (by active management)
can be substantial due to the inefficiency of the market, it is best to keep the benchmark as pure, and low risk as possible. In this way, managers are encouraged,

and clients can observe, high information ratio value added through modest duration and relative value positioning of the ILB portfolios.

By contrast, if currency exposure is imbedded in the benchmark, large moves in exchange rates will result in the benchmark and portfolio returns from an ILB mandate to fluctuate somewhat dramatically. This will tend to overwhelm alpha generated through ILB management, making it difficult for clients to identify, and difficult for managers to focus upon.

STRUCTURING A PORTFOLIO

Passive Benchmark Replication: Dedicated and Immunized Portfolios

The first step in structuring an actively managed portfolio with measured and conscious deviations from the benchmark is the ability simply to replicate the benchmark. Conceptually this involves buying securities in exactly the market value proportion of the benchmark that they represent. This is often possible in ILB benchmarks because of the small number of securities involved. Passive investors, or "indexers," use such an approach. Unfortunately it does include frequent rebalancing in a predictable manner every time a new ILB is issued (or matures).

The perfect benchmark replication resulting from this product does not make up for the transaction costs involved. Further, the small number of ILBs outstanding lead to large gaps in the yield curve and the inability to take off index positions targeting parts of the yield curve where no ILBs exist. Thus, most active managers eschew this approach in favor of one that consists of matching the benchmark in terms of a limited number of risk factors.

One step removed from pure indexing is portfolio immunization. The simplest example of this is matching the duration of the benchmark by purchasing a single security. While this could match the benchmark's interest rate exposure, it could not match exposures to the shape of the yield curve or convexity. In order to accomplish these goals, one could match the benchmark on an increasing number of "key-rate durations" (sensitivity to changes in specific portions of the yield curve), starting from a limited number of intuitive key rates such as "2s to 10s duration" (measuring sensitivity to changes in yield curve slope between 2 and 10 years) "10s to 30s duration" (measuring sensitivity to changes in the slope between the 10- and 30-year point). Alternately, one could immunize against a benchmark in terms of factor loadings[3] by matching the first, second, and perhaps higher-order factor loadings. Increasing the granularity and number of key-rate durations or factor loadings will ultimately result in perfect benchmark replication as discussed above. The number of risk factors to use depends

---

3. Factors, and factor loadings, can be defined based on various statistical approaches. For example the first factor could be defined as real duration, the second factor as real curve slope, and the third factor as real curve bowing. Some researchers would follow this general framework, however redefine these three factors to be "orthogonal," which would result in slight modifications to the mapping of real durations into the first factor, and so on for the second and third factors.

on the portfolio manager's intuition and could change depending on the economic landscape and views to be implemented.

Process for Structuring an Actively Managed Portfolio (Portable Alpha)

So far, we have simply talked about how to implement passive or immunized ILB portfolios. Here we talk about how to implement active views. We discuss this in terms of both the complementary approaches to replication discussed above: in terms of deviations from the market value weights represented by securities in the benchmarks as well as in terms of deviations from the benchmark's risk factors.

A portfolio can be defined by the weightings of each security held in that active portfolio. Consider a simplified example in which there are 50 potential securities. In that case we can define a portfolio as weights $W(1)$ through $W(50)$. The sum of these weights is necessarily 100%.

Similarly we can define the weights of those same securities in the benchmark as $B(1)$ through $B(50)$, weights that also sum to 100%. If a security is held in benchmark, but not in the portfolio, that security's portfolio weight W, would simply be zero.

One can easily redefine a new set of relative weights, $w(1)$ to $w(50)$. In particular $w(i) = W(i) - B(i)$. Note that the relative weights, w, will sum to exactly 0%. *This set of relative weights, w, we can simply call the "active portfolio."*

The alternative approach would be to optimize a portfolio of "risk factors." Different marketable securities have different weightings to the different risk factors, so as such, targets for risk factors can generally be obtained by constructing a portfolio of securities. Under this framework a portfolio manager develops views regarding the various factors, and overweights or underweights them.

At PIMCO we favor the approach using risk factors, and relative portfolios and their implied views are expressed in terms of these. Some of the more important ones are: nominal duration, real duration, various key-rate durations (introduced in the previous section), corporate spread duration (sensitivity to changes in corporate bond spreads), convexity—all broken down by economic region. Given a view on each of these factors we can conceive a portfolio of security weights, positive and negative totaling 0%, that implements these views.

Given such weights, they can be applied to any benchmark. This is likely to result in all client portfolios, regardless of benchmark, having approximately the same alpha in any given day, month, quarter, or year. To use a simple example: if the portfolio manager expects interest rates to fall, he/she will structure all portfolios to have a longer duration than the benchmark, *regardless of what the benchmark is. Thus, all "active portfolios" look identical in terms of their deviations from their respective benchmark.*

This framework is not bulletproof. We must be quick to point out that it is difficult to underweight a security if the benchmark has a zero weighting in that security. If that is the case, underweighting would involve shorting a security, which might be prohibited by the client, and in any case would involve some risk of being squeezed (that is not being able to borrow the security so that a short position could be maintained) and transactions costs.

A client hires an active manager with a number of objectives in mind. First, the manager is to provide a client with exposure to the benchmark. Second, the manager is to add value, or "alpha," above and beyond the benchmark. Third, the manager is to manage risk relative to the benchmark. In the pursuit of alpha, the manager should not take an undue amount of risk.

Now the definition of risk is subjective, but one definition of appropriate risk that a manager is taking is known as tracking risk. Tracking risk is the standard deviation, either historical or expected, of the alpha. One can then elegantly define the active management as maximizing alpha subject to a constraint of keeping tracking error to less than some maximum targeted tracking error. If some clients desire a more aggressive active management implementation, or a less aggressive implementation, this would result in an increase or decrease in their tracking error budget, and a larger or smaller portion of the relative portfolio can be applied to their benchmark.

This exercise tells us two things.

First, that the optimal portfolio of overweights and underweights is largely independent of benchmark.

Second, that success of active management relative to a benchmark simply amounts to being able to identify opportunities that best generate risk-adjusted absolute return.

Since this may be a bit abstract, let us now turn to tools specific to the ILB market that add value to a portfolio. We will present the arsenal, if you will.

TECHNIQUES USED BY MANAGERS TO ADD VALUE

There are many similarities and some subtle differences between determining ILB value in an absolute sense as a proprietary trader might and determining value in the context of an ILB portfolio, as a portfolio manager would. The main difference, as discussed above, is that portfolio managers generally operate in the context of a benchmark and, therefore, value is added by altering the portfolio composition from that of the benchmark.

To the extent that which these deviations from benchmarks are prescient in terms of identifying characteristics that will subsequently be valued by the market, and are not excessively onerous in terms of execution costs, determine if the actively-managed portfolio efforts will be a success. We will go further into the process of structuring inflation-linked portfolios in later sections; however, in this section we discuss specific weapons in the portfolio manager's arsenal.

Real and Nominal Duration Management

Investors familiar with fixed income portfolio management know that one of the most fundamental measures of a fixed income portfolio is duration. The same is true for portfolios of inflation-linked bonds.

One of the ways inflation-linked bond portfolios can outperform their benchmarks is through active duration management. Since the price of an inflation-linked bond is driven by the interaction of real yields and real duration, portfolio managers can outperform their benchmarks by having a longer-than-benchmark real duration if they forecast that real yields are likely to fall and a shorter-than-benchmark duration if real yields are expected to rise. Their success will of course be a function of the accuracy of their forecasts, and the effectiveness of their implementation.

Various techniques can be used to forecast real-yield moves. Our favorite is macroeconomic fundamentals. Other techniques are charting, technical analysis, and perhaps even computer-driven quantitative black-box techniques. The top-down, macroeconomic-driven forecasting we rely on heavily starts with consideration of global concepts, such as global growth and global monetary conditions. It also includes considerations best assessed from a local perspective. Each country's ILB market will be influenced by that country's real GDP growth, productivity, inflation, and central bank policy, and the nuances of those measures in that country.

Forward Real Yields

Previously we suggested that the forecast of falling real yields calls for extending durations and vice versa for rising real yields. That is not precisely correct, however, because one must also incorporate the concept of forward real yields. In particular since forward real yields are typically higher than spot (current) real yields, it follows that if one forecasts that the real yield curve will remain unchanged, that is, neither rising or falling, one is generally advantaged by extending durations to be above benchmark.

To see this, consider the following example. Assume that 5-year real yields are 1.50% and 1-year real yields are 0.50%. You are contemplating extending your portfolio duration approximately 0.5 years by taking 10% of your portfolio out of 1-year ILBs and extending them into 5-year ILBs.

The decision-making process would have to incorporate forward real yields. Given the above parameters, the 1-year forward real yield on a then 4-year ILB would be almost 1.75%. (Extending the portfolio from 1 to 5 years would pick up about 1% in real yield. At the end of the 1-year horizon, a rise in yields of 0.25% to 1.75% would result in approximately 1% capital loss. The 1% in incremental yield picked up by extending equates to the 1% capital loss suffered due to the slight, 0.25%, rise in interest rates. This implies that the forward real yield is 1.75%.)

Consequently, if you forecast a yield rise, but less than 25 basis point rise, extending durations is called for. Even though you might have contemplated real yields rising, if you expect them to rise less than 25 basis points, you are actually forecasting horizon real yields "falling" from the level implied by the forward real yield.

This manager is, therefore, actually forecasting a fall in real yields (from their forward level) and, as a result, would outperform his benchmark by (a) extending duration, and (b) being correct in his real interest rate forecast. A subtlety in calculating forward real yields is that they depend on the inflation accrual realized over the term in consideration, so that one can accurately calculate the real rate at which forward purchases are financed. This would not only include correctly predicting future inflation but also correctly accounting for any lags in inflation indexation.

Curve Positioning

Though real yield duration management is the first tool in a bond manager's arsenal, curve positioning may be as important. Curve positioning describes how a manager structures a portfolio *of a given duration*. The three basic curve structures are bulletized, barbelled, and laddered.

Bulletized

A bulletized portfolio is an overweighting of intermediate ILBs relative to benchmark, and an underweighting of the shorter and longer ILBs. Bulletized portfolios are noteworthy in that, under normal circumstances, they provide the most yields and the most roll-down[4] among the three curve structures. They yield additional profits in a steepening real-yield curve environment. Bulletized portfolios, however, tend to underperform other curve structures if the real yield curve is flattening, volatility is increasing, and in certain other scenarios.

Barbelled

The opposite of a bulletized structure is a barbelled structure. A barbell, as its name implies, involves overweighting of short- and long-maturity sectors, and an underweighting of intermediate instruments. Barbell structures generally underperform the benchmark in a stable environment. In trader parlance, they exhibit "negative carry." They outperform when the real yield curve flattens.

Laddered

A third curve structure, which is something of a compromise between a bulletized and a barbelled curve structure, is a laddered portfolio structure. A laddered structure involves roughly equal exposure to each maturity sector. Many less active bond investors utilize laddered portfolios extensively, given their ease of construction and elegant aging dynamic. Consider a $500,000 laddered portfolio of bonds between 1 and 10 years. It could involve $50,000 of bonds of each

---

4. Roll-down is a fixed income concept involving capital gains that occur because of a bond aging in the presence of a stationary and positively-sloped yield curve.

maturity between 1 and 10 years. An easy way to create such a portfolio, for a patient investor, is to simply buy $50,000 of a 10-year bond each year. After 9 years, the first bond purchased will be a 1-year bond, the second a 2-year, and so on. Once a laddered portfolio is structured it is easy to maintain. Each year as the shortest maturity bond matures, the proceeds are simply reinvested in the longest maturity.

Benchmarks are similar to laddered portfolios in structure, though they are not exactly alike. Most benchmarks are capitalization weighted. Given that issuers (the US Treasury for example) issue more shorter-maturity bonds, benchmarks have additional exposure to shorter-maturity bonds as compared to a laddered portfolio. (For example, the 1-year sector would include both a 10-year bond issued 9 years ago, and a 5-year bond issued 4 years ago.)

Break-Even Inflation Trading

A common strategy employed by portfolio managers is break-even inflation trading. Such trades involve owning ILBs, and being short (or hedging) with nominal bonds. Such portfolio positioning makes sense when one foresees inflation expectations increasing, and doing the opposite when one foresees inflation expectations decreasing.

Recall that you can calculate the break-even inflation rate for a given maturity by finding the yield on a treasury of that given maturity, and subtracting the real yield of an ILB with that maturity. So for example if 10-year Treasuries yield 4.25% and 10-year TIPS yield 1.75% then the break-even inflation rate is 2.50%.

What that means is that if over the next 10-years inflation averages above 2.50%, the TIPS return, that is its real yield plus inflation accruals, will amount to more than the nominal bond's fixed yield of 4.25%. Of course, nuances involving the compounding of coupon income received and the trajectory of inflation rates means the simple arithmetic subtraction of real yields from nominal yields is only an approximation. Market participants still tend to prefer an approximation that is easy to calculate over a complex formula that needs a computer to calculate and is not easily comprehended. This is particularly true since market traders are focused more on changes in break-even inflation rates, or comparisons of break-even inflation rates, than they are in attributing a literal hold-to-maturity outcome to a given market relationship.

If break-even inflation rates imbedded in the ILB and associated nominal markets are low, then a trader may put on a break-even inflation trade. They would buy ILBs and sell nominals. If subsequently their assessments were right and validated by the market, their position would profit, as ILB yields performed well relative to nominal yields.

Though accurately forecasting inflation is an important aspect of such success, what is as important, particularly over shorter horizons, is forecasting what market perceptions of long-term inflation might do. As Keynes describes in his beauty contest example, one is not forecasting which contestant is most attractive; one needs to forecast which contestant will be chosen by the other judges to be most attractive. (And so on, *ad infinitum*.)[5]

The following section drills down into nuances involving the concept of break-even inflation.

Relative Volatilities and Real Yield Beta

The Basic Inflation-Linked Valuation Equation

Few notions in the inflation-linked market have contributed so much to confusion and misvaluation as the notion of naïve break-even inflation. First things first: how does the risk of inflation-linked bonds stack up against the risk of nominal bonds? With so many moving parts there is no single answer to this question, but the most common way to approach the ultimate answer is to start by looking at the fixed-rate nominal bonds in the same currency, with the same issuer credit risk, and the same maturity as the inflation-linked bond we are considering. By subtracting the real yield of our chosen inflation-linked bond from the nominal yield of the nominal bond with the above characteristics we get a very close proxy for break-even inflation.[6]

Time Horizon   Now, for investors with time horizons exactly equal to the bonds' maturity, this number provides a useful first gauge of value between nominal and inflation-linked bonds when compared to the investor's own expectation of average inflation over the chosen time period. In practice, most investors evaluate return and risk of their portfolios on a much more frequent basis, effectively shortening their time horizons. One example of such short horizon is an investment manager whose performance is evaluated by the client on an annual, semi-annual, or even a quarterly basis.[7] Over such short time horizons, market volatility plays the key role in the relative value consideration.

Capital Market Line and Yield Curves   The most popular way of looking at risk and reward was developed by Harry Markowitz who won a Nobel Prize in 1990 for his pioneering work. He suggested that if we plot risk on the horizontal axis of a chart and expected return on the vertical axis, we get an upward sloping line

---

5. J.M. Keynes, 1936, General Theory of Employment Interest and Money, 1st Ed., 156 Macmillan, London.
6. Some observers go further and use the so-called Fisher formula to derive break-even inflation. Fisher break-even inflation = (1+nominal yield)/(1+real yield). While the Fisher break-even formula lends the number an aura of scientific respectability, at current low single-digit real yields and inflation rates, it makes little material difference.
7. While most investment management mandates have considerably longer time spans, end investors, or sponsors, tend to have considerable uncertainty about whether the manager is doing a good job. One way to reduce this uncertainty that many sponsors employ is to increase the frequency of monitoring portfolio performance. Whether more frequent monitoring generates higher information content about the quality of investment management is debatable, but that debate is beyond the scope of this chapter.

with portfolios bearing higher expected risk generating higher expected return, as shown in Exhibit 3–2.

In fixed income, one of the most popular graphical representations is the yield curve, where maturity is plotted along the horizontal axis and yield along the vertical axis, as shown in Exhibit 3–3. It is so popular, in fact, that most practitioners look at it as the substitute for the capital market line, making habitual mental adjustments for the fact that maturity and yield are nonlinear approximations of risk and return respectively. This mental shortcut works fine, and most bond portfolio managers and traders have developed lightning-quick intuition for dealing with this imperfect approximation.

Relative Volatilities   Where the intuition fails is when this framework is used for comparing two debt instruments with different relationships between risk and

E X H I B I T   3–2

Capital Market Line

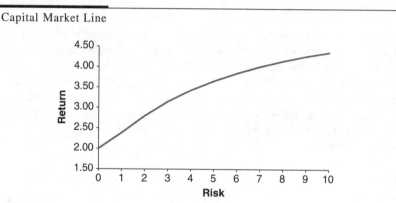

E X H I B I T   3–3

Yield Curve

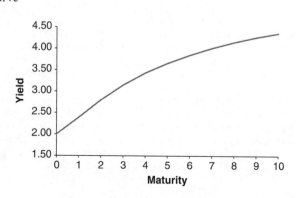

maturity. There is significant empirical evidence, supported by solid economic logic, that real yields of inflation-linked securities are less volatile than the nominal yields of conventional bonds. The logic rests on the basic equation made famous by Irving Fisher,[8] that a nominal interest rate can be decomposed into the real rate and expected inflation. In the typical economic environment, higher expected economic growth leads to increases in both the expected inflation rate and real interest rate. The latter is driven by higher demand for capital from corporations (itself the function of higher expected returns on capital investment) as well as the expectations of the central bank increasing short-term interest rates in response to higher inflation.[9] This positive correlation between real rates and expected inflation arithmetically leads to higher volatility of nominal vis-à-vis real rates.

Over the modern era of inflation-linked bonds (i.e., since 1997), real yields have been only about 60% as volatile as nominal yields. This number is a key element in what is referred to as real yield beta. Real yield beta quantifies changes in real yield for a given change in the nominal yield of the same maturity. Mathematically, this is a product of the correlation between changes in the real and nominal yields with the ratio of their volatilities. Under the assumption that real and nominal yields are perfectly correlated, beta reduces to the simple ratio of volatilities. Betas tend to be higher when changes in nominal rates are driven by changes in real-rate expectations, and lower when they are driven by changes in inflation expectations. Theoretically, under our typical economic scenario, this should result in a downward-sloping term structure of betas, with shorter maturity linkers having higher betas than longer maturity linkers. For any maturity point, the beta is neither stable nor easy to estimate looking forward, but under most economic environments, it is less than one.

Real-Yield Beta Adjustments   This basic observation leads to the demise of break-even inflation as a meaningful measure of value when comparing nominal and inflation-linked bonds. Instead of a clear and unambiguous picture presented by the naïve break-even inflation, we end up having to deal with the additional complexity of both adjustments to scale risk.

---

8. One of the first neoclassical economists, Irving Fisher, also introduced the curve showing the inverse relationship between inflation and unemployment long before it was named the Phillips curve following Alban Phillips' 1958 paper. Unfortunately, he is best known not for his contribution to theoretical economics, but for pronouncing that "Stock prices have reached what looks like a permanently high plateau" in 1929.
9. The two "atypical" economic environments are stagflation and what came to be known as "goldilocks economy." Under stagflation, higher and more volatile inflation decreases expected growth by lowering capital investment (due to greater uncertainty about expected returns) and depressing consumer spending (due to greater uncertainty about the saving rate required to secure future consumption). Under "goldilocks," higher expected growth is driven by increases in productivity that drive down the costs of goods and services, thus lowering expected inflation.

One way to adjust for this is by comparing the real yield of an inflation-linked bond to the nominal yield of a bond with shorter maturity (and comparable risk). A more yield-curve-neutral approach is to compare the real yield of ILB to the total yield of the package comprised of 60% (or whatever the estimated beta may be) nominal bond with the same maturity and 40% money-market deposit. Whatever the method chosen, in the environment of positively-sloped yield curves, naïve break-even inflation would tend to overstate the true future inflation rates necessary to equate risk-adjusted returns of nominal and inflation-linked portfolios.

The optical illusion of naïve break-even inflation tends to create opportunities for investment managers to improve risk-adjusted portfolio returns before even having to predict macroeconomic shifts in real growth and inflation landscape across the global economies.

However, this is not all. Previous paragraphs sailed very quickly over the complex subject of estimating real-yield beta. Exhibit 3–4 presents empirical evidence by plotting effective 3-month betas obtained by regressing daily changes in real yields on changes in nominal yields along the vertical axis, and absolute levels of nominal yields along the horizontal axis. The data was collected between November 2000 and November 2003 using the real yields of 3⅝% TIPS maturing in 2008 and the nominal yields of 5½% Treasury also maturing in January 2008.

Convexity Implication: Tendency for Betas to Increase as Nominal Yields Decrease

In addition to the previously-made observation that betas are lower than 1, there is a clear tendency for betas to increase as the level of rates decreases and to go

E X H I B I T   3–4

TIPS 2008 3m yield beta vs. T 2008

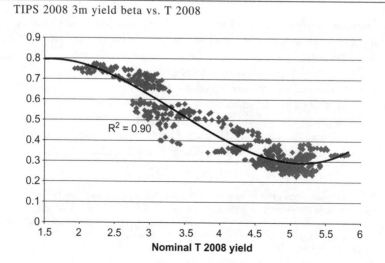

in the opposite direction as the rates go up.[10] Apart from providing a framework for making forward-looking beta estimates, this relationship reveals another hidden pocket of value—inflation-linked bonds tend to exhibit positive convexity as compared to nominal bonds.

One way of looking at convexity is by tracing what happens to the inflation-linked bond portfolio when rates change. As rates decrease, the sensitivity of real rates to nominal rate changes increases as well; so inflation-linked portfolios gain additional duration. This can be thought of as the portfolio acquiring additional bond exposure just when it is profitable—when the yields are falling. Likewise, with rising yields, the portfolio is shedding bond exposure, thus reducing the losses from rising yields. This is clearly a very valuable characteristic—effectively investors are given both call and put options on interest rates.

Valuing these options in practice is a rather technical math- and data-intensive exercise that relies on Monte Carlo techniques. In September 2004, for US TIPS maturing in 2029, we estimate this effective convexity was worth 0.30% more in yield, compared to the 2029 nominal Treasury issue. What this means is that even investors looking at risk-adjusted break-even inflation still overestimated true break-even inflation by 30 basis points, if they failed to take into consideration the value of inflation-linked bonds' effective convexity.

Convexity value just discussed depends on a number of different variables, including maturity of the bonds under consideration, yield curve shape, and the market price of traded options on interest rates. It is also dependent on the market's perception of macroeconomic conditions going forward. So the systems and experience requirement for trading it can be quite onerous. Investors with the necessary resources are able to pick up yet a few more pennies on the way, still before getting to the heart of global macroeconomic forces that affect interest rates and inflation rates.

Inflation Capture

Apart from the real-rate beta, and the corresponding risk parameters of nominal and real durations in investment portfolios, one other metric is unique to inflation-linked bond portfolios. At PIMCO it is known as "inflation capture." While the portfolio exposures to real and nominal rates manifest themselves via changes in value that can be roughly approximated by multiplying the relevant duration measure by the change in rate, inflation capture stems from the very transmission mechanism that "protects" inflation-linked bonds against inflation. Most inflation-linked bonds follow the capital-indexation model, meaning that the face value of the bonds is adjusted based on the changes in the underlying price index.

---

10. Unlike with the assessment that betas should generally lie between 0 and 1, there is no univer-
    sally-applicable theory explaining the downward slope in the beta curve vs. the level of nom-
    inal rates. Since it appears to mostly rely on investor expectations of the central bank policy
    function, there is no guarantee that the relationship will not change as the views driving the
    formation of central bank policies evolve.

We define inflation capture as the percentage of the portfolio that is indexed to the respective inflation index.

Historically, there has been a trade-off between inflation capture, real-rate duration, and real-curve position in portfolios: higher-duration exposure to longer-maturity inflation-linked bonds led to reduced inflation capture in portfolios with overall duration constraint. With the inflation derivatives markets gaining in liquidity and depth, such trade-offs are gradually disappearing, paving the way to more efficient portfolios.

Seasonality

Most of the inflation-linked bond universe is linked to unrevised not-seasonally adjusted price indices.[11] In practice, this results in monthly index changes that are very different from the smooth annual changes divided by twelve. For managers able to forecast and correctly measure the impact of volatile monthly inflation numbers and seasonal effects, appropriate inflation capture in the portfolio can generate additional alpha. Apart from seasonal variations, real-world inflation numbers are exposed to shocks that affect the price level permanently as one-off price level changes, or lead to mean-reversion over some time horizon.

One-Off Price Shocks and Mean Reversion

Examples of one-off price level changes that can be considered permanent for most investment time horizons are changes in value-added taxes or changes in underlying inflation index calculation.[12] Furthermore, given the size and importance of the energy sector, price spikes in this sector can often partially be accommodated with a drop in real monetary policy.

A good real-life example of mean-reverting changes can be found in Sweden: a large share of the country's electricity need is served by hydropower. After a drought in 2002, the water level in the main reservoir decreased, causing the electricity prices to spike sharply. The situation was reversed in 2003, with very small net effect on cumulative inflation, but certainly a short-term effect on inflation accruals.

---

11. Non-seasonal inflation series are utilized presumably for two reasons. First, unlike seasonally adjusted inflation, NSA inflation is not normally revised, which is very important. Second, being a more raw data item, it is conceptually less subject to any bias, or official interpretations.

12. Index changes are a controversial topic, with views that range from dismissing them as immaterial, to treating changes that lead to lower reported inflation as breaches of contract. Of the major ILB markets, UK Gilts are the only ones where there is an actual written contract in the form of new issue prospectus, which used to offer to buy the bonds back if there was "a fundamental change in the Index which would be materially detrimental to the interest of the stockholders." The language was changed with the 2002 issue of the 2035 linker. Now if the index "continues the function of measuring changes in the level of UK retail prices" any change "shall be conclusive and binding on all stockholders."

Somewhere in the middle is an oil patch inflationary shock. While it is reasonable to expect that over medium-to-long time horizons the capital investment cycle in the oil industry would lead to some mean-reversion in prices, neither speed nor magnitude of this mean reversion are obvious.[13]

One way of dealing with temporary price level shifts is to look at relative value via forward real yields, calculated as far forward as known monthly inflation numbers allow or even beyond, using forecasted monthly inflation. Once the forward real curve is constructed, unencumbered by the distortions caused by temporary shocks, it can be evaluated in the context of cyclical and secular forces affecting real yields and inflation.

Global Sector Rotation

One effect of increased integration among the global financial markets manifests itself via the smaller role that geographic segmentation plays in defining relative valuations. Still, certain sectors of the inflation-linked universe do provide tangible risk-reduction or tax benefits to selected investors. Three examples stand out.

UK Linkers

Long-dated UK linkers have for a long time provided almost the perfect hedge for UK pension plans whose liabilities to retirees are typically indexed to inflation.

Unlike other major markets, UK private investors are not taxed on inflation accretion. This has historically meant that the shortest maturity UK linkers have traded expensively to the rest of the market. Private investors flock into them, and bid their price up and their yield down, given that the short-dated UK ILBs are a very tax-efficient equivalent to cash deposits for UK based taxable investors.[14]

French Livret A

Interest paid on a very popular tax-free savings account in France is by law partially linked to French domestic inflation, making short-maturity bonds linked to French inflation a very good hedge for banks offering such accounts.

Managers whose accounts do not benefit from these effects to the same degree should pay close attention to the valuations of the affected market segments. What may seem like an attractive real yield on a riskless asset to one investor is a market dislocation to another.

---

13. In economic terms, mean-reversion can be expected where long-run elasticity of supply and/or demand is greater than near-term elasticity. However, the effects of changing elasticity are often overshadowed by the secular shifts in the supply/demand balance.
14. The authors are not authorized to provide tax advice. Please consult your tax attorney for such advice.

Eurozone

Euro-denominated inflation-linked markets provide an additional layer of complexity that can spell opportunity to managers with the right tools and skills. Unlike other homogenous currency zones, the Euro market offers several different inflation indices. Two indices dominate, however: European Monetary Union (EMU), CPI excluding tobacco (known as HICP—Harmonized Index of Consumer Prices), and the already mentioned French CPI ex-tobacco.[15]

Core and Periphery Eurozone

At the advent of the EMU it was common to divide its member countries into "core," or countries with low and stable pre-EMU inflation (the group that included France), and "peripheral," countries that experienced higher and more volatile inflation rates. Depending on how one defines the latter group, around one-third of the HICP index is based on inflation rates in the peripheral countries. Three main factors contributed (and to some extent continue to contribute) to the higher inflation rates in the peripheral countries after the start of the EMU:

> Inflation expectations tend to be sticky, with firms deciding on pricing policy often using last year's inflation as a guide.

> With high inflation expectations based on experience, generally lower EMU interest rates resulted in very loose local monetary conditions. Expectations-based low or even negative real rates stimulated growth in the peripheral economies that provided upward impetus to the actual realized inflation.

> Peripheral countries entered the Monetary Union at exchange rates that were significantly undervalued on the purchasing power basis. With free trade in product markets, price convergence pulled price levels in peripheral countries up, closer to the EMU average.

While some of these effects have diminished over the years, the impact on the pricing of long-dated bonds linked to HICP and French CPI is far from over. Potential entry of new European Union member states into the Monetary Union will likely provide further dislocations and opportunities. By analyzing the factors influencing future inflation paths for the respective price indices, managers can improve portfolio performance with relative value trades on bonds linked to these indices.

Currency Management

When considering inflation-linked bonds denominated in foreign currencies, the question of whether to hedge or to tactically add value through currency management needs to be considered. Generally, given the currency position's risk

---

15. The ex-tobacco feature is due to the French statue prohibiting any indexation to tobacco prices.

dominating all other risk factors, hedging currency exposure to be 100% identical to benchmark currency exposure is a good place to start.

If the manager has the skills to add value by taking currency positions, active positions should be considered independently of the bond holdings based on the currency's risk and expected return contributions. This approach, dividing the bond and currency decisions into two distinct decisions, is not historically how bonds, or ILBs, have always been managed. However given the evolution, and increased efficiency, of global currency, bond, and collateral markets, there is no longer a need or advantage to combining the two decisions.

Currency hedges have another effect on the inflation-linked portfolio—by effectively translating foreign nominal short-term interest rates into domestic rates, some of the foreign inflation indexation is transformed into domestic inflation.[16] In some instances, particularly for small open economies,[17] total-return volatility from investment in local inflation-linked bonds may be minimized with less than 100% currency hedge.

This is due to the linkage between the value of the country's currency and the cost of imported goods—a depreciating currency would lead to higher domestic inflation, which would in turn translate into higher total return for inflation-linked bonds.

Corporate Inflation-Linked Bonds

Most fixed income portfolios, notably those benchmarked against aggregate indices, have to deal with the issue of credit risk. While government issuers dominate inflation-linked bond markets, some corporate issues have been marketed over the years as well. For managers with the capacity to analyze and manage credit risk, this can be an added source of alpha in the portfolios. There are three basic ways to create inflation-linked credit exposure in portfolios:

First, you can buy inflation-linked bonds issued by corporations. This is usually the least attractive option. Most companies are not natural payers[18] of inflation. They issue inflation-linked bonds merely to tap a new investor segment in order to lower their cost of funds vis-à-vis their nominal debt. In calculating their cost of funds the companies also need to take into account the cost of the inflation swap hedge. Perhaps the most important argument is that the very narrow universe of corporate ILB issuers strips away most benefits of diversification and active credit-risk management.

The next two strategies require greater investment by the manager in derivatives infrastructure, the cost that for all but the smallest of managers is dwarfed

---

16. This statement relies on the assumption that short-term nominal interest rates are correlated to inflation over long periods. The holding horizon over which this correlation becomes visible through short-term noise is neither constant nor known in advance.

17. Iceland is probably the only country with an inflation-linked bond market where this effect is material at present.

18. "Payers" is a term used to describe an entity that receives inflation-linked revenues from its business and, therefore, is well positioned to pay inflation-linked coupons on its debt.

by the portfolio management efficiencies they create. The choice between the two depends on the relative liquidity and supply-demand imbalances in the credit and inflation derivatives markets:

Choice 1:   Buy government inflation-linked bonds and overlay credit-default swaps (selling credit protection).

Choice 2:   Buy nominal corporate bonds and overlay inflation swaps (receiving inflation vs. paying fixed).

Recently, Choice 1 has been more efficient; though the technicalities of the credit-default swap markets are highly intricate.

Out-of-Benchmark Opportunities

Most investors can benefit by allowing their managers substantial discretion in exploiting opportunities throughout the fixed income market within an ILB mandate. Such positions would be described as out-of-benchmark. There are a number of reasons this might make sense. Doing so allows a client to have the full discretion-active management alpha applied to 100% of their fixed income allocation, rather than just their CorePlus allocation. Furthermore if they were to limit each mandate to its own sector there would be no tactical relative-value evaluation being performed to exploit cross-sector disparities in return outlooks. They could, of course, perform such cross-sector evaluations themselves. However, unless they were on the ground and focusing on such efforts, they might be better off delegating such efforts to a manager, or managers.

Case for Full-Discretion Graphic

Meanwhile, by allowing the manager the freedom to access the full range of fixed income tools, the portfolio will achieve a greater "efficiency." Let us first look at the example of a view which could conceivably be taken in underlying index-linked, but can be more efficiently reflected using another part of the fixed income universe. Consider the situation where the manager wishes to reflect a positive view on the likely path of short-term interest rates—in his view the market has become overly bearish on the future level of short-term interest rates. In a world in which trades are permitted only via underlying index-linked bonds, the portfolio manager would take an overweight allocation to short-dated index-linked bonds. These typically perform well when short-rate expectations fall. However, falling real rates in such a situation may be associated with falling inflation. Thus, investing in short-term linkers at such a time would negatively impact the inflation capture (as discussed earlier). Rather, the manager with a full array of fixed income instruments at his/her disposal could reflect this view directly via short-dated nominal bonds or, indeed, via the futures market by purchasing futures contracts which pay out short-term interest rates based on the current market level.

Whilst this example merely shows how investment views can be structured more efficiently using a broader range of investment views, it does not highlight the ability to access a much wider set of investment views than is possible by merely using benchmark assets. Let us take a second example relating to the shape of the fixed-rate curve. Given discretion to transact in futures (where contracts exist at 5-, 10-, and 30-year maturities) or interest rate swaps (where all maturities are available), views on the likely shape of the yield curve become easy to implement. In the case of an expected yield curve steepening, the portfolio manager could purchase 5-year futures contracts (or receive short-dated fixed rate via the interest rate swap market) and sell against it the 30-year futures contract (or pay long-dated fixed rates via the interest rate swap market). In no way is the intention to replace investment views on the underlying benchmark assets class (index-linked), but rather to augment these views to create a more efficient portfolio.

There are some very large, and very sophisticated, institutions that do appropriately discourage out-of-benchmark positions. They segment their investment process down into dozens, or in some cases many dozens, of fine cells. (Given the size of such institutions each cell may still involve hundreds of millions in assets.) Within fixed income they may have a dozen different sectors (Global Governments, US Mortgages, ILBs, Currency, High Yield, etc.) and sometimes two or more managers within each strategy, as well as an in-house team.

Such investors can successfully discourage out-of-benchmark position taking by their outside managers, since they allocate among such segments ahead of time with a top-down internal process in mind. Furthermore, given their size, level of sophistication, and full-time focus on tactical allocations within their home office, they can and do exploit sector opportunities by shifting allocations among managers, or by altering their substantial in-house managed portfolios.

REMAINING QUESTIONS
How Big an Allocation?

In our view, sovereign ILBs are the ultimate risk-free asset. Even sovereign nominal treasuries incorporate inflation risk that is absent from ILBs. Thus, ILBs should be the asset of choice to the extent that an institution's (or individual's) future liabilities can be defeased by investing in them. Given the relatively recent introduction of ILBs and the prior existence of allocations to nominal bonds and equities—we demonstrate in Exhibit 3–5 using a simple mean-variance optimization that introducing global ILBs to an existing mix of global equities and global nominal bonds results in a significant improvement in the efficient frontier. The assumptions used below are that a "Global Portfolio' consists of 50% allocation to the US, 25% to the EMU and 25% to the UK. Historic data are used for variance and correlations, while future return assumptions are simply a hypothetical 6% for equities, 4% for nominal bonds, and 4.4% for ILBs. Adding ILBs to a portfolio under these hypothetical conditions might expand the efficient frontier, especially for investors with lower levels of risk tolerance.

EXHIBIT   3–5

Global Asset Allocation

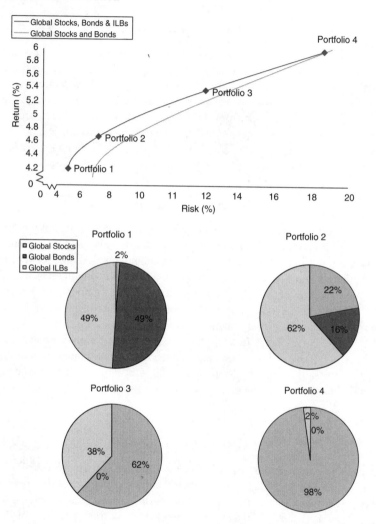

Active vs. Passive

Once the decision to make a strategic allocation is made, the investor is faced with the choice of using a passive strategy or an active one. We do not wish to belabor this point too much except to point out the obvious fact that skilled active managers more than earn the marginally higher fees they charge over passive managers. The popular financial press often cites studies on the average equity manager and whether they outperform a passive manager net of fees. The keyword in these studies is "average." While the average ones may not be worth it, it is worth the investor's time (and most importantly money) to seek out the above-average portfolio managers who consistently outperform the benchmark.

Internal vs. External

This is a key question facing investors deciding to make a strategic allocation to ILBs and does not have a clear answer. Investors with significant fixed income expertise and a successful track record of managing non-ILB portfolios should certainly consider in-house management. It is likely that such an investor would profit in their ILB portfolios from the successful prediction of macroeconomic trends. However, without a team of dedicated ILB specialists, it is unlikely that even an institution such as this could successfully exploit the inefficiencies and idiosyncrasies that still exist in the ILB market.

Overlay Strategies

Some institutional investors choose to invest in ILBs on an essentially unfunded basis utilizing what is known as an "overlay strategy." This could be implemented by maintaining a portfolio of ILBs all of which are purchased on a forward basis, and continuously rolled to a future date without ever allowing them to settle. The recent development of the inflation swap market allows an alternative implementation via maintaining a portfolio of inflation swaps. The overlay portfolio can be managed by boutique overlay managers who specialize in the margin and collateral management inherent in such a levered strategy, but may or may not be specialists in inflation-linked bonds. Given the risks incorporated in an unfunded strategy such as this, and the subtleties of the ILB market, we recommend that managers chosen to implement such strategies should have substantial expertise in *both* collateral and ILB management.

CONCLUSION/RECAP

This chapter is intended to give the reader an overview of the process of actively managing portfolios of ILB's—both from the view of the investor (strategic vs. tactical, benchmark selection) as well as the portfolio manager—tools used to add value—both generic to the fixed income markets as well as specific to ILBs. We have focused on our approach to investment management—based on dominant secular and cyclical macroeconomic themes and implemented via measured deviations from the benchmark's risk factors in a way that is essentially independent of the benchmark used. We have then given some specific examples of tools in an ILB manager's arsenal that differ from those of a core bond manager. Finally, we concluded with some questions a fiduciary thinking of implementing an allocation to ILBs might have. With this we hope to have provided the reader with a starting point for evaluating a decision to invest in ILBs, as well as a better understanding of the portfolio management process once this decision is made.

CHAPTER 4

EXCHANGE-TRADED INFLATION FUTURES

Sayee Srinivasan and Richard Co
Chicago Mercantile Exchange

INTRODUCTION

Over the past four decades, economists have been urging regulatory authorities and the derivatives exchanges to launch inflation futures contracts. An early paper titled "A CPI futures Market" was published by Michael C. Lovell and Robert C. Vogel in 1973 in the Journal of Political Economy.[1] Since then various arguments have been proposed in favor of central banks making active markets in such contracts.[2] Though these concepts might be theoretically sound, the feasibility of such contracts depends on more mundane issues like the presence of an underlying cash or derivatives market where market makers can hedge their futures positions.

Fast-forward to the late 1990s, and it appears as if conditions supportive of such contracts were finally being created. The growth of the inflation-linked asset class has led to multiple efforts to launch exchange-traded derivatives tracking some measure of inflation. The world of futures is littered with failed contracts, but the exchanges continue to innovate.

In this chapter, we describe the evolution of the general concept of inflation futures contracts. We attempt to analyze market structure issues that led to the demise of past efforts, and hypothesize how ongoing changes in underlying markets hold the promise for the eventual success of this concept. We will describe current products, focusing on the US CPI futures and potential European HICP futures. We will explain the intricacies of the current contract designs, their uses, and survey alternate pricing models.

BRIEF HISTORY

The concept of futures on economic indicators is not new. It dates back to at least the mid-1980s, with the Coffee, Sugar, and Cocoa Exchange's failed attempt to

---

1. Lovell, Michael C & Vogel, Robert C, "A CPI futures Market," 1973, Journal of Political Economy, University of Chicago Press, vol. 81(4), pages 1009–12.
2. See Abraham Lioui and Patrice Poncet, "Revealing Inflation Expectations: Let the Markets do it," 2002, Bar Ilan University and ESSEC Working Paper. A related paper is by Tyler Cowen, "Should central banks target CPI futures? (consumer price index)," August 01, 1997, Journal of Money, Credit & Banking.

establish futures based on the CPI-W (based on wage earners and clerical workers). More recently, in the late 1990s, the Chicago Board of Trade listed Inflation-Indexed Treasury Note futures. While the contract itself was not based directly on the inflation numbers, trades could be constructed to isolate certain inflation-related concepts. For example, when trading the TIPS futures against, for example, cash nominal Treasury notes or Treasury note futures, one can isolate the expected inflation component embedded in the TIPS. Similarly, when trading the TIPS futures against underlying cash TIPS notes, one can isolate the short-term inflation accretion component. Therefore, the contract very well could have served as a surrogate for CPI futures.

The effort also failed. Looking back at these attempts, we believe that they were too far ahead of their times. Fast-forward to 2003, and there seemed to be abundant indications that the factors contributing to the demise of these previous efforts had been mitigated, and that the current environment would be more favorable than ever for exchange-traded inflation-derivative products. Accordingly, the Chicago Mercantile Exchange (CME) launched a CPI futures contract in February 2004.

CPI Futures at the Coffee, Sugar, and Cocoa Exchange

The Coffee, Sugar, and Cocoa Exchange (CSCE) attempted launching futures on economic indicators in the mid-1980s. While CSCE contemplated futures on four categories of economic indicators, namely the consumer price index (CPI-W series, based on wage earners and clerical workers), housing starts, automobile sales and earnings, only the CPI futures contract was actually listed for trading in 1985. The product traded 10,102 contracts over a 2-year period. With no trading and open interest after April 1987, the contracts were later delisted.

We can attribute the demise of the product to the fact that though there was nothing wrong with the basic concept, the marketplace was not yet ready for it. The product traded as a stand-alone instrument, a straight bet on (short-term) inflation. While inflation is a key economic statistic for the financial markets, in the absence of inflation-indexed instruments, it was unclear how the futures contract could be utilized within the context of a broader financial strategy.

Though memories of the high inflation rates in the 1970s would have been relatively fresh in investors' minds, seeking protection against this risk does not seem to have been very high in the list of investment objectives. Thus the contract was never able to attract sufficient trading interest and failed to appeal to traders once the novelty effect wore off.

A more critical issue that might have sealed the fate of the CSCE contract was the lack of a clear pricing relationship. Given the absence of correlated financial instruments at that time, it was unclear how a trader might price the contract. The inflation-linked security market had yet to emerge.[3] Given the absence of a complementary cash market that would have helped sustain this contract on

---

3. The British government started issuing inflation-linked Gilts in 1981. The inflation-linked market worldwide was still in its infancy in 1985. The comparable market in the US would not make its debut till 1997 when the US Department of Treasury issued its first inflation-linked security.

a longer-term basis, it had a tough time competing with more traditional—and a lot more liquid—inflation plays involving crude oil, precious metals and interest rate contracts.

Inflation-Indexed Treasury Note Futures at CBOT

The Chicago Board of Trade listed for trading futures on the Inflation-Indexed Treasury Notes in June, 1997. Unlike conventional bonds that have fixed nominal coupon rates, coupon payments of inflation-indexed bonds are fixed in real terms at the time of issuance. The par value is adjusted for inflation, as measured by changes in the benchmark price index, on coupon dates and at the maturity. Coupon payments are calculated by applying the coupon interest rate to the inflation-adjusted principal. Though the nominal value of the coupon payments will fluctuate with inflation, investors are assured that the purchasing power of their interest and principal is protected from inflation, although with a slight delay.

As we explained earlier, while the product itself was not based directly on inflation, i.e., on the CPI number, it was a *de facto* inflation-futures contract because of its pricing relationship with the cash market. The product managed to trade only 22 contracts in total, all in 1997, and was also eventually delisted. In contrast to the CPI futures at CSCE a decade ago, a different set of factors appeared to have contributed to the demise of this contract.

The timing of the product was perhaps slightly too early. The US Department of Treasury had auctioned its first ever Inflation-Indexed Treasury Note (TIPS) in January of the same year. At the time of the launch of the futures contract, there was only one issue of the 10-Year TIPS outstanding.[4] This aspect had numerous consequences adversely impacting the near-term prospects for this contract.

First, given the short history of the TIPS program, the distribution of the security was concentrated in relatively few hands. This restricted distribution of the cash security meant a very limited audience for the futures contract. Very few investors—of both institutional and individual varieties—had started following this then brand-new asset class.

Second, with so few interested parties, the futures contract was in direct competition with the cash TIPS instrument for liquidity. It lost the battle.

Moreover, broad groups of market participants tend to be reluctant to support products that lack sufficiently long track records. With the TIPS launch taking place just 6 months before the launch of the futures contract, there was hardly any price history. Traders in this market were still learning about the properties of TIPS, and were not ready to commit much effort to support the new futures contract.

US CPI FUTURES

Futures contracts are by their nature short term instruments. On the other hand, from a (long-term) investor's perspective, there is limited interest to concentrate

---

4. For a physically-settled contract with just one series of the underlying bond having been issued, figuring out the cheapest-to-deliver bond was trivial.

on the short-term inflation. At first pass, these two factors appear to be incompatible. However, futures may be able to serve as a common denominator for other instruments. From a market-evolution perspective, the existence of a CPI futures instrument designed to suit different applications will likely help in the development of the broader market for inflation-index instruments.

One of the main obstacles to earlier attempts at inflation-related futures had been the dearth of natural users for both sides of the contract. In the absence of end-user participation, these attempts were destined to fail, but by 2003–2004, the landscape seemed to have changed significantly:

the notion of inflation-linked (IL) financial instruments had gained broad acceptance;

participation in the cash TIPS market had grown in both breadth and depth;

OTC (over-the-counter) IL derivatives had emerged (first in Europe, and later in the US);

in a TIPS survey published[5] by the US Bond Market Association, 72% of the respondents said they would be interested in trading a US CPI-based futures contract;

active derivative markets have developed based on nonfinancial underlying quantities such as electricity, weather, catastrophes; market participants are more comfortable pricing and trading derivatives on economic indicators.

As there are no cash products indexed solely to inflation, the default underlying market for this contract is the TIPS market. These bonds have gained considerable traction these past few years, and have now become a very important asset class. Their main attraction is the protection afforded from inflation; but this protection is not perfect—indexation lag and taxation of inflation accruals reduce their effectiveness as hedging devices for inflation-linked derivatives. A liquid inflation-futures product could provide a cleaner hedge.

As such, the Chicago Mercantile Exchange (CME) concluded that, given the presence of a broader class of natural users for the contract, the obstacles that had plagued earlier attempts had been breached. And a new CPI futures contract was listed for trading on CME's Globex® electronic trading platform on February 9, 2004.

Contract Design

When developing the CPI futures, a conscious effort was made to retain a contract design that would appeal to a broad class of market participants. A summary of the contract specifications is in Appendix 1.

---

5. "Most Investors Want More TIPS Across the Maturity Spectrum with Demand Especially Strong for Longer-Dated Inflation-Indexed Treasury Securities," TIPS Survey, Bond Market Association, December 2003.

Successful futures contracts tend to be very simple instruments. There are only a couple of reasonable designs for such a contract based on the CPI numbers. One possibility is to fashion the contract like stock-index futures, i.e., based on a fixed dollar value per CPI index point. The other design is to fix the value of the contract based on the percentage accretion of the consumer price index, i.e., a fixed dollar value per percentage point of inflation over a predefined period of time. In the case of the US CPI futures, the current design calls for an accretion period of three months. Such a design will lead to a structure similar to that of a short-term interest rate contract, for example Eurodollar futures.

A closer look at the two candidate designs will lead to a conclusion that they are really not very different. Once the CPI number for the base period is determined, the latter design is effectively the same as the former—the dollar value per index point is fixed. Therefore, one can easily translate from the latter to the former. In other words, there is a one-to-one correspondence between the two designs.[6]

In addition to retaining simplicity and general applicability, the exchange also attempted to avoid direct competition with TIPS. The goal has been to maintain a complementary relationship with TIPS and the nascent inflation swap in the US. In some sense, the approach mirrored the CME Eurodollar futures contract, where the growth of Eurodollar futures coincided with the emergence of the interest rate swap market in the United States.

Basic Design

Analogous to the Eurodollar futures contract, the design of CPI futures is a cash-settled futures contract, with the usual IMM-style[7] quoting convention of 100 minus the contracted annualized rate of inflation over a 3-month period.[8] Each 0.01 IMM point is worth $25.[9] So the contract is shortterm in nature, designed to attract speculative trades on the inflation number as well as hedging interests from the active cash TIPS market as well as the growing US inflation swaps market.

Trading Hours and Venue

CPI futures are listed for trading on CME Globex® on Sundays from 5:30 p.m. to 2:00 p.m. the following day; on Mondays through Thursdays from 5:00 p.m. to 2:00 p.m. the following day (all times refer to local Chicago times).

---

6. In an example below, we illustrate the use of the latter design to hedge inflation accretion risk in TIPS. By trading a calendar spread of a contract of the former design, one can isolate the inflation accretion over a specified future period.

7. IMM stands for the International Money Market, an old division within CME.

8. If your view is that inflation will be higher than market consensus as implied by the CPI contract, you will sell the contract and vice versa.

9. The implied $25 value for each 0.01 Index point is identical to that of the Eurodollar futures. Thus, one may interpret the contract as futures on a 3-month instrument with a notional value of $1,000,000.

Final Settlement Procedure

On expiration, settlement of the CPI futures contract is effected by cash settlement against the final settlement price of 100 minus the annualized inflation in the latest three months[10] implied by the Consumer Price Index–US city average for all urban consumers, all items, not-seasonally adjusted series (CPI-U). For example, the Reference CPI Futures Index for a hypothetical June 2003 contract would be computed using the annualized percentage change from the CPI-U for February 2003 (released in March 2003) to CPI-U for May 2003 (released in June 2003). The CPI-U for February and May 2003 were 183.1 and 183.5, respectively, the Reference CPI Futures Index for the June 2003 contract would have been 100.00 less the following value,

$$4 \times 100.00 \times \frac{183.5 - 183.1}{183.1} = 0.873839432$$

rounded down to 0.8738. The Reference CPI Futures Index as well as the final settlement price was $100.00 - 0.8738 = 99.1262$. The final settlement price is rounded to the nearest 1/10000th of a percentage point, a convention similar to that for Eurodollar futures.

So as we pointed out earlier, an expiring futures contract is settled against the inflation history of the recent past. To the extent that the actual compilation of the CPI-U requires time, it is not possible to utilize the contract month as the concluding calendar month for the 3-month period for which inflation is determined. In other words, given the standard lag in the release of inflation numbers, a contract expiring in March will always settle to the February inflation number and so on.

Last Trading Day

Trading for an expiring contract terminates at 7:00 a.m. Chicago time on the day CPI announcement is made in the contract month. For example, the March 2005 contract stopped trading at 7:00 a.m. Chicago time on March 23, 2005, the scheduled date for CPI release. If the announcement is postponed beyond the contract month, trading ceases at 7:00 a.m. Chicago time on the first business day following the contract month.

As shown in Table 4–1, CPI numbers for a particular contract month are always released with a lag. As release dates are published to cover the immediate following calendar year, it is very likely that when a deferred contract month is

---

10. A couple of comments are in order: (i) unlike the Eurodollar, the CPI futures are necessarily backward looking; the expiring futures contract is settled against the inflation history of the immediate past; (ii) as there is a slight lag in the release of the CPI numbers associated with the calendar month; thus, the 3-month period covered by a quarterly contract month is not a calendar quarter; (iii) short-term interest-rate futures seldom, if ever, trade "overpar," i.e., at prices over 100.00. However, overpar valuation of CPI futures is a distinct possibility. A price of over 100.00 in CPI futures reflects a deflation in the 3-month period covered by the contract.

T A B L E   4–1

Scheduled CPI Release Dates for 2005

Reference Month	Release Date	Reference Month	Release Date
December-05	Wednesday, January 19, 2005	June-05	Thursday, July 14, 2005
January-05	Wednesday, February 23, 2005	July-05	Tuesday, August 16, 2005
February-05	Wednesday, March 23, 2005	August-05	Thursday, September 15, 2005
March-05	Wednesday, April 20, 2005	September-05	Friday, October 14, 2005
April-05	Wednesday, May 18, 2005	October-05	Wednesday, November 16, 2005
May-05	Wednesday, June 15, 2005	November-05	Thursday, December 15, 2005

Source: www.bls.gov/cpi

listed for trading, the precise expiration date may not be known. In such instances, the last trading day of the contract month is set as the tentative expiration date, and finalized once the Bureau of Labor Statistics (BLS) publishes its release schedule.

Changes to Price Index—Revisions

Though revisions to previously released CPI numbers are always a possibility, the CPI data as originally released shall be referenced in the calculating the final settlement price. Subsequent revisions to the CPI data shall not be recognized. For example, the CPI for February 2003 as originally released in January 2003 is referenced in the calculation of the Reference CPI Futures Index for the June 2003 contract. Any subsequent revision to the CPI for February 2003 shall not be recognized.[11]

Readers should note that this policy helps avoid the issue of having to reopen contracts that have already been settled. It also helps maintain consistency across the settlement prices for consecutive contract months. In the example above, the adoption of revised February inflation numbers for settling the June contract but not the March contract (any revision would surely have happened after the final settlement of the March contract) would imply that two successive

11. It should also be noted that there have been rarely any revisions of CPI data to date. So the risk of having to deal with such revisions is quite remote, but given that the exchange in the business of helping firms manage their risks, it was deemed appropriate to have rule language to handle any such an eventuality.

contracts refer to two different inflation numbers for the same month—original for the March contract and revised for the June contract—thus introducing jumps in the inflation price series implied by the settlement prices of these contracts.

Changes to Price Index—Base Dates
In the event that the BLS changes the base period, the Reference CPI Futures Index and the final settlement price for the nearby contract month shall be determined by referencing the CPI-U calculated using the old base period.

Any index measures changes in prices in comparison to a reference date. It is typically the case that the value of the index on this reference or base date is set to 100.0. The base date for the CPI-U is the period 1982–1984. The CPI-U for the month of July 2003 was 183.9. This indicates that prices for the basket of goods and services underlying the index have risen 83.9% since the base period of 1982–1984. In other words, if one unit of this basket cost $10.00 in 1982–1984, the same basket would cost $18.39 in the month of July 2003.

In order to keep the index relevant, the BLS could change the base date at any time in the future. Given the impact of the change, the agency would tend to give sufficient notice before implementing it. Based on prior experience, even after the change it will continue to publish the index using both the old and new base dates. Following current rules, the final settlement price of our CPI futures for the nearby contract month will refer to the index value computed using the old base. All succeeding contract months will be based on the new index series.

Handling Delays in Data Release

Though CPI-U release dates for different contract months are known in advance, unforeseen delays are possible. In the event that the scheduled release is postponed, trading may be extended until whichever is the earlier, the actual announcement, or the end of the calendar month. As long as the applicable CPI-U value is released before the end of the calendar month, the usual procedure for determining the final settlement price for the expiration remains applicable. If the delay extends beyond the calendar month, the final settlement price for the affected contract will be calculated using a specific procedure similar to the inflation accretion determination in TIPS trading.

In case the CPI-U numbers have not been released by the end of the contract month, the Reference CPI Futures Index and the final settlement price shall be computed using the CPI-U value calculated based on the last 12-month change in the CPI-U available. If the CPI for month M is not reported by the end of the next month, the Exchange will use the following formula to calculate the index number (assuming the last reported CPI-U was N months prior to month M)

$$\mathrm{CPI}_M = \mathrm{CPI}_{M-N} \times \left[\frac{\mathrm{CPI}_{M-N}}{\mathrm{CPI}_{M-N-12}} \right]^{\frac{N}{12}}$$

Suppose the August 2005 CPI-U has not been released by the end of the September 2005 contract month. The last released CPI-U for May 2005 was 120.1; the CPI-U for May 2004 was 105.0. The CPI-U for August 2005 shall be

$$120.1 \times \left[\frac{120.1}{105.0} \right]^{\frac{3}{12}} = 124.2028137$$

rounded down to 124.2. Such CPI-U calculations in the case of delays by the Bureau of Labor Statistics in the release of CPI-U data beyond the contract month, shall reference only CPI-U data released by the Bureau of Labor Statistics or any other US governmental agency or body. Calculated values shall be referenced only for the purpose of determining the Reference CPI Futures Index and the final settlement price for contract months for which relevant CPI-U data have not been released.

This interpolation technique is similar to that adopted by the US Treasury for its TIPS securities to compute coupon payments for months for which the Bureau of Labor Statistics has delayed the released of the CPI-U numbers. Inclusion of this rule helps the Exchange avoid the less-preferred option of keeping the contract open beyond the contract month.

Choice of Price Index

Of the many Consumer Price Index series published by the Bureau of Labor Statistics (BLS), one price index emerges as the natural candidate for the futures contract; the Consumer Price Index–US city average for all urban consumers, all items, not-seasonally adjusted (CPI-U).[12] The inflation-indexed Treasury securities, TIPS, employ the same price index series for determining inflation accretion on the face value of the securities.

CPI-U is based on a market-basket of goods "consumed" by a wide spectrum of households (adding up to about 87% of the total US population) and reflects the buying habits of wage-earner and clerical-worker households, groups such as professional, managerial, and technical workers, the self-employed, short-term workers, the unemployed, and retirees and others not in the labor force. The market basket comprises goods and services that these households purchase for day-to-day living. The basket includes food, clothing, shelter, fuels, transportation, charges for doctors' and dentists' services, and drugs. The BLS tracks changes in consumer spending patterns and accordingly modifies the contents of the market basket as well as the weights assigned to individual items.

The sample area of the CPI-U survey covers 87 urban areas across the country, and includes about 50,000 housing units and approximately 23,000 retail establishments. Prices are collected from various retail outlets and service centers; for example, department stores, supermarkets, hospitals, and filling stations. All prices are inclusive of any taxes on the purchase and use of goods and services in the index. Except for fuels and a few other items whose prices are

---

12. All through this chapter, we ignore the suffix 'U' and refer to this price index as simply 'CPI.'

obtained every month in all 87 locations, price information for other items in the index market basket is typically collected every month in the three largest geographic areas and every other month in other areas. These surveys are conducted by BLS representatives either by personal visit or by telephone.

The Bureau publishes both seasonally-adjusted and -unadjusted price index series. The futures contract is based on the latter. The unadjusted CPI-U is actively tracked by consumers concerned about the prices they actually pay. Inflation-based escalation clauses in various contracts are typically based on the unadjusted price index series. Compensation adjustments agreed to as part of collective-bargaining contracts, as well as the payment liabilities of pension plans are indexed to price changes reflected by the CPI-U unadjusted for seasonal variation. Most important, TIPS are indexed to this price series. Having a futures contract tracking the same series makes it easier for TIPS investors to participate.

The Bureau of Labor Statistics usually publishes the index for the calendar month on a preannounced day towards the middle of the following month. For example, the CPI figure for the month of January 2005 inflation number was released on February 23, 2005. The following table shows the release dates or scheduled release dates of CPI statistics from January 2005 to December 2005. The December 2005 CPI number will be released on January 18, 2006. Note that the release dates do not necessarily fall on a particular weekday. Generally speaking, the Bureau sets the release dates for the immediately following year towards the end of the current calendar year.

Applications

By providing a common hedging instrument, the CPI futures contract is designed to create synergies with the cash TIPS securities, OTC inflation swap, and other OTC inflation derivatives markets. Given a listing of consecutive quarterly months, various applications are possible.

With a single contract month, users can hedge short-term inflation risk. Examples may include the inflation risk in the accretion of TIPS principal.

With a strip of consecutive contract months, users can hedge longer-term inflation risk. In particular, OTC swap dealers can price inflation swaps based on strips of CPI futures and hedge their risks with it.

Issuers of inflation-linked securities may reengineer their exposure to inflation, once again by trading strips of CPI futures. Alternatively, issuers and buyers of nominal-rate debts can synthetically create an inflation-linked security with the CPI futures.

Portfolio managers and pension funds with substantial positions in regular dollar-denominated nominal corporate debt issues or conventional US Treasury notes could create synthetic inflation-indexed securities by initiating a short position in the CPI futures coupled with a portion of their long cash position.

Arbitrageurs could trade strips of consecutive quarterly CPI futures expirations against strips of 3-month Eurodollar futures to create forward real-rate positions.

Though these and other interesting applications have been proposed by market participants, it is not clear if firms have currently figured out the mechanics (or even more, the merits) of structuring such trades. Accordingly, in the sections below, we will illustrate the use of the inflation futures contracts by means of simple hedging examples involving the following risks: inflation-accretion risk, portfolio risk, and inflation swap reset risk.[13]

Example 1: Hedging inflation-accretion risk

This example demonstrates the mechanics of a technique to hedge the impact of inflation on the par value of TIPS securities.

Calculating Incremental Inflation Accretion in TIPS

Consider the case of a 10-year $3\frac{7}{8}$ TIPS maturing on January 15, 2009. As of March 1, 2003, a trader is holding a short position that will be reversed on May 1, 2003. On that date, the $100 million principal will be adjusted for inflation accrued since the issue date, January 15, 1999.

The January 2003 CPI was at 181.7 and the market expects it to remain constant at that level; in other words, zero inflation in February 2003. Based on this information, the trader knows that the inflation accrual will be computed as illustrated below.

The total inflation accrual adjustment as of February 1, 2003[14] is given by the following index ratio[15]

$$\frac{CPI_{NOV02}}{Ref\ CPI_{JAN99}} = \frac{181.3}{164.0} = 1.10549$$

for a total of $10,549,000. This amount will be added to the $100 million principal value.

Given market expectation of constant inflation between January and February 2003, the incremental inflation accrual adjustment on May 1, 2003 is expected to be

$$\frac{expected\ CPI_{FEB03}}{Ref\ CPI_{JAN99}} = \frac{181.7}{164.0} = 1.10793$$

---

13. A swap reset risk hedge example is included in the section on Euro HICP futures.
14. The two-step calculation procedure illustrated is consistent with the quarterly expiration cycle of the CPI futures contract. For instance, the March 2003 contract settles based on the November 2002 and February 2003 CPI.
15. Historical *Ref CPI* numbers and *Index Ratios* are available at http://www.publicdebt.treas.gov/of/ofhiscpi.htm. The index ratio for February 1, 2003 is available at ftp://ftp.publicdebt.treas.gov/of/of022003cpi.pdf.

$100 million $\times (1.10793 - 1)$ results in total accrued amount of $10,793,000. The incremental inflation accrual adjustment between February 1, 2003 and May 1, 2003 is expected to be $244,000 (= 10,793,000 - 10,549,000).

Given that the market is expecting inflation to remain constant at 181.7, a 0.1 change in CPI-U will cause the accrued value to change by

$$\left(\frac{0.1}{164.0} = 0.00061 \right) \times \$100,000,000 = \$61,000$$

The trader would like to hedge the impact of any such change by using CPI futures. As the trader has a short TIPS position, he/she would like to protect against an increase in CPI (which would cause the incremental inflation accrual adjustment to be greater than the current expectation of $244,000).

This can be done by going short on CME CPI futures. If inflation is higher than expected, the short futures position will generate a profit that will offset the higher[16] inflation accrual adjustment on TIPS.

Hedge Ratio
Based on the market expectation of February CPI at the same level as January CPI, i.e., at 181.7, the March 2003 CPI futures are trading at

$$100 - 400 \times [(\exp CPI_{FEB03} \div CPI_{NOV02}) - 1]$$
$$= 100 - 400 \times [(181.7 \div 181.3) - 1] = 99.1175$$

If the February 2003 CPI comes in higher by 0.1 at 181.8, the March contract will settle at

$$100 - 400 \times [(181.8 \div 181.3) - 1] = 98.8969$$

As each 0.005 change in final settlement price is equivalent to $12.50, a long CPI futures position will result in a loss of

$$\frac{(99.1175 - 98.8969 = 0.2206) \times \$12.5}{0.005} = \$551.5$$

per contract. So a trader looking to hedge against an increase in the CPI from January to February 2003 can sell 111 contracts ($\approx 61,000/551.5$).

Impact of the Hedge
In this case, the February 2003 CPI was reported at 183.1, resulting in a final settlement price for the March 2003 CPI futures at 96.0287. Assuming the trader had sold 111 contracts at 99.1175 when he/she initiated the hedge, the gain from the futures position would have been

$$\frac{(99.1175 - 96.0287 = 3.0888) \times \$12.5 \times 111}{0.005} = \$857,142$$

---

16. On the other hand, if the trader was long TIPS, then he/she would go long CPI futures to hedge against any losses if inflation is lower than current market expectation.

The inflow would have financed the additional inflation accrual adjustment on May 1, 2003 of $853,000[17] (in excess of the incremental adjustment of $244,000 as of February 1, 2003).

If the February 2003 CPI had been reported lower at 180.5 instead, the CPI futures position would have resulted in a loss of $734,681 which would have been offset by a negative accrual of $732,000 to the TIPS principal on May 1, 2003.

Example 2: Hedging portfolio risk

The CPI contract as well as the HICP futures contract described later in the chapter can be used by fund managers to hedge their portfolios from any inflation exposure. The first step in this task would be to figure out the potential exposure to inflation risk. To keep things simple, in the example below we consider the case of a TIPS trader who should have a better sense for the impact of inflation risk on his/her position.[18]

Let us consider the case of a trader who is short inflation indexed bonds, and would like to hedge some of this exposure. The short position has been put in place with a view that actual inflation would be *lower* than current market expectation or that real rates would rise. Given a $10,000,000 notional short TIPS position, the trader would like to protect his/her portfolio from the risk of *higher* inflation over the next few months, while retaining a positive exposure to a rise in real rates.

On May 14, 2004, the June 2004 CPI futures contract is trading at 95.73. Given a February CPI of 186.2, this would imply that the market expects the May 2004 CPI number to be around 188.2.

The trader figures that a 0.1 change in CPI-U will result in a gain or loss of $250,000 to his/her short position.

If the May 2004 CPI comes in *lower* by 0.1 at 188.1, the June 2004 contract will settle at

$$100 - 400 \times [(188.1 \div 186.2) - 1] = 95.9184$$

As each 0.005 change in final settlement price is equivalent to $12.50, a *short* CPI futures position will result in a gain (or loss if the number comes in lower by 0.1) of

$$\frac{(95.9184 - 95.73 = 0.1884) \times \$12.5}{0.005} = \$471.00$$

per contract. So the trader looking to hedge against potential losses from higher inflation will sell 531 contracts ($\approx 250,000/471$).

The actual May 2004 CPI number was higher than market expectation at 189.1. The CPI futures contract settled at 93.7701. The trader pocketed

---

17. Total inflation accrual as of February 1, 2003 was $10,793,000. Total inflation accrual as of May 1, 2003 was $11,646,000. The difference between these two values is $853,000. The May 2003 index ratio is available at ftp://ftp.publicdebt.treas.gov/of/of052003cpi.pdf.

18. Please note that for purposes of this example, we are ignoring the source of this loss–inflation accrual and/or changes in market expectations.

a gain of $2,601,767.25, offsetting the loss ($2,250,000)[19] from the short TIPS position.[20]

Example 3: CPI futures for asset/liability management

In this example, we will illustrate how a pension fund manager can use CPI futures to acquire inflation exposure on the "asset" side of the balance sheet so as to offset the fund's inflation-indexed liabilities. In other words, the fund wants long-term exposure to CPI to match its liabilities, but without exposure to the changes in real rates that come from owning TIPS.

The fund would typically take a short position in CPI futures, so that if the actual CPI comes higher than contracted, gain in the futures position will fund the higher than expected payments to pension holders, and vice versa.

Assuming a long term average inflation rate of say, 3% p.a., the fund has projected quarterly payments of $100,000,000 over the next 5 years. As these payments are indexed to inflation, a 0.1-percentage-point *annualized* incremental increase in *quarterly* inflation (in comparison to the average rate assumed in making the projections) will result in additional payments of

$$\frac{0.1}{100} \times \frac{3}{12} \times \$100,000,000 = \$25,000$$

per quarter. This risk exposure on the liability side can be hedged by selling appropriate numbers of CPI futures contracts with expirations coinciding with the quarterly payment schedule.

Each 0.1-percentage-point annualized gain in quarterly CPI will reduce the final settlement price of the contract by 0.1000. As each 0.005 change in the final settlement price is worth $12.50, we can calculate the hedge ratio by dividing the expected additional payment of $25,000 per quarter by (0.1/0.005 = 20 × $12.50 =) $250, which will equal 100 contracts.

So assuming the pension fund has made realistic projections of its future quarterly payments, the manager can sell 100 contracts each of the 12 listed CPI futures contracts. Gains or losses on each expiring contract should offset the additional payments or savings to its pension holders. After each such contract expiration, the manager will sell 100 contracts of the newly-listed (twelfth) quarterly contract. For instance, on the expiration of say, the June 2005 contract, the exchange will list the June 2008 contract; the pension fund in this example, will then sell 100 contracts of this contract.

---

19. CPI was higher by 0.9 percentage points; at $250,000 per 0.1 per cent point change in CPI, the loss from the short TIPS position is (250,000 × 9 ≈) $2,250,000.

20. This hypothetical gain would also have offset any potential losses from a drop in real yields. For instance, the real yield on the 10-year 2% TIPS maturing in January 15, 2014 dropped by about 1.9 basis points between May 14, 2004 and June 15, 2004; as bond prices move in the opposite direction, the trader would have recorded a small capital loss if he/she had attempted reversing his/her short position on the latter date.

Contract Performance

As of April 2005, the CPI futures contract had recorded total volume of 5,508 contracts. Most of the volume was traded in the first few months. Though the lion's share of trading volume in any given day tends to be concentrated on the first expiring contract, open interest has consistently extended across all listed contract months.

Before we start analyzing reasons for the relatively lackluster performance of the contract past the initial euphoria phase, there are a few points worth mentioning. First, the contract is reported to have improved the level of transparency in the US inflation-derivatives market. The contributing factor has been the presence of a dedicated market maker continuously showing two-way prices across all the 12 contract months. These tradable prices tend to reflect current market expectations of average inflation for each of the next 12 quarters as determined in the underlying inflation-linked cash and derivatives markets. Trades can thus use this information to price their trades in related instruments.

Second, the fact that open interest tends to be distributed (though in a highly skewed manner) across most of the 12 listed contract months indicates that it is being utilized by inflation swap dealers to hedge their inflation-risk exposures. Finally, the contract continues to attract the interest of hedge funds and other similar players speculating specifically on the inflation numbers.

Contract Structure Issues

Questions have been raised on the structure of the contract. As trading interest has dwindled, market participants have suggested that the exchange consider changing the structure tracking quarterly inflation to one tracking annual inflation. Given that firms face inflation risks every month, arguments have been put forward in favor of an annual inflation contract expiring every month, rather than once a quarter. The exchange has been studying the issue, and as we discuss below, has decided to adopt this suggested structure for a new contract tracking inflation in the Euro-zone.

A Still-Nascent Inflation-Derivatives Market

One of the reasons for the lackluster trading in the CPI futures contract in the first half of 2005 could be the still-nascent nature of the US inflation-derivatives market. Though the TIPS market continues to grow, both in issuance and in trading volume, the US inflation-linked derivatives market does not appear to have grown at the same rate.

In its February 2005 Research Quarterly, the Bond Market Association reported that the US Treasury issued $63.4 billion TIPS securities in 2004. The agency has also expanded its product offerings by introducing $1 billion of 5- and 20-year TIPS maturities in 2004. Daily trading volume in TIPS averaged $6 billion in 2004, compared to $3.7 billion traded daily in 2003. Unfortunately, there is very little published data on trading activity in the US inflation-derivatives markets.

Anecdotal evidence indicates that the derivatives market has not kept up with the growth rates of the cash bond market.

The December 2003 TIPS Survey from the Bond Market Association quoted earlier also reported that a majority of market participants were of the view that the launch of a CPI futures contract would increase corporate issuance of inflation-linked debt. Unfortunately, this prediction has not been realized as the US corporate inflation debt market remained dormant through 2004.

To summarize, continuing with our earlier argument that markets tend to feed off each other, further growth of the US inflation-derivatives market will most likely increase arbitrage opportunities and hedging needs involving the CPI futures contract. The exchange is weighing the prospects of a contract tracking annual inflation with monthly expirations. Finally, although inflation concerns persist at some level in the economy, they have not yet risen to a point where firms have to actively hedge their inflation exposures. If this changes, then the contract could attract more trading interest in the marketplace.

EURO-ZONE HICP FUTURES

At the time of this writing, CME is planning the launch of a futures contract on European inflation. The new contract will complement the existing futures contract on US inflation, and extend coverage to the nations in the European Union which have adopted the euro as the common currency (or Euro-zone).

The cash-settled HICP futures contract will track annual changes in the Harmonized Index of Consumer Prices, excluding tobacco (HICP), for the Euro-zone, as calculated by the European Statistical Institute (Eurostat). It measures the level of prices for market goods and services consumed by households in the Euro-zone.

The contract would be similar in concept to the CPI contract, with one crucial difference. Unlike the US contract, which tracks *annualized percentage change in the price index over a 3-month period*, the European version would track *annual inflation with monthly settlement*. It will be sized to represent inflation on a notional value of €1,000,000 for a period of 12 calendar months, as implied by the HICP. The exchange plans to list up to 12 consecutive monthly contracts on its Globex electronic trading platform. Following are some of the differences between the US and European IL-derivatives markets.

A Different Market Structure

Based on a widely prevalent view that the inflation-derivatives market in Europe is deeper and more advanced than the US market, in some sense, the HICP contract ought to have preceded the US CPI futures contract. For instance, the first inflation-indexed (or IL) bond in the US was launched in January 1997. The first IL bond in Europe was issued by the UK Debt Office in March 1981. With France's first IL debt issuance in 1998, the inflation swap market in Europe was soon the most active in the world.

European Inflation Swap Market

The growth in the IL bond market has driven exponential growth in the European OTC inflation-derivatives market. Though we have not seen any credible published data, the Euro-zone inflation swap market is reported to have a turnover four times higher than the US; this despite the fact that the US IL bond market is twice the size of the Euro-zone market. While the US inflation swap market did not see much activity until the middle of 2003, the market in Europe had been active for over 3 years. Some swaps books are more than 5 years old.

The derivatives market offers sovereign issuers the means to customize their inflation exposures in their liability portfolio to a greater extent, and to have more flexibility to take advantage of opportunities as they arise. The inflation-derivatives market has developed to a point where structured contracts exist which can be tailored to almost any requirement, and can step in where index-linked bonds are unavailable or unsuited for a particular environment. In Europe, the derivatives market has grown to such an extent that it is said to be growing faster than the physical equivalents (namely the IL cash bonds), and are offering opportunities that are not otherwise available.

Retail Interest

In contrast to the US, activity in the European market is partly driven by retail demand for structured notes. Banks in Europe have developed novel structures to distribute inflation risk to European investors. Dealers have created structured notes specifically to meet the needs of small or medium-sized retail and private bank customers. Some of these notes are in form of Euro medium-term notes (MTNs) linked to inflation. The individual size of such transactions might be modest, but collectively they are thought to account for a sizeable proportion of the Euro-based inflation derivatives market.

To illustrate this trend, nearly every bank in Italy sells inflation-protected bonds today. In 2003, Poste Vita, the life insurance arm of the Italian post office, which has a large structured retail products business, issued €500 million bonds that incorporated an option paying investors the best of inflation or a basket of securities. The French post office has also issued similar products.

Another demand feeding into the European IL market's dynamic growth is the banking-related reform in countries such as France. From July 2004, interest rates offered by local French deposit accounts—Livret A and Codevi accounts, in which about €350 billion is already invested—have been linked to Euribor and French inflation. This is reported to have created a huge demand for IL securities from banks wanting to match their liabilities in such deposit accounts. The expectation is that increased activity in the IL cash market will translate into greater demand for inflation derivatives, particularly inflation swaps.[21]

---

21. Though these accounts are linked to French and not Euro-zone inflation, developments here are expected to cause an increase in trading activity in the inflation swaps market.

Market reports also indicate that hedge funds and proprietary trading desks at various large investment banks are increasingly looking to Euro-zone IL bond and derivative securities to generate higher returns. This is partly driven by the fact that, in a broad sense, these markets, though quite liquid, are still relatively underdeveloped, thus offering the lure of profits from inefficient pricing practices.

Short-Term Instrument

Summarizing the foregoing discussion, one can conclude that the financial landscape in Europe is quite different.

The inflation derivatives market in the Euro-zone region is deeper and more mature.

These instruments are distributed more widely in Europe. Unlike the US, there are many more natural issuers (paying inflation) in this region.[22]

Dealers in this market appear to be looking towards exchange-traded contracts to hedge their short-term inflation risks.[23]

An active short-term inflation hedge will allow dealers to free-up their capital to create more structured products of medium- and longer-term tenures, thus contributing to the further growth of the inflation-derivatives market.

Hedge funds looking for new trading opportunities might be willing to trade short-term instruments to exploit pricing inefficiencies, as well as to place bets on inflation numbers. Their active trading strategies might be more receptive to a short-term instrument than one with a longer maturity structure.

Contract Design

Rules pertaining to contract size, final settlement price, quote specification, and tick size, mirror those for the CPI futures contract.[24] Reflecting the specific elements of the European market, unlike the CPI which is a 3-month instrument, the HICP contract tracks inflation over a 12-month period, and hence, is an annual contract.

It will have the usual IMM-style quoting convention of 100 minus the contracted annual rate of inflation, where each 0.01 IMM point will be worth €100.

---

22. Banks in Europe, for example, have created special purpose entities (SPEs) to help firms in specific sectors—for instance, water-supply companies and public property development firms in the UK—raise debt in the inflation-linked bond market. Though the German government has yet to issue any inflation-indexed debt, such bonds have been issued by at least 14 private German entities, indicating the diverse issuer base in Europe. These nongovernment issuers typically have returns linked to inflation, and hence prefer issuing debt linked to it too. Réseau Ferré de France, the entity that owns and manages the French rail network, for example, has issued debt linked to both UK RPI and HICP.
23. Refer to the discussion preceding the swap hedge example below.
24. A summary of the contract specifications is in Appendix 2. A comparison of the clause for last trading day for the two contracts will indicate that, unlike the CPI futures contract, trading in HICP futures will not reopen in case of any delays in release on the data. This restriction was imposed in response to feedback from market participants.

Annual vs. Quarterly Inflation

Users can hedge short-term inflation risk exposures for every calendar month. Given that a single contract will track year-on-year (or annual) inflation, swap desks can hedge their reset risks for any single month.

Traders can execute hedges, or express views over finer gradations, something not possible with the CPI contract which settles only once a quarter. This is especially important as institutions face inflation risks throughout the year.

CPI users can also track annual inflation, but only by trading consecutive strips of four quarterly-expiring contracts, and that too for only 4 out of the 12 calendar months in a year.

With a focus on near-term (i.e., the next 12 months) rather than longer-term (3 to 5 years), the contract seeks to fill a crucial gap due to the absence of short-term IL debt instruments.

Speculative trading interests tend to be short-term in nature. Monthly-expiring contracts could, in theory, increase trading opportunities for active traders such as hedge funds.

Trading hours and venue

HICP futures will be listed for trading on CME Globex® from 8:00 a.m. to 4:00 p.m. (London time) on Mondays through Fridays.[25] In other words, except when Daylight Savings Time is in effect in either, but not both, London or Chicago, HICP futures will be listed for trading on Globex® from 2:00 a.m. to 10:00 a.m. (Chicago time) on Mondays through Fridays.

Final Settlement Procedure

Similar to the CPI contract, the final settlement price of HICP futures shall be 100 minus annual inflation rate in the 12-month period preceding the contract month. For a July 2004 contract, the relevant inflation rate would be determined by the HICP for the months June 2003 and June 2004 (released in July 2003 and July 2004, respectively).

Last Trading Day

Trading for an expiring contract terminates at 4:00 p.m. (London time) on the business day preceding the scheduled day of the HICP announcement. For the July 2005 contract, trading will stop at 4:00 p.m. (London time) on Friday July 15, 2005.

As shown in Table 4–2, HICP numbers for a particular contract month are always released with a lag. As release dates are published to cover the immediate following calendar year, it is very likely that when a deferred contract month is listed for trading, the precise expiration date will not be known. In such instances, the last trading day of the contract month will be set as the tentative expiration date, which will be finalized once Eurostat publishes its release schedule. The exception would be the February contract, for which the tentative last trading day

---

25. Though these hours seem shorter than for the US CPI futures contract, the market maker for the latter typically shows continuous two-sided prices from just 7:30 a.m. to 2:00 p.m. (Chicago time).

T A B L E   4–2

Scheduled HICP Release Dates for 2005

Reference Month	Release Date	Reference Month	Release Date
December-05	Thursday, January 20, 2005	June-05	Monday, July 18, 2005
January-05	Monday, February 28, 2005	July-05	Thursday, August 18, 2005
February-05	Wednesday, March 16, 2005	August-05	Friday, September 16, 2005
March-05	Monday, April 18, 2005	September-05	Tuesday, October 18, 2005
April-05	Thursday, May 19, 2005	October-05	Wednesday, November 16, 2005
May-05	Thursday, June 16, 2005	November-05	Friday, December 16, 2005

Source: http://epp.eurostat.cec.eu.int/pls/portal/url/page/PGP_RELEASE/PGE_DS_RELEASE

shall be the first business day following the second Tuesday of the following month.[26]

Other Contract Terms

All other terms are similar to that for the US CPI futures contract described earlier.

Choice of Price Index

The reference index for the futures contract is the Harmonized Index of Consumer Prices, excluding tobacco (HICP), for the Euro-zone, as calculated by Eurostat. It measures the level of prices for market goods and services consumed by households in the Euro-zone. The Euro-zone HICP is an aggregate of the member states' HICPs. It is targeted to cover almost 99.1% of all Euro-zone household consumption.

The major traded inflation indexes are the US CPI-U (the basis of the existing CPI futures contract), the UK RPI(X) (Retail Price Index excluding mortgage

---

26. February is a special case, as the scheduled release date tends to be close to the last trading day of the month. In 2004, the January HICP number was released on Friday, February 27, 2004, and the 2005 number came out on February 28. Extending the forced final settlement date until the business day following the second Tuesday of March allows the market to accommodate any delayed releases by Eurostat.

interest payment), French CPI ex-tobacco, and the HICP ex-tobacco. The UK IL issues and the first French IL bond issues were indexed to respective domestic price indexes. While the UK continues to issue bonds linked solely to its domestic price index (RPI), France has decided to split issuance between domestic and Euro-zone inflation indexes.

France took the lead in issuing the first euro-denominated product linked to Euro-zone inflation, the OAT€i 2012. By being the first Euro-zone issuer of IL bonds, the French debt management agency, Agence France Trésor, has been able to define the indices it wanted to use. The decision to use an ex-tobacco index, which is now commonly used by other Euro-zone sovereign issuers such as Italy and Greece, was related to French laws forbidding linkage to tobacco prices. Although a combination of inflation swaps linked to the Euro-zone HICP (all items) and the HICP (ex-tobacco) had been trading several months prior to the 2001 issue of the OAT€i 2012, the Trésor-favored ex-tobacco index has effectively become the market benchmark. Once Italy decided to join the club of IL bond issuers and chose the same HICP (or ex-tobacco) index, no doubt was left about the index that future Euro-zone sovereign issuers would choose.

Germany recently announced that it is likely to enter the IL market in 2005. Though plans have still not been finalized, market participants anticipate that Germany will choose the HICP in order to benefit from existing market liquidity.

There continues to be speculation that the UK might switch to the use of the HICP index. In June 2003, the British Chancellor announced that while the country is not yet ready to join the euro, it was considering adopting the HICP measure of inflation as its inflation target in place of the RPI(X) (Retail Price Index excluding mortgage interest payment). HICP is the definition of inflation that is targeted by the European Central Bank (ECB). Analysts believe that should the UK move to a new inflation target, future UK IL bond issues are likely to be linked to Euro-zone inflation represented by HICP rather than domestic inflation.

Harmonized Index

Harmonization refers to the fact that the same methodology and nomenclatures are adopted for the index of prices for all the countries in the Euro-zone and the European Union. This enables comparison of inflation among different member states in the Union.

Aggregation involves the use of weights which equal each country's share in the Euro-zone final household consumption. These weights are calculated every year. The 2004 weights were based on consumption numbers from 2002, and went into effect with the calculation of the HICP numbers for January 2004. Annual change is facilitated due to the fact that the index is an annual chained-index. New entrants to the Euro-zone are added the same year to the HICP.

Eurostat usually publishes the index for the calendar month on a preannounced day, typically between the 16th and 18th of the following month. For example, the HICP figure for the month of June 2004 was released on July 16, 2003. Table 4–2 shows scheduled release dates of HICP statistics for 2005. Note that the release dates do not necessarily fall on a particular weekday. Generally speaking, Eurostat sets the release dates for the immediately following year towards the end of the current calendar year.

Applications

Speculative and Tactical

HICP inflation swaps in Europe have monthly resets rather than daily inflation reference (as in the case of the US TIPS-based market). The addition of monthly-expiring HICP futures contracts to the product mix could offer a potential for tactical trading during the months. This would supplement any speculative trading interests demonstrated by hedge funds and other active risk players.

Also, there is a relatively active market for break-even trades (see the pricing section below for a definition of the term "break-even inflation"), including spread trades targeting the differentials between two different inflation indexes. Using the HICP and a modified version of the US CPI contract, traders could implement spread trades tracking the relative changes in expected US and Euro-zone inflation as implied by the prices of respective contracts.

Hedging Swap Risks

Based on feedback from traders in some of the key banks in the European inflation-derivatives business, the main source of demand for the inflation-futures contract is expected to be inflation swap desks looking to hedge their swap reset risk. In the current environment, in the absence of natural payers of inflation, banks have started underwriting, as principal, the inflation risk in Europe—either outright, or by warehousing it against other inflation risks they might have, such as French and Italian IL bonds.

Also, Euro-MTN bonds issued by governments or supranational entities-such as the European Investment Bank tend to be swapped into nominal floating rates by the bookrunner, which takes on the inflation risk via an inflation swap.

Banks that lack proprietary-risk appetite could use HICP futures to hedge the inflation risks incurred in making payments on euro inflation swaps. When paying in an inflation swap with a given underlying index and maturity, the simplest hedge is to buy the equivalent index-linked bond, rather than using nominal bonds as a swap hedge. For those dealers who find the IL bond market to be too illiquid and hence, unreliable, the inter-dealer swap market is the main recourse. Analogous to the relationship between Eurodollar futures and interest-rate swaps, inflation swap dealers could use an exchange-traded instrument to lay-off any net inflation exposures they do not wish to carry in their books.

Even if they are sufficiently liquid, as IL cash instruments tend to be of longer durations (typically 5 years or more), they might not make very good short-term hedges. The swap desks could hedge some of their longer-dated reset risks in the cash market, but appear to be looking for an alternate hedge, especially for reset dates that fall within the first 12 to 18 months.

Example 4: Hedging swap reset risks

Background

The most commonly used inflation-derivative, inflation-linked (or IL) swaps, offer an alternative to, and an effective way of, matching IL liabilities. In a basic plain vanilla swap, two counterparties exchange an agreed payment for the compounded annual inflation rate at maturity. Because the swap is tailor-made, it can be used to match the end-user's liabilities more closely than an IL bond. For example, the period over which inflation is received can be extended, or the shape of inflation receipts can be tailored to the shape of the liabilities.

The plain vanilla contract, also known as a zero-coupon or break-even swap, has become the standardized instrument for transferring inflation risk among dealers. OTC swap-market volumes are difficult to estimate, but based on press reports, the turnover in Euro-zone inflation swaps adds up to around €10 billion a month in 2004, more than twice the €2 billion from a year prior.

The example below illustrates the mechanics of a hypothetical swap hedge using HICP futures. Though there are alternative ways of structuring a swap, the basic approach demonstrated can be easily adapted to figure out hedge ratios for other structures.[27]

Swap dealers can buy HICP futures as a hedge if they are receiving inflation in a swap or, conversely, sell HICP futures if they are paying inflation in an OTC swap—similar to the way participants in the interest-rate swap market hedge their transactions using strips of consecutive Eurodollar futures.

Swap Structure

Notional amount = €100 million

Trade date = January 3, 2005

Maturity date = December 16, 2005

Fixed side

  Fixed rate = 2.5% payable monthly

  Payment dates = HICP release dates

  Day-count convention = Actual/360

Floating side

  Reset dates = HICP release dates

  Payment dates = HICP release dates

  Day-count convention = Actual/360

  Floating rate = Year-on-year (or annual) Euro-zone HICP ex-tobacco

  Spread over floating reference rate = 0 basis points

---

27. Readers should note that this hedge example can be executed using US CPI futures too, though the application will be limited by the quarterly expiration structure.

Swap Transaction
The dealer has agreed to receive fixed rate and pay the floating rate. If you compare the fixed rate with the average rate implied by the HICP futures numbers below, the former is priced at about 10 basis points over the average or break-even rate.

Calculating the Hedge Ratio

Table 4–3 illustrates how the dealer can assess the expected gain or loss from the transaction, by referring to the HICP futures contract. Please note that the numbers are all completely hypothetical.

Column (iv) above presents the future inflation rates as implied by the hypothetical HICP futures contract trading on January 3, 2005. If these expectations turn out to be correct, then the dealer can expect to pocket a net gain of €85,000.

Knowing that the expected gain can be protected by using HICP futures, the dealer can calculate the hedge ratio using a procedure similar to that illustrated in earlier examples. As the dealer has agreed to pay the floating rate on the swap, he/she will be selling the HICP futures contract to hedge against the risk of rates increasing from the current expected levels.

T A B L E   4–3

Assessing Expected Gain or Loss from the Swap Trade

Cash Flow Dates	# of days	Rates % Fixed	Rates % Expected*	Cash flows Fixed	Cash flows Expected	Net Cash Flow Expected
(i)	(ii)	(iii)	(iv)	(v)	(vi)	(vii)
20/01/2005	17	2.5	2.1	118,055.56	99,166.67	18,888.89
28/02/2005	39	2.5	2.2	270,833.33	238,333.33	32,500.00
16/03/2005	16	2.5	2.4	111,111.11	106,666.67	4,444.44
18/04/2005	33	2.5	2.6	229,166.67	238,333.33	(9,166.67)
19/05/2005	31	2.5	3	215,277.78	258,333.33	(43,055.56)
16/06/2005	28	2.5	2.5	194,444.44	194,444.44	–
18/07/2005	32	2.5	2.7	222,222.22	240,000.00	(17,777.78)
18/08/2005	31	2.5	2.3	215,277.78	198,055.56	17,222.22
16/09/2005	29	2.5	2.4	201,388.89	193,333.33	8,055.56
18/10/2005	32	2.5	2.5	222,222.22	222,222.22	–
16/11/2005	29	2.5	2.1	201,388.89	169,166.67	32,222.22
16/12/2005	30	2.5	2	208,333.33	166,666.67	41,666.67
					Total	85,000.00

* implied by HICP futures as of Jan 3, 2005

In Table 4–4 we compare cash flows using the futures implied rate and the implied rate less 0.1. As each 0.1 change in HICP futures price[28] is worth €1,000, column (viii) above gives the hedge ratio for each of the 12 contract months.

Table 4–5 displays the net impact of the hedge. Assuming the actual rates are as shown in column (ii) above, the swap contract will generate a gain that is less by €30,555.56 than expected. But this opportunity loss is compensated by a corresponding gain from the futures hedge.

PRICING ISSUES

Researchers have just begun exploring the problem of pricing such contracts. So the discussion that follows is basically a description of models to extract expectations of future inflation embedded in the prices of traded financial instruments.

The literature on estimating expected inflation is vast. These efforts follow either of two basic approaches. The traditional macroeconomic approach has been to construct structural models of the economy to estimate inflation. With the development of inflation-linked financial instruments, a second approach has evolved. Here forecasters attempt to analyze the spread between nominal and real interest rates for estimates of expected inflation.

The structural model approach, one instance of which is the traditional Philips curve, has been shown to produce unreliable estimates of inflation.[29] The rest of this section will focus on approaches to derive inflation expectations from market prices, and in turn, using these expectations to price the CPI futures contract.

Going into the intricacies of each approach would be beyond the scope of this chapter, particularly due to the fact that the state-of-art is still work-in-progress. Accordingly, we provide brief descriptions of the purported solutions, with one exception. In order to highlight to readers some of the issues involved in working with inflation-linked and nominal bonds, we will demonstrate the methodology to compute break-even inflation, an estimate of market consensus of average inflation over a specific period of time.

Economist Surveys

We will start with an approach which could be the end-result of a process involving either one or both of the two forecasting methods listed above. Since 1968, one popular source of information on US inflation expectations has been the Federal Reserve Bank of Philadelphia's quarterly Survey of Professional Forecasters. This quarterly survey relies on a pool of about 30 forecasters, professionals who

---

28. Please note that a 0.1-percentage-point change in the annual inflation rate will translate into 0.1 (or 10 basis points) change in the HICP futures final settlement price.

29. The main complaints have been regarding the applicability of these models across different countries and their stability over time. See R. Gordon, 1998, "Foundations of the Goldilocks Economy: Supply Shocks and the Time Varying NAIRU," Brookings Papers on Economic Activity, 2, 297–333.

T A B L E   4-4

Computing Hedge Ratios

| Cash Flow Dates | # of days | Rates% | | Cash flows | | | DV01 | Hedge Ratio |
| | | Expected | (iii)−0.1 | Expected | (iii)−0.1 | | (v)−(vi) | (vii)/1000 |
		(iii)	(iv)	(v)	(vi)		(vii)	(viii)
20/01/2005	17	2.1	2	99,166.67	94,444.44		4,722.22	4.72
28/02/2005	39	2.2	2.1	238,333.33	227,500.00		10,833.33	10.83
16/03/2005	16	2.4	2.3	106,666.67	102,222.22		4,444.44	4.44
18/04/2005	33	2.6	2.5	238,333.33	229,166.67		9,166.67	9.17
19/05/2005	31	3	2.9	258,333.33	249,722.22		8,611.11	8.61
16/06/2005	28	2.5	2.4	194,444.44	186,666.67		7,777.78	7.78
18/07/2005	32	2.7	2.6	240,000.00	231,111.11		8,888.89	8.89
18/08/2005	31	2.3	2.2	198,055.56	189,444.44		8,611.11	8.61
16/09/2005	29	2.4	2.3	193,333.33	185,277.78		8,055.56	8.06
18/10/2005	32	2.5	2.4	222,222.22	213,333.33		8,888.89	8.89
16/11/2005	29	2.1	2	169,166.67	161,111.11		8,055.56	8.06
16/12/2005	30	2	1.9	166,666.67	158,333.33		8,333.33	8.33

TABLE 4-5

Evaluating the Net Impact of the Futures Hedge

Cash Flow Dates	Rates %		Net Swap Cash Flow			Futures	
	Expected	Actual	Actual	Expected	Surprise	# of Contracts	Gain (Loss)
(i)	(ii)	(iii)	(iv)	(v)	(vi)	(vii)	(viii)
20/01/2005	2.1	2.1	18,888.89	18,888.89	–	5	–
28/02/2005	2.2	2.2	32,500.00	32,500.00	–	11	–
16/03/2005	2.4	2.3	8,888.89	4,444.44	4,444.44	4	(4,000.00)
18/04/2005	2.6	2.8	(27,500.00)	(9,166.67)	(18,333.33)	9	18,000.00
19/05/2005	3	3.2	(60,277.78)	(43,055.56)	(17,222.22)	9	18,000.00
16/06/2005	2.5	2.6	(7,777.78)	–	(7,777.78)	8	8,000.00
18/07/2005	2.7	2.6	(8,888.89)	(17,777.78)	8,888.89	9	(9,000.00)
18/08/2005	2.3	2.4	8,611.11	17,222.22	(8,611.11)	9	9,000.00
16/09/2005	2.4	2.4	8,055.56	8,055.56	–	8	–
18/10/2005	2.5	2.5	–	–	–	9	–
16/11/2005	2.1	2	40,277.78	32,222.22	8,055.56	8	(8,000.00)
16/12/2005	2	2	41,666.67	41,666.67	–	8	–
				Total	(30,555.56)		32,000.00

work for Wall Street firms and other businesses producing forecasts of different economic variables.

Although these survey results receive headline coverage in the mainstream media, they are viewed with a high level of skepticism by both academics and market practitioners.

> It is not clear how these economists produce their forecasts—do they follow an econometric model, do they analyze nominal and real yields, or do they simply extrapolate the recent past?

> Since these survey respondents represent just a small fraction of the affected population, their views might not be representative of actual market expectations.

> The survey is conducted on a quarterly basis, a frequency level that might not be convenient for pricing short-term instruments.

Based on published research,[30] given the poor quality of these numbers, it is evident that they cannot be relied upon solely to price financial contracts like CPI futures. In contrast to this approach, however, the trend illustrated below is to base inflation expectations on yield spreads[31] determined by investment decisions of large numbers of traders.

Analyzing Financial Asset Prices

Since the first issuance of inflation-indexed bonds in the UK in 1981, models have been developed to extract inflation expectations from prices of these bonds. With the development of the inflation-indexed bond market, traders now have access to market-determined real interest rates which can be compared with nominal Treasury rates to develop a measure of expected inflation.[32]

Prior to the launch of these bonds, researchers had to rely solely on nominal bonds. Subject to certain assumptions, the new models are reported[33] to produce forecasts that tend to be more accurate than those that rely solely on nominal yields. One common approach depends on the famous Fisher hypothesis on the relationship between real and nominal interest rates.

---

30. See F.X. Diebold, A. Tay and K. Wallis, 1999, "Evaluating Density Forecasts of Inflation: The Survey of Professional Forecasters" in R. Engel and H. White (eds.), Festschrift in Honor of C.W.J. Granger, 76–90. Oxford University Press.

31. One should note a caveat here. While the inflation forecast published by the Philadelphia Fed is a well-defined number, as we explain in the discussion below, the expected inflation values derived from yield spreads could in theory be more realistic, but in practice be relatively opaque.

32. One could argue over the claim that these new measures reflect people's expectations for inflation. An alternate view would be to reason that these measures reflect the arbitrage relationship among inflation-linked bonds, inflation swaps, and other assets which can be used to hedge against inflation risk.

33. See D. Barr and J. Campbell, 1997, "Inflation, Real Interest Rates, and the Bond Market: A Study of UK Nominal and Index-Linked Government Bond Prices," Journal of Monetary Economics, 39 (3), 361–383.

Estimating Break-even Inflation

Fisher Equation

The Fisher equation states that the nominal interest rate is composed of the real rate plus a compensation for inflation

$$(1 + \text{Nominal Rate}) = (1 + \text{Real Rate})(1 + \text{Inflation Compensation})$$

The equation predicts that if there is no uncertainty in the economy, a one-to-one relationship exists between nominal rates and expected inflation. Irving Fisher developed this theory in 1930, and since that time inflation compensation has been further categorized into expected inflation and a risk premium.[34] This risk premium is a compensation for any differences between predicted or expected and actual or realized inflation. Exhibit 4–1 depicts the decomposition of the nominal yield.

Alternatively, if one assumes that inflation risk is minimal, and hence the risk premium is close to zero, the Fisher equation implies that market expectations of inflation can be derived from yields on nominal (or conventional) bonds and inflation-indexed bonds such as TIPS.

The analysis below uses the yield from TIPS as the real interest rate, and computes expected inflation assuming that the inflation-risk premium is low. A key reason for this assumption (one also made by numerous researchers) is that separating expected inflation from the risk premium is a nontrivial task.[35] If inflation risk is significant, the Fisher equation will deliver a noisy estimate of expected inflation.

---

34. As UK inflation-indexed bonds have an indexation lag of 8 months, the break-even inflation will be synthesized into expected inflation, the inflation-risk premium, plus an indexation-lag premium. For purposes of this example, as we are working with US rates, where reported inflation impact TIPS coupon payments with a 3-month lag, we can safely ignore this lag premium.

35. For a study on the estimation of inflation risk premium and inflation expectations using UK data, see Stefano Risa, 2001, "Nominal and Inflation Indexed Yields: Separating Expected Inflation and Inflation-Risk Premia," Working Paper, Lehman Brothers.

E X H I B I T   4–1

Decomposing Nominal and Real Yields

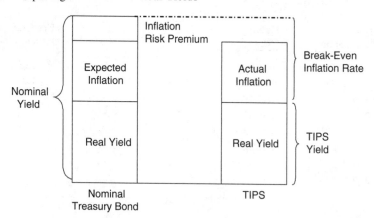

The table below lists the real yields as of close on September 1, 2003 for a set of TIPS issues expiring over the next 10 years, along with corresponding yields for nominal US Treasury issues of similar maturity. It also displays the break-even inflation for each of the TIPS securities calculated using the formula above.

Deriving an Inflation Curve

The data presented above can be used to derive a break-even inflation curve.

Exhibit 4–2 displays the inflation curve estimated using the cubic spline interpolation method. The highlighted values include the annualized inflation rate for the March to May 2003 quarter (0.87%),[36] and the break-even inflation numbers from Table 4–6.

---

36. The latest available quarterly change in CPI value—March to May 2003 in this case—is used to set the y-intercept for the estimated break-even inflation curve. The low value of 0.87% reflects the fact that inflation fell for two consecutive months in that quarter, April and May 2003.

E X H I B I T   4–2

Break-Even Inflation Curve (09-01-2003)

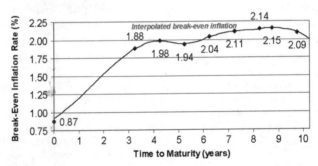

T A B L E   4–6

Computing Break-Even Inflation (09-01-2003)

TIPS Series	Maturity Date	Yield to Maturity (%) Nominal	Real	Break-Even Inflation (%)
10 Yr 3 3/8	1/15/07	2.75	0.86	1.88
10 Yr 3 5/8	1/15/08	3.23	1.24	1.98
10 Yr 3 7/8	1/15/09	3.52	1.58	1.94
10 Yr 4 1/4	1/15/10	3.87	1.82	2.04
10 Yr 3 1/2	1/15/11	4.12	2.00	2.11
10 Yr 3 3/8	1/15/12	4.30	2.15	2.14
10 Yr 3	7/15/12	4.37	2.21	2.15
10 Yr 1 7/8	7/15/13	4.39	2.29	2.09

Source: Bloomberg.

Using the Implied Break-even Inflation Numbers to Price CPI Futures

As the final settlement price of CME CPI futures is computed as 100 minus the annualized change in the CPI over the specific quarter, following the spline interpolation technique above, the estimated annualized percentage change in the CPI for the months June, July, and August 2003 is 0.9231%.

If one were to take the view that this break-even inflation rate is a valid prediction of the inflation rate over the June to August 2003 period, then the estimated final settlement price for the September 2003 contract would be $100 - 0.9231 = 99.0769$, and the contract would be priced for trading at this level.

Caveats

Break-even inflation is considered a long-term fundamental indicator. As such, it is not always a useful measure when forecasting 3- to 6-month inflation expectations. Though relatively easy to compute, its usefulness as a short-term pricing and trading tool can be negatively impacted by the following shortcomings.

> We earlier alluded to the zero-inflation-risk assumption underlying the break-even calculation methodology illustrated above. The pricing of nominal bonds includes compensation for inflation risk as well as for expected future inflation. If inflation risk is significant, the break-even inflation rate will overestimate expected future inflation.

> The calculation above also ignores the issue of bond convexity and the impact of relative differences between nominal and real bonds on break-even estimates.[37] For instance, Deacon, Derry, and Mirfendeski (2004, pages 84–85) observe that though the risk premium and convexity effects are normally assumed to cancel each other out, there is some uncertainty surrounding both the size and sign of these two effects. Estimating the net impact is still an open problem as the individual effects tend to vary with time.

> Though governments in both the US and Europe have increased the number of maturities of inflation-indexed bonds, this number is still small compared to the number of points generally required for the derivation of the whole term structure. Some suggested solutions to deal with this issue are discussed in the next subsection.

> The break-even inflation rate calculated for any particular maturity is an estimate of the average future inflation rate. As the next TIPS contract will not mature till January 2007, the break-even measure might not be a useful indicator of inflation over the next few months or quarters.

> This average-inflation prediction also ignores cyclical aspects of the inflation rate, especially in the context of the US CPI futures contract where, given its short-term structure, seasonality is a critical factor in its pricing.

---

37. Mark Deacon, Andrew Derry and Dariush Mirfendeski, Inflation-Indexed Securities: Bonds, Swaps and Other Derivatives, 2004, 2nd Ed., John Wiley & Sons.

The CPI is not adjusted for seasonal changes in the price level in the US economy. This means that seasonal changes will impact the price index. Although estimates based on average inflation rates will smooth out all seasonal changes, caution should be exercised while using the break-even inflation rate for short-term forecasts.[38]

Given the indexation lag referred to earlier, a trader looking to price the September 2003 contract using the break-even inflation value should adjust the TIPS yield to reflect the lag in the impact of reported inflation values on coupon payments. The need for such adjustment increases the noise level in using break-even inflation to forecast short-run expected inflation.

As TIPS tend to be less liquid that the nominal US Treasury bonds, any difference in respective yields could include a liquidity premium, a factor not related to expected inflation, but one that will introduce a bias in the break-even estimate.

The US Treasury has promoted TIPS as a potentially important component of an alternative asset class of inflation-indexed instruments. In recent years, various mutual fund companies as well as various banks have started aggressively marketing inflation-indexed savings products to retail investors. As investors develop a better understanding of this new asset class and allocate more money to it, if the increased demand—not necessarily due to any new concerns about inflation or real yield, but simply to accommodate a new asset class—is not met by increased issuance activity, these bonds will be bid up in price.[39] Thus any differences in the returns investors expect from the inflation-indexed and nominal bonds will tend to diminish the relevance of break-even inflation as a predictor of future inflation.

Differences in the expected real interest rate arising from differences in the duration of nominal and indexed securities will impact the differences in their yields.

To the extent that investors focus on real after-tax cash flows, taxation of the inflation accrual on the principal could potentially distort the relative movements of nominal and real yields, and thus the quality of the break-even as an estimate of expected inflation.[40]

---

38. For a description of the impact of seasonality and some suggestions on how to factor it while pricing inflation-linked products, see Eric Benhamou and Nabyl Belgrade, "Smart Modeling of Inflation Markets: Taking Seasonality into Account," 2004, CDC Ixis Capital Markets Working Paper, and Nabyl Belgrade, "Market Inflation Seasonality Management," 2004, CSC Ixis Capital Markets Working Paper.

39. This demand-induced increase in prices could in the short-run, push down real yields away from their equilibrium levels, thus artificially boosting break-even inflation (constant nominal yields and lower real yields will translate into higher implied inflation).

40. See Cedric Scholtes, "On Market-Based Measures of Inflation Expectations," Spring 2002, Bank of England Quarterly Bulletin.

Modeling the Term Structure

In countries with a more developed index-linked debt market, methodologies[41] have been developed where the estimated term structure of break-even inflation is consistent with term structures of nominal and real interest rates. To solve the problem caused by the shortage of available maturity dates for inflation-linked bonds researchers calibrate structural models of the term structure to fit actual bond prices. The goal is to infer inflation expectations by processing prices of nominal and index-linked bonds through these models. This approach can also be used to estimate the size of the effects of inflation-risk premium and convexity.

The general approach is to first construct nominal and real interest-rate term structures, and then use these as the basis for estimating future expected inflation. By using curve-fitting techniques, traders can estimate expected inflation for any target date.[42] Hence these numbers could, in theory, be used to price short-term contracts like inflation futures.

Though these models eschew the reliance on pairs of nominal and inflation-indexed bonds with similar maturities, their estimates of inflation expectations are prone more or less to the same set of shortcomings as the simple break-even methodology illustrated earlier. Adjustments have to be made to isolate the effects of inflation-risk premium, convexity, taxation, and indexation lag. The particular techniques adopted for this purpose could introduce biases in the estimated expected inflation rate.

General Equilibrium Pricing Models

Standard general equilibrium models have been in use for the pricing of stocks and nominal bonds. Lioui and Poncet (2005)[43] construct one such model of an economy subject to both real and monetary shocks, where money is a risky asset.[44] By making a simplifying assumption that all processes are lognormal, they derive closed-form solutions to price inflation on forwards and futures as well as options.

The price of the forward contract in their model "is equal to the ratio of the nominal price today of a real discount bond maturing at the maturity of the forward contract over the price of a nominal discount bond maturing at the same date." In this sense, this pricing model relies on the same asset-pricing information as the break-even and inflation-term structure models discussed above.

---

41. See Deacon, Derry, and Mirfendeski (2004), pages 85–92 for a summary description of the various modeling strategies.
42. The break-even inflation curve illustrated earlier is, on the other hand, a set of estimates of average expected inflation from calculation date to the maturities of different inflation-indexed bonds.
43. See Abraham Lioui and Patrice Poncet, "General Equilibrium Pricing of CPI's Derivatives," 2005, Journal of Banking and Finance, 29(5), 1265–1294.
44. This is in contrast to traditional monetary models where money is neutral—in other words, it does not impact real wealth and real interest rates.

More research has to be conducted into the merits of these models, especially their robustness over time and across countries. It is not clear that any practitioners use these more complex CPI futures pricing models which can lose their tractability once stochastic nominal interest rates are introduced.

Conclusion Regarding Pricing Issues

Though there might some value to the use of estimates of expected inflation, either via the Fisher hypothesis or by analysis of the term structure of nominal and real rates, for the purposes of long-term forecasts, reliable models to forecast short-term inflation do not yet exist. Lioui and Poncet propose a relatively well-specified approach to pricing CPI derivatives, but it is not clear that their model can be applied to the pricing of short-term contracts. Further research and, more importantly, the growth of an actively-traded inflation futures contract could help in the development of improved estimation and pricing models by enhancing the ability of researchers to better calibrate their models.

OTHER PRODUCT CONCEPTS

The concept of markets in economic indicators is not new. We described the early effort by the Coffee, Sugar, and Cocoa Exchange (now a division of the New York Board of Trade (NYBOT)) to launch an inflation index, despite the absence of "a primary market for inflation to trade against the futures."[45]

Inflation-Indexed Bond and/or Bond-Index Futures

Though the Chicago Board of Trade's first attempt at an inflation-indexed bond futures contract failed, given the increased trading volumes[46] in the cash TIPS market, it might be time to explore the possibility of resurrecting the contract. Index futures tracking a basket of IL bonds is a possibility, especially with the launch of numerous mutual funds benchmarked to IL bond indices.

In order for one such contract to come to fruition, certain structural improvements will have to take place in the TIPS market.

> For instance, the fact that large proportions of these bonds are kept in buy-and-hold portfolios might increase the cost of making physical deliveries in an IL bond contract. A relatively active TIPS repo market is reported to exist, but the market has not yet been stress-tested for efficiency.

> In the case of the Euro-zone inflation-indexed bond market, the feasibility of one such contract is adversely impacted due the distribution of liquidity

---

45. The explanation provided by the exchange for the failure of the contract, as quoted by J. Wrase, 1997, "Inflation-Indexed Bonds: How do they Work?" July/August 1997, Business Review, Federal Reserve Bank of Philadelphia.
46. Please refer to our earlier quote from the Bond Market Association that TIPS volumes nearly doubled in 2004.

across multiple sovereign issuers of varying credit quality. Though a physically-delivered contract tracking just one issuer might not be viable (amount outstanding for each issuer will not be sufficient to support an actively-traded futures contract), one could envision a futures contract on an index composed of multiple sovereign issues.

Index-futures contracts tend to be cash settled. This in turn requires the availability of noncontestable prices to compute the cash or spot value of the index at expiration. These bonds tend to be traded in the OTC market, making the determination of their fair values relatively difficult. However, this issue might be resolved as trading in the underlying bonds eventually moves to electronic platforms. This shift would enable exchanges to observe current market prices based on actual transactions.

Break-even Inflation Futures

There has been some talk on the possibility of break-even inflation futures. Banks do trade the break-even curve by taking opposite positions in inflation-linked and nominal bonds. For instance, if a firm is of the view that the market is overestimating inflation (based on break-even inflation), it can attempt to profit from its view by executing a short position in an inflation-linked bond and a long position in a matching nominal bond used to calculate the break-even inflation.

The feasibility of a futures contract on this metric depends on the same set of issues as the inflation-linked bond futures discussed above. Moreover, it is not clear if there is a large audience for this metric, especially in view of all that is known about the issues related to the calculation methodologies. An exchange could use a transparent set of rules to calculate the break-even rate; but it is not clear if this product cannot be replicated more easily by having a futures contract on the inflation-linked bond itself. A simpler product might be able to support break-even trades as well as other trading strategies involving the bond contract and other instruments.

SUMMARY

This chapter examined the concept of exchange-traded inflation futures. We reviewed the historical experience of these contracts and described current efforts to design contracts that are improvements in the sense that they attempt to better integrate with underlying inflation-linked cash and derivative markets. This asset class is relatively new, and growing at a rapid pace. Interestingly, the respective markets in the US and in Europe appear to be proceeding along different tracks. Differences in market structure could impact the design as well as the success of inflation-futures contracts targeting each market. We summarized the approaches to estimating future expected inflation. This is a growing area of research and should deliver tractable models which can be used to price inflation futures and other related derivative instruments.

APPENDIX 1

CPI Futures—Contract Spec Summary Sheet

Consumer Price Index Futures
Contract Specification Summary

Ticker Symbol	CME Globex® = CPI; Clearing = CU
Contract Size	Contract valued at $2,500 × Reference CPI Futures Index
Reference CPI Futures Index	100.00—annualized inflation rate in the 3-month period preceding the contract month based on the Consumer Price Index—US city average for all urban consumers, all items, not-seasonally adjusted ("CPI-U" or "CPI")
Contract Months	12 consecutive "March quarterly" contract months
Trading Venue and Hours	Traded on CME Globex® on Sundays from 5:30 p.m. to 2:00 p.m. the following day; on Mondays through Thursdays from 5:00 p.m. to 2:00 p.m. the following day (All times refer to local Chicago times)
Minimum Price Fluctuation	0.005 Index points or $12.50
Price Limit	No price limits. Price banding will be in effect as follows: On non-CPI announcement/release dates, the price band will be set at 0.20, i.e., 40 ticks, for both outrights and calendar spreads. On CPI announcement dates, 1 hour before and 1 hour after the scheduled announcement time (7:30 a.m. Chicago time), the price band will be widened to 2.00, i.e., 400 ticks, for both outrights and calendar spreads
Last Trading Day[47]	7:00 a.m. Chicago time on the day CPI announcement is made in the contract month. If the release of the relevant CPI data by the Bureau of Labor Statistics is postponed beyond the contract month, trading ceases at 7:00 a.m. Chicago time on the first business day following the contract month
Final Settlement Price	By cash settlement on the last day of trading. The final settlement price shall be calculated as 100 less the annualized percentage change in CPI-U over the past 3 months, rounded to four decimal places, or $100 - [400 \times ((CPI_t \div CPI_{t-3}) - 1)]$

APPENDIX 1

Continued

	E.g., for the June 2003 contract, the applicable CPI-U figures are those for May 2003 (183.5, released on June 17, 2003) and February 2003 (183.1, released on March 21, 2003). The final settlement price shall be $99.1262 = 100 - [400 \times ((183.5 \div 183.1) - 1)]$ Note that a price of over 100.0 suggests deflation during the 3-month period.
Position Limits	5000 CPI futures contracts, net long or short in all contract months combined

[47] At the initial listing of a contract month, if the scheduled date of the release of the CPI for the contract month is undetermined, the last trading day shall be tentatively set to 7:00 a.m. Chicago time on the first business day following the contract month. Upon the announcement of the CPI release schedule for the contract month, the last trading day shall be reset to 7:00 a.m. Chicago time on the scheduled day of CPI release.

APPENDIX 2

HICP Futures—Contract Spec Summary Sheet

Euro Consumer Price Index (HICP) Futures
Contract Specification Summary

Ticker Symbol	CME Globex® = HC; Clearing = HC
Contract Size	Contract valued at €10,000 × Reference HICP ex-Tobacco Futures Index
Reference HICP Futures Index	100.00—annual inflation rate in the 12-month period preceding the contract month based on the Euro-zone Harmonized Index of Consumer Prices excluding tobacco (HICP) published by the European Statistical Institute (Eurostat).
Contract Months	12 consecutive calendar months
Trading Venue and Hours	Available for trading on CME Globex® from 8:00 a.m. to 4:00 p.m. (London time) on Mondays through Fridays[48]
Minimum Price Fluctuation	0.01 Index points or €100.00 (this will render the contract equivalent to €1,000,000 notional)
Price Limits	No price limits. Price banding will be in effect as follows: On non-HICP announcement/release dates, the price band will be set at 0.20, i.e., 20 ticks. On HICP announcement dates, the price band will be widened to 2.00, i.e., 200 ticks.
Last Trading Day[49]	4:00 p.m. (London time) on the business day preceding the scheduled day the HICP announcement is made in the contract month
Final Settlement Price	By cash settlement on the day the HICP announcement is made. The final settlement price shall be calculated as 100 less the annual percentage change in HICP over the past 12 months, rounded to four decimal places, or $100 - [100 \times ((HICP_t \div HICP_{t-12}) - 1)]$ E.g., for the March 2005 contract, the applicable HICP figures are those for February 2005 (115.1, released on March 16, 2005) and February 2004 (113.5, released on March 17, 2004). The final settlement price shall be $98.2379 = 100 - [100 \times ((115.5 \div 113.5) - 1)]$

A P P E N D I X   2

Continued

Position Limits	Note that a price of over 100.0 suggests deflation during the 12-month period. 5,000 HICP futures contracts, net long or short in all contract months combined

[48] In other words, except when Daylight Savings Time is in effect in either, but not both, London or Chicago, HICP futures will be listed for trading on CME Globex® from 2:00 a.m. to 10:00 a.m. (Chicago time) on Mondays through Fridays.

[49] At the initial listing of a contract month, if the scheduled date of the release of the HICP for the contract month is undetermined, the last trading day shall be tentatively set to 4:00 p.m. (London time) on the last business day of the contract month. The exception would be the February contract, for which the tentative last trading day shall be the first business day following the second Tuesday of the following month. Upon the announcement of the HICP release schedule for the contract month, the last trading day shall be reset to 4:00 p.m. (London time) on the business day preceding the scheduled day of HICP release.

CHAPTER 5

COMMODITY INDEXES FOR REAL RETURN

Robert J. Greer
PIMCO

"Economic forces are not understood well enough for predictions to be beyond doubt or error… We are expecting too much if we require the security analyst to predict with certainty." Harry Markowitz, Portfolio Selection.

Investment in commodities is an idea that has been around since the 1970s,[1] but only recently has it become popular with institutional investors. Perhaps that is because traditional stocks and bonds have done so poorly in the last few years. Perhaps it is because investors have recently become more concerned about inflation, and they recognize that their liabilities will go up as inflation increases. Perhaps it is because investors are recognizing the potential diversification benefits that commodities offer. Or perhaps it is because they see other reputable investors who have committed to the asset class in search of potential benefits, which include:

Positive correlation to inflation and to *changes* in the rate of inflation

Diversification from stocks and bonds (zero or negative correlation)

Long-term returns and volatility comparable to equities

Protection from some economic "surprises" that is not offered by stocks and bonds.

This chapter will explain the fundamental reasons why those benefits have occurred in the past and why they might persist in the future. It is nice to see historical results, but an investor cannot rely on historical results without understanding why those results occurred. First we will explain why commodities are a distinct asset class. Then we will think of the various ways that an investor might obtain exposure to the asset class, concluding that a commodity index is the best measure of the inherent investment characteristics of the asset class. We will then explain why there are, in fact, inherent returns to the asset class, and why those returns should be expected to have the characteristics described above. We will consider historical results and discuss how an investor might incorporate commodities in a portfolio.

All of the discussion above will be without consideration of a specific outlook for commodities. However, we will then consider what economic factors over a secular timeframe will most impact the returns to commodity investment.

---

1. The first description of an investable commodity index was in the Journal of Portfolio Management, Summer 1978, "Conservative Commodities: A Key Inflation Hedge," by Robert J. Greer.

COMMODITIES AS A DISTINCT ASSET CLASS[2]

Commodities are fundamentally different from stocks and bonds. While they are investable assets, they are not capital assets. Commodities do not generate a stream of dividends, interest payments, or other income that can be discounted in order to calculate a net present value. The Capital Asset Pricing Model does not apply to a bushel of corn. Rather, commodities are valued because they can be consumed or transformed into something else which can be consumed. Their value at any time is determined by basic laws of supply and demand. Analytically, it is the intersection of supply and demand curves that determines their price. And it is the expected intersection of those supply and demand curves in the future that will affect (but not totally determine) the price of a commodity futures contract. This is the unifying feature of commodities that distinguishes them as an asset class different from the other investable assets in a portfolio. These commodities include energy products, livestock, food, fiber, and industrial and precious metals. Unlike financial assets, commodities are *real* assets, also known as "stuff." Stuff which can be used, touched, seen, and consumed; hard assets as opposed to paper assets. Not only are commodities a distinct asset class, but they are an important asset class in the world economy. The commodities included in some of the most popular investable indexes represent about $1.5 trillion of *annual* global production. This is important stuff.

WAYS TO GET COMMODITY EXPOSURE

If an investor wants exposure to commodity prices, the first thing he might think is that he should own commodities. Conceptually, he should have a warehouse where he stores some barrels of crude oil in one corner, bushels of wheat in another corner, and a pen of live cattle in the middle of the space. Wrong! Not only is this obviously impractical, but in fact *the price of actual commodities has not even kept up with inflation since World War II.* Even if it were possible to own the physical commodity (as a "consumable asset"), this would not have provided an attractive return in the post-war period.

Some investors think they can get adequate exposure to the distinct asset class of commodities by investing in the equities of commodity producers. By creating a portfolio of oil and gas companies, mining companies, agribusinesses, and the like. This is not the same thing as getting direct exposure to commodity prices (and changes in those prices). Once you own stock of a commodity producer, you are exposed to the financial structure of that company, exposed to other businesses in which the company might be involved, exposed to changes in accounting practices of that company, and exposed to the management talents of that company. Perhaps most important, you are also exposed to the possibility that the management might, for valid reasons, hedge its commodity production, so that you do not receive the full benefit of changes in commodity prices.

---

2. These thoughts on commodities as a distinct asset class are more fully expressed by the author in "What Is an Asset Class, Anyway?" in the Journal of Portfolio Management, Winter 1997.

For instance, in one study, 78% of surveyed financial executives said they would give up economic value in exchange for smooth earnings.[3] Perhaps that is why, in a study by Gorton and Rouwenhorst, it was shown that the equity of commodity producers is more highly correlated to the S&P 500 than to the price of the commodity which the company produced.[4]

To experience complete and direct exposure to changes in commodity prices, an investor must go directly to the commodity futures markets. At this point, he faces the question of "active" or "passive." That is, does he hire an active manager (a commodity trading advisor, or "CTA") to give him the exposure to the asset class, or does he use a passive index. Some active managers might indeed create value; but the investor must ask the question, "Does this truly give me exposure to the asset class?" The best way to answer that question is to ask an active manager, "If I wake up one morning six months from now, and I see that the price of wheat has gone up, can you assure me that this will be positive for my portfolio?" Most CTAs will have to answer, "I don't know. I can't tell you if, six months from now, I'll have a long position in wheat, a short position, or perhaps no position at all." (Most CTAs will also have to tell you that they are likely to be holding positions in noncommodity futures, such as currency and other financial futures, so that they have exposure to a lot more than just commodity prices.) For these reasons, a typical CTA does not give consistent positive exposure to the asset class of commodities. Instead, just like hedge funds, the CTA is providing exposure to *the asset class of gray matter* (brain power). If the CTA in fact has good gray matter, in the form of technical systems or fundamental judgment, the investor might get good returns, but this is not the same thing as exposure to the asset class of commodities. That is why the typical CTA will not offer an incentive fee based on outperforming a published commodity index.

Unlike active management, a commodity index can serve as the mechanism for investment in this long-only exposure, or it can serve as the benchmark for active management of commodity futures. As such, an index will capture the inherent returns that have been there in the past.

DEFINITION OF A COMMODITY INDEX

A commodity index measures the returns of a passive investment strategy, which has the following characteristics:

Holds only long positions in commodity futures.

Uses only commodity futures ("consumable assets").

Fully collateralizes those futures positions.

---

3. "The Economic Implications of Corporate Financial Reporting," by John Graham and Campbell Harvey of Duke, and Shiva Rajgopal of the University of Washington (Working Paper #10550), as summarized by Peter Bernstein in his newsletter, Economics and Portfolio Strategy, 1 August 2004.

4. Gorton, Gary, and Geert Rouwenhorst. 2004. "Facts and Fantasies about Commodity Futures." Unpublished working paper.

Passively allocates among a variety of commodity futures, taking no active view of individual commodity prices.

By holding only long positions, the investor will be required to "roll" his/her positions forward over time—unless he/she wants to own the physical commodity, which we have already established is both impractical and uneconomic. In other words, if he/she owns, say, the March crude oil contract, he/she will sell that contract and buy the April contract before delivery begins on the March futures. Then he/she will later roll from April into May. This process means that the investor will always be exposed to *changes in the expected future price of the commodity.*

The second bullet point is obvious. We are talking about the asset class of "consumable assets," not capital assets. No financial futures are included.

By "collateralizing" the futures positions, the investor will set aside collateral equal to the notional value of his/her long-only contracts. Going back to crude oil, if he/she owns one crude contract at, say, $60 per barrel × 1000 barrels per contract, he/she will have exposure to changes in the expected future price of $60,000 worth of crude. Therefore, he/she will set aside that amount of collateral to support his/her long-only position. This means two things. First, the investor will not get a margin call—unless the price of crude drops below zero. More important, the investor's total return will equal the return on collateral plus or minus the change in the expected future price of the commodity. The collateral assumed in most published commodity indexes is T-Bills.

Finally, the investor will not try to predict which commodities will perform the best. Rather, he/she will allocate his/her portfolio to a broad range of commodities based on some predetermined algorithm, which typically will cause him/her to have more of his/her portfolio exposed to commodities that are more important in world trade. This is clearly not like managed futures. When using a commodity index, an investor does not try to be smarter than the market; he/she merely extracts the inherent return that the market offers—and he/she restricts herself just to commodity markets. In this sense, a commodity index indeed provides exposure to a distinct asset class. The components of that asset class, as defined by the more popular indexes, are shown in Table 5–1.

COMMODITY FUTURES PRICING MODEL

Some people argue that, if the commodity futures markets are efficient, then there is no inherent return from consistently and passively owning long-only futures. Not only do historical results prove those people wrong, but so does fundamental economic and financial logic, as the model described below explains.

It seems that most commentators like to talk about energy markets. To be different, this chapter will explore another market, live cattle, to explain the source of returns. Most commentators also like to talk about "contango," "backwardation," and "roll yield." In this chapter we will try to avoid those terms.

Let us assume that I am a cattleman, and you, the reader, are a long-only investor in the commodity futures market. You have long-only fully collateralized

T A B L E   5–1

Commodity Index Components

As of 4/30/2005	DJAIGCI	GSCI	DBLCI*
Natural gas	12.34%	9.34%	n/a
Crude oil	13.21%	42.32%	35.00%
Unleaded gas	4.53%	8.61%	n/a
Heating oil	4.00%	13.18%	20.00%
Live cattle	5.47%	3.75%	n/a
Lean hogs	4.11%	2.22%	n/a
Wheat	4.72%	3.59%	11.25%
Corn	5.57%	2.54%	11.25%
Soybeans	8.20%	1.85%	n/a
Aluminum	6.51%	2.85%	12.50%
Copper	5.75%	2.41%	n/a
Lead	n/a	0.30%	n/a
Zinc	2.64%	0.56%	n/a
Nickel	2.62%	0.87%	n/a
Gold	5.67%	1.79%	10.00%
Silver	1.97%	0.20%	n/a
Sugar	2.59%	1.25%	n/a
Cotton	3.69%	1.20%	n/a
Coffee	3.67%	0.95%	n/a
Cocoa	n/a	0.23%	n/a
Soybean oil	2.75%	n/a	n/a

*These are target weights for the DBLCI as of 12/31/04.
Source: Goldman Sachs, AIG, Deutsche Bank.

positions in cattle, crude oil, wheat, and all the other commodities of an index. Further, let us assume that your friend, Jackson, is neither a cattleman nor an investor. He is a meatpacker, and he has a commitment to supply, say, a million pounds a day of steak and hamburger to Safeway. Safeway will pay him the market price, but he has to be sure that he has the meat to deliver.

We are assuming efficient markets, which means that we all agree, at least at the margin, on what prices will be in the future.

Let us assume we (you, Jackson, and I) are in February, and are looking out to October. We all agree that we think the price of live cattle in October will be 72 cents per pound, but we cannot be sure. We might have the entire world go on the Atkins diet, driving up the price of cattle to 84 cents. Or we might have a "mad-cow scare" causing everyone to shun beef, and driving the price to 60 cents. We do not know. However, there is one thing we do know about the future. We know that I have cattle coming to market in October, and when cattle are ready to come to market, they will be marketed, regardless of price. I also know that I have certain costs of production tied up in my cattle, say 65 cents per pound. I will need to sell my cattle for more than 65 cents in October if I am going to stay in business as a cattle producer. So I approach you, the reader/investor, with a proposal: Since we both agree that the price of cattle is likely to be 72 cents in October, can we agree right now, ahead of time, that I will deliver my cattle to you at that price in the fall? I doubt you would accept my proposal, because I have just asked you to take on all of my price risk for a zero expected return. However, you are a smart investor. You decide to counter my offer with a proposal of your own. You will agree to buy my cattle in October, but at a price of 70 cents—2 cents lower than where you or I think the price will really be. I will be happy to take you up on your offer. I have just paid 2 cents to ensure that I will remain in the cattle business! This is a key feature of commodity futures markets (unlike financial futures markets), which are often considered a "zero-sum game." There are participants in the commodity futures markets who have objectives different from the investment objectives of you, the long-only investor.

Why, you might ask, do I not just go to Jackson the meatpacker and contract with him for October delivery of my cattle. Simply put, Jackson, as a processor, does not need the price protection that I require. He will be selling beef to Safeway in October at market prices. If they are high-priced cattle, then he will be selling high-priced steak. If they are low-priced cattle, then he will sell low-priced steak. Either way, his inventory, on which he has price risk, is only a few days of supply. If Jackson locked in his cost of materials in February, without locking in his final selling price in October, he would actually be increasing his business risk. On average, over the wide range of commodities produced every year, the producer has larger inventories and higher fixed costs than the processor, who is the natural buyer of his products. Therefore the producer needs price insurance more than the processor.

The model that I have described is shown in Exhibit 5–1. This "insurance premium" is not the only source of return to an index, but it is part of the picture.

Now time passes and we get to October. In all likelihood, the price of cattle will not be 72 cents. Something unexpected will have occurred. This is shown by Exhibit 5–2, which demonstrates that actual prices will have varied from our expectations. If we are really rigorous about our assumption of efficient markets, then we have to say that, over time, the two shaded areas will even out. On average, we will guess too high as often as we will guess too low. However, in any one month, or any one year, this variance from expectations will likely dominate short-term returns. So this "expectational variance"[5] will not, in the long run, be a source of return, but it will affect the *pattern* of returns in a very important way, as we will see.

As we approach October, Jackson the meatpacker looks at the supply of cattle in feedlots in his market, and he begins to realize that there are not as many cattle there as he had expected. Maybe a drought has reduced supplies, as cattle failed to

---

5. A term coined several years ago by Grant Gardner of the Frank Russell Company.

E X H I B I T   5–1

Commodity Futures Pricing Model

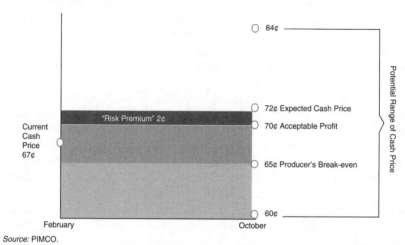

Source: PIMCO.

E X H I B I T   5–2

"Expectational Variance"

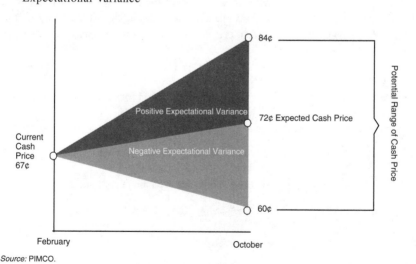
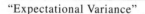

Source: PIMCO.

fatten up quite as quickly as expected. Or, if this had been December, perhaps an early freeze would have diminished supplies. For whatever reason, Jackson begins to worry. What if there are no cattle there to be bought in the next few weeks? What if they are there only at a very high price? What is he supposed to do?

Simple: Jackson buys the October live cattle futures contract. This way, at worst, he can take delivery of cattle at one of several designated locations, to ensure that he will have animals to process; or, more likely, if this anticipated shortage drives up prices in the cash market, he will at least have profits from his long October position to help finance the purchase of cattle. Either way, at all costs he must meet his commitment to supply a million pounds a day of beef to Safeway, and Safeway will be paying market price, even if that price has gone up.

What is this likely to do to the futures prices, as Jackson pays for the *convenience* of knowing that he will have cattle to process through his plant? You are likely to see the price of the nearby contract go up, as Jackson and other meatpackers pay for the certainty of immediate supply. Economists call that "convenience yield." Perhaps Jackson's view of longer-term prices (and your view as well, since the markets are efficient) has not changed? We have already established that if he took a long term futures position, he would actually be increasing his business risk. As a result, we could have a situation where the longer-dated futures prices are lower than current prices. (Now imagine that Jackson had been working at a refinery where he was responsible for procuring crude oil. One day without a crude supply would not just disappoint customers; the cost of shutting down and restarting a refinery is tremendous. How important is the *convenience* of supply in that situation? Very important.)

Exhibit 5–3 is a schematic of forward prices for a commodity. The situation just described is represented by the top curve. Future prices are lower than the current price. For analysts who have grown up on the study of only financial futures, this makes no sense. For instance, how could the future price of the S&P 500 be lower than the current price? It cannot, because there is an arbitrage

EXHIBIT 5–3

Examples of a Forward Curve

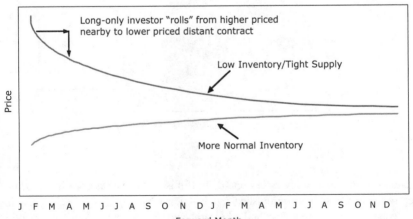

Source: PIMCO.

opportunity—you could short the stocks of the S&P and buy the futures. Commodities are different. Can you sell short live cattle? Unlikely; this downward-sloping pattern of forward prices is called "backwardation," but I promised I would not use that word.

Consider what this does to your portfolio of futures positions, since you are a passive long-only investor. As October arrives, you sell the nearby contract at a higher price and replace it with a lower-priced December contract. Then, if in December there are still low inventory and tight supplies, Jackson may be paying again for the convenience of being able to meet his contractual commitment to Safeway. That could cause the December contract to rise to the same level as the expired October contract and you might have made money even if the cash price of cattle did not change between October and December.

At other times, when inventories are more plentiful, you are more likely to see a pattern of futures prices like the bottom line on this chart. A pattern called "contango."

Let us begin to analyze where your inherent return comes from, shown diagrammatically in Exhibit 5–4. There are several components to the return of the long-only investor.

The first and easiest component of return is the return on your collateral, since your futures positions are fully collateralized. Published futures indexes typically assume that this collateral is invested in T-Bills, which over a long period of time (for instance, 1970 to 2004, according to Bloomberg) have returned an expected rate of inflation plus a real rate of return.

The next component of return is the risk premium that has already been described.

Now its time to talk about another source of return offered by the commodity markets. This return comes from the fact that you would not expect

E X H I B I T   5–4

Commodity Indexes: Basis for Returns

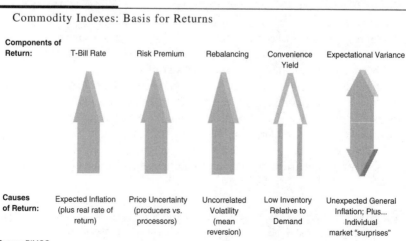

Components of Return:	T-Bill Rate	Risk Premium	Rebalancing	Convenience Yield	Expectational Variance
Causes of Return:	Expected Inflation (plus real rate of return)	Price Uncertainty (producers vs. processors)	Uncorrelated Volatility (mean reversion)	Low Inventory Relative to Demand	Unexpected General Inflation; Plus... Individual market "surprises"

Source: PIMCO.

commodity prices to be highly correlated with each other. Each commodity responds to a supply/demand model, with unique supply/demand factors for each commodity market. The key factors that change our expectation about the price of oil are different from the key economic factors that change our expectation about the price of copper, which in turn are different from the key factors that affect our expectation about the future price of coffee. We take advantage of this fact by constructing a commodity index in the same way that Harry Markowitz taught us was the efficient way to construct a portfolio of uncorrelated assets. An index can be designed to have weightings that force it to buy what goes down and sell what goes up. It can rebalance. This rebalancing can give you a third aspect of return to your commodity index—the return that can come from rebalancing a portfolio of assets that are not highly correlated with each other.[6]

The next arrow in Exhibit 5–4 shows the source of return labeled "Convenience Yield." You will see that this arrow is a little lighter. That is because it is there sometimes in some markets, and is dependent on the relative tightness of supply and demand. It is also more important to processors in some commodities than in others.

Finally, let us go back to the "expectational variance" we talked about earlier. In most cases, the factors causing a change in expectations of future commodity prices have little or nothing to do with our expectations about stock or bond markets. A freeze in Brazil might dramatically affect our expectations about future coffee prices, but it will not affect the movement of the S&P 500, or the bond markets. Likewise, with a strike in the copper mines in Chile, or a threat of mad cow disease. This fact supports the idea that movements in commodity futures prices should be generally uncorrelated with stock and bond returns, with one important exception: Suppose that we all began to expect higher inflation.

If that happened, if in fact the world began to expect higher inflation, bonds would be dropping in price as interest rates rose. Many people would expect stock prices to drop as well. Yet a commodity index, because it reflects our changing expectation of future prices of $1.5 trillion per year of "stuff," might be expected to rise in response to an expectation of higher inflation. This response to changes in inflation expectations actually gives us some reason to expect negative correlation between a commodity index and stocks or bonds.

Note that this last arrow points both up and down. Over a long time period, it may not be a source of return, as the market might guess too high as often as it guesses too low, but it is the major determinant affecting the *pattern* of returns to a commodity index over shorter periods of a week, a month, or even a year.

As an aside, ask yourself what kind of "surprises" are likely to affect futures. Most likely are unexpected reductions in supply. We seldom are surprised

---

6. For a formula that might be used to measure the value of rebalancing in certain instances, see "The Nature of Commodity Index Returns," by Robert J. Greer, in the Journal of Alternative Investments, Summer 2000.

by a bumper corn crop or by additional supplies of crude oil, or cattle that suddenly appear and demand is reasonably stable, unless there is a shock, such as the threat of mad cow disease. So if supply shocks are more likely than demand shocks, then surprises should tend to be to the upside, which creates positive skew—certainly better than volatility to the downside.

Does a commodity index have an inherent return? Yes, though there can be extended periods of negative performance. That return consists of:

Expected inflation

Plus (or minus) unexpected inflation

Plus a real rate of return

Plus an insurance premium to producers

Plus another risk premium—sometimes—paid by processors for convenience

Plus a rebalancing yield, if you choose to rebalance.

Because of the phenomenon of expectational variance, the pattern of index returns should be at least uncorrelated with stocks and bonds, or somewhat negatively correlated to stock and bond returns to the extent that unexpected inflation affects returns of all these asset classes. And the returns might have positive skew.

HISTORICAL RESULTS

We have just reviewed the fundamental theory regarding the drivers of commodity index returns, and why those inherent returns should be expected to show a desirable pattern. It is as fundamental as Economics 101 and Finance 101. History also supports these arguments. Table 5–2 shows the correlations and skews of the most well-known investable commodity indexes since their inceptions.

Indeed, for each of the time periods shown, they all have negative correlation to stocks and bonds and positive correlation to inflation.

The longest time series for these indexes is that of the Goldman Sachs Commodity Index, a product which has been calculated live since 1991 and on a back-tested basis since 1970. This is a time which covers periods of increasing inflation, decreasing inflation, expansion, recession, war, and peace. Over this extended period of time, the index has not only shown negative correlation to stocks and bonds, but has also shown a small positive correlation to inflation—and a larger positive correlation to *changes* in the rate of inflation. Those changes in the rate of inflation are more likely to hurt stock and bond returns. For instance, if we had a *stable* 10% rate of inflation, bonds could conceivably yield 12% to 13%, and stocks might not do so badly either. However, what is disastrous for bonds and stocks is the move from a low rate of 3% up to a 10% rate of inflation, which is when commodity pricing theory says that a commodity index should do well. In fact, especially over longer measurement periods, there is higher correlation to changes in the rate of inflation than to the level of inflation. If you used annual returns instead of quarterly, this improved correlation to changes in inflation would be even

T A B L E   5–2

Commodity Index Statistics

	DJ-AIG[1]	GSCI[2]	DBLCI[3]
Begin date	31-Dec-1990	31-Dec-1969	31-Dec-1988
End date	31-Dec-2004	31-Dec-2004	31-Dec-2004
Annualized return	6.87%	12.00%	12.67%
Annualized volatility	11.66%	19.59%	23.67%
Skew	–0.15	0.99	2.10
Correlation to S&P500	–0.19	–0.28	–0.34
Correlation to LBAG[4]	–0.09	–0.07	–0.13
Correlation to CPI	0.17	0.17	0.32
Correlation to changes in CPI	0.12	0.33	0.37

[1]Dow Jones-AIG Commodity Index.
[2]Goldman Sachs Commodity Index.
[3]Deutsche Bank Liquid Commodity Index.
[4]Lehman Brothers Aggregate Bond Index.
Source: PIMCO.
Past performance is no guarantee of future results.

more pronounced (see footnote 4). Furthermore, in only 2 years from 1970 through 2004 did both stocks and the GSCI drop in value. This is true diversification.

To see what actual returns might have been in that wide range of economic environments from 1970 to the present, look again at Table 5–2. From 1970 through 2004, the GSCI actually had higher returns than the S&P 500, with only slightly higher volatility—and with that diversifying aspect of negative correlation. An examination of returns of the various commodity indexes over shorter periods of time would also show higher returns in the last few years, while returns in the 1980s and 1990s were not much better than just the return on T-Bills (a time period when paper assets were benefiting a portfolio). It was not just in the 1970s that they did well. Over the most recent 5 years ending in 2004 this asset class also performed well, as equity returns disappointed.

One can begin to see why asset allocation models like commodities. With a return related to inflation, which drives the liabilities of many investors, asset-liability models like commodities even more.

It looks as if commodities might indeed shelter a portfolio from inflation, and also provide useful diversification in a wide range of economic environments. Meanwhile, they still provide positive exposure to some unexpected events that might affect individual markets.

This could be shown if you looked at commodity index returns when we had the unexpected start of the first Gulf War. A commodity index went up as stocks declined. Even more interesting is to see the performance of a commodity index during the equity market meltdown of October 1987—commodities were flat. Why? People kept eating their Wheaties and drinking their coffee. No changes in supply and demand for commodities. That is the kind of fundamental economic diversification that makes this asset class so important.

In summary, a commodity index has an inherent return that can be expected to provide diversification in a variety of economic scenarios, when we do not know what scenario to expect.

Before concluding, let us consider one more issue. Let us say that you like the asset class. That must mean that, besides diversification, you want some inflation protection. Remember that the published indexes, and all the data used in this chapter, assume that T-Bills are collateralizing long-only commodity futures. If you really want inflation protection, why would you use T-Bills as your collateral if you could use inflation-linked bonds (ILBs) instead?

Think about it. Real return characteristics of commodities backed by the real return aspects of inflation-linked bonds. ILBs might capture higher inflation as it actually occurs in higher reported CPI, while the commodity futures exposure might provide protection from rising inflationary *expectations*. And an investor might also consider, over a complete economic cycle, which might be expect to outperform—ILBs or T-Bills. If the former, then an investor could look for a way to collateralize futures with inflation-linked bonds. Just one more attractive feature of commodity indexes is that they can be implemented using a variety of styles for collateral management, including ILBs, or LIBOR, or some other style, as long as that style has a certain amount of liquidity.

IMPLEMENTATION

Once an investor decides to include commodities, as an asset class, in his/her portfolio, he/she faces the questions of how and how much. That second question is dealt with in a later chapter of this handbook. There are a variety of ways to answer the first question.

An investor might decide to purchase contracts on all the individual commodities underlying an index. However, unlike buying and holding the stocks that make up a stock index, these futures contracts cannot just be bought and put away. They will expire as they approach maturity, and therefore must be replaced by other contracts. In the cattle example given earlier, you, the investor, must "roll" the October live cattle contract into a December contract. Not only that, but you have collateral to manage, and that typically means active management. Furthermore, as you hold futures positions, you would have to manage margin flows as contract prices moved up and down.

There are futures contracts on two of the more popular indexes, but managing a position in these index futures still requires monthly trading and management of margin. Furthermore, these index futures markets are not highly liquid, especially outside the predefined roll period of the given index.

Because of this requirement for active administration of a set of futures positions, most investors elect to utilize derivatives to get commodity index exposure. Some use structured notes. Some of these notes may include principal protection (at a cost, of course). Other investors use total return swaps. These swaps typically work as follows: On a stated notional amount, the counterparty (typically the commodity desk of an investment bank) agrees to pay the total return of the published index. Note that this return includes the embedded T-bill rate described earlier. In return, the investor agrees to pay back that same T-bill rate plus a negotiated fee. That fee is supposed to cover the transaction costs of the counterparty, who must manage positions in all the underlying futures markets. This agreement also maintains the ownership, control, and management of the collateral in the hands of the investor, who is then able actively to manage those fixed income assets to gain additional value.

OUTLOOK

To this point we have made a case for commodity index investment as a strategic allocation. Diversification, potential protection from unexpected events, hedging from the inflation that affects our liabilities; these arguments were made while being agnostic about the economic outlook. In fact, as evidenced by the opening quotation from Markowitz, it is that agnosticism, that recognition that we cannot "predict with certainty," which creates the need for the benefits that commodity indexes offer. For a brief moment, as this is written in the first half of 2005, let us take a look at a possible scenario for the next few years; a secular timeframe.

Commodity demand has been rising over the long term, driven by continued growth in the global economy. This is likely to continue. Short-term reductions in demand, perhaps resulting from a slowdown in China's economic growth, will likely be temporary and have a limited effect on the long-term upward trend. As a result, demand should remain a positive contributor to the factors that drive commodity index returns. During this time, there will likely be constraints on supply—supply of commodities, supply of storage, supply of processing capacity, and supply of transportation. In other words, the entire infrastructure for many commodity industries will be strained.

Specifically, there are three trends that will support long-term growth in commodity demand. First, expansionary policies in the US and elsewhere will stimulate growth, increasing the demand for goods and services and the raw materials (i.e., commodities) used to manufacture and produce those goods and services.

A second, equally important trend is China's (and, to a lesser extent, India's) effort to export low-cost labor, which will likely have an inflationary impact on commodity prices. To export its cheap labor, China will have to purchase raw materials. Therefore, to the extent that cheap labor makes China's exports of finished goods more attractive in the global marketplace, demand for cheaper finished goods would tend to support the price of commodities used to produce those goods. China is also importing raw materials (metals, energy) to expand its manufacturing capacity, which should provide additional support to commodities prices overall.

The third, and perhaps most important trend, is a rising standard of living in China, India and other emerging economies. If these nations succeed in exporting their cheap labor, the standard of living in those countries will rise, which will increase the net global demand for commodities. Higher living standards in emerging economies would likely increase demand for commodities in a number of ways:

More energy will be consumed. Before 1993 China was a net exporter of crude oil; since then, it has been a net importer.

More cars will be purchased, increasing global demand for gasoline and the raw materials used in vehicle production. For example, car ownership in China is growing at a rate of 1 million per year, according to J.D. Power and Associates.

More housing, of higher quality, will be built, increasing the demand for copper, lumber, and other building components.

Diets will improve over time, increasing the global demand for meat protein (livestock), which will in turn increase the demand for feed grains.

More broadly, a rising standard of living in emerging markets is a positive factor for commodity index returns because a dollar of wages in the hands of workers in emerging economies will buy more commodity content than an incremental dollar in the hands of US, European, and Japanese workers. Workers in developed economies already have their cars and houses, and their diets already are above subsistence, so they are more likely to spend that dollar on services or discretionary items. A dollar spent at the movies, in a restaurant, or for health services does not increase commodity demand as much as a dollar spent on a car, a refrigerator, or a house.

While these factors should support commodity demand over a secular, 3- to 5-year horizon, we need to consider the possibility that shorter-term factors could influence demand. In particular, a slowdown in China's economic growth could have a negative effect on global demand for certain commodities. When economists speak of either a "soft" or a "hard" landing for the Chinese economy, they are really talking about the rate of growth slowing to a mere 3% to 4% annual increase (for a "hard" landing). Such an extreme slowdown might in fact curtail some of the industrial and infrastructure development in that country. That could in turn reduce the demand for commodities like concrete and steel, to the extent that these commodities are used to build infrastructure.

However, a slowdown in China's economy will likely have only a limited effect on the factors driving commodity index returns. Most of the components of popular commodity indexes are "consumption commodities" such as energy, agricultural products, and livestock, which should be less sensitive to a slowdown in China's economic growth. If the Chinese economy grows at a "mere" 4%, then you might expect their energy consumption to grow by a "mere" 4% as well. In addition they will continue to consume more food, as there are more mouths to feed, some of which are demanding upgraded nutrition.

To meet increasing demand for commodities, there must also be an increase in supply, storage and transportation capacity. Currently, production capacity is not keeping pace with the rise in commodity demand. Development of infrastructure for processing, storage, and delivery of commodities is also lagging. As a result, a lack of supply flexibility in many commodities has been another positive contributor to the factors that drive commodity index returns.

This situation is not likely to change quickly, because demand does not, by itself, generate additional supply. Additional supply requires substantial investment in the infrastructure for production, transportation, and storage, which in turn requires the incentive of higher prices, and the expectation of some stability in those higher prices. In addition, it requires time—several years—to build the necessary infrastructure.

Today's supply constraints can be traced back to the boom in commodity prices in the 1970s. As prices rose, investment in infrastructure surged globally, leading to surplus capacity in the 1980s and 1990s. This excess capacity caused commodity prices to lag general price increases in the economy and lowered the return on capital invested in commodity infrastructure. As a result, investment in commodity production and infrastructure declined, the effects of which we are now seeing on a global basis. The emphasis is on global, since most commodities are consumed globally, with pricing differentials based mainly on transportation costs. (Natural gas, which, for the most part, is limited to pipeline transportation, is an exception.)

Paradoxically, the lack of infrastructure development in some commodities has led to price volatility, further inhibiting investment in needed infrastructure, since returns on investment become more variable. This chapter does not go into great detail about the supply/demand balance and production capacity of every commodity sector, since each sector has its own unique factors to consider. However, we offer a few highlights to illustrate the fact that commodity production and capacity are not keeping up with demand.

Crude oil refining capacity: US consumers are keenly aware that no new refining capacity has been built in the US for many years, due to environmental restrictions and insufficient return on capital. However, it is not just in the US Chart 5–1 shows that, globally, refineries are running at the highest utilization rate that they have experienced in the last 25 years—close to 100%. There is little room for any mishaps that could affect this global capacity.

Crude oil production capacity: For the last 20 years most of the world believed that OPEC had sufficient excess crude oil production capacity to prevent a true shortage. As Russia and other areas also developed their production capacity, energy consumers fell into the comfortable notion that the world had sufficient crude oil supplies. It would just be a question of how to pay OPEC's price and whether we would be subject to political action from an OPEC that controlled less of the total global production. As Chart 5–2 shows, however, the world, after years of excess capacity, is now consuming almost as much as it is capable of producing; and it gets worse. An oil well (or field) will have declining production as it ages. Consequently, as estimated by Barclays Capital, the world must find and develop new crude oil production of about 3.5 million barrels per day just to make up for the depletion of existing fields. On top of that, the world needs to develop another 1.5 million bpd to support global growth in demand. This requires a great

CHART 5-1

Global Refining Capacity and Crude Oil Demand

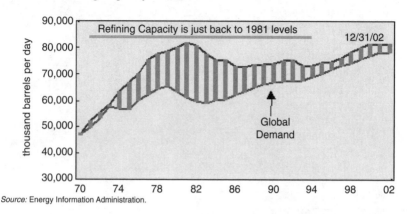

Source: Energy Information Administration.

CHART 5-2

World Oil Production and Total Capacity

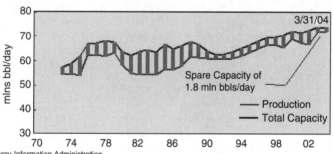

Source: Energy Information Administration.

amount of capital and many years to develop and bring into production new projects that are at higher cost and more difficult to complete.

Grain inventories: It is not just energy; grain production, while growing, is in some cases not keeping up with demand. Measured in terms of days of supply, Chart 5–3 shows that global inventories of wheat and corn are at historically low levels. Soybeans are also at about the same level, though this is not such a new phenomenon for that crop. The USDA also reports that global planted acreage for wheat and corn has declined recently, while yields per acre have leveled off.

Metals inventory: Inventories of industrial metals are almost as low as anytime in the last 20 years, as measured by days of global supply (Chart 5–4).

In summary, global demand will likely increase for most commodities, especially the "consumable" commodities that typically comprise the bulk of commodity indexes. Global supply and infrastructure capacity will take several

C H A R T   5–3

Days of Inventory

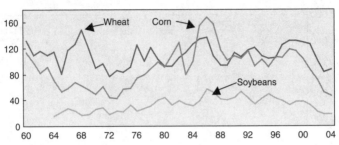

Source: USDA.

C H A R T   5–4

Aluminum, Copper, Nickel—Days of Forward Consumption

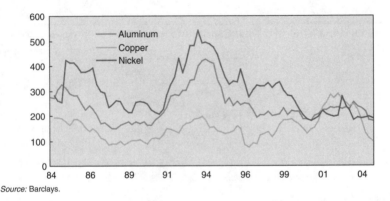

Source: Barclays.

years to catch up. This tightness means that unexpected events are likely to be positive for commodity returns, unless the surprise results in an unexpected drop in absolute demand, as happened for instance, with jet fuel soon after September 11, 2001. This combination of rising demand and insufficient supply means that the factors driving commodity index returns will likely remain positive contributors.

That means three things: First, there are more likely to be bottlenecks, or supply disruptions, which means that "surprises" ("expectational variance") might more likely be to the upside. Second, tight supply and limited infrastructure might also mean, in some industries, that commodity processors will more freq-uently demand the *convenience* of having access to commodities until supplies are more plentiful. Third, to encourage the flow of capital into commodity industries, the commodity producers need an expectation of stable prices, which means that the demand for producer "insurance" may continue.

FIT IN A PORTFOLIO

Commodities serve the dual purpose of providing an inflation hedge (when we are not sure what the inflation outlook is, but know that we have liabilities linked to inflation) and also providing essential diversification. Many investors utilize a mean-variance optimizer to determine their optimal asset allocation, while some also use an asset-liability allocation model. In the former MVO model, the inherent diversification characteristics of a commodity index will often cause the model to call for a 15% to 30% commodity allocation. An ALM model often likes commodities even more due to their inflation hedging characteristics. Many investors, after seeing these results, decide that commodities can improve their portfolios, but they typically will constrain the allocation to this asset class to be in single digits. To show how commodities might have the potential to improve the efficient frontier of a portfolio, consider the hypothetical case described below.

Think of a portfolio that has only stocks, bonds, and TIPS. Table 5–3 shows purely hypothetical return assumptions, as well as volatilities and correlations for these asset classes. Graph 5–1, which includes an efficient frontier, focuses on the least risky part of that curve (i.e., the leftmost part of the frontier). The lower curve in Graph 5–1 represents the riskier of the two efficient frontiers in that, for every level of return, a portfolio can be found on the upper curve with lower risk. Now consider adding commodities. Again, Table 5–3 shows hypothetical return assumptions for this new asset class. This hypothetical return for commodities was calculated as 2% over the hypothetical TIPS return, with the idea that TIPS might be used as collateral to collateralize commodity index exposure. The higher curve shows the efficient frontier which results from adding commodities to the universe of choices available to the portfolio manager. This conclusion is not too surprising, since an investor usually expects some expansion of the efficient frontier from adding more asset classes. What is instructive, however, is to look at the

TABLE 5–3

Stocks, Bonds, TIPS, Commodities

	Stocks	Bonds	TIPS	Commodities
Stocks	1.00			
Bonds	0.10	1.00		
TIPS	0.00	0.50	1.00	
Comm	–0.30	–0.20	0.10	1.00
Hypothetical return	7.0%	4.3%	4.36%	6.6%
Risk	20.2%	7.6%	5.6%	24.5%

GRAPH 5–1

Stocks, Bonds, TIPS and Commodities

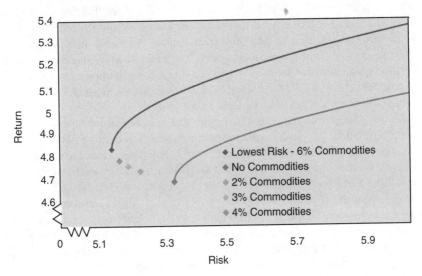

minimum risk portfolio that results from adding commodities. As commodities are included, first at 2%, then 3%, then 4%, and finally 6%, the calculated risk actually decreases while the calculated return increases. That is, with these particular assumptions, there is not a trade-off between risk and return. The portfolio benefits by achieving lower calculated risk and higher calculated return up to an approximate 6% commodity allocation.

In this hypothetical example, commodities, which can be a volatile asset class on a stand-alone basis, may actually be beneficial to those investors who are seeking the minimum volatility for their total portfolio.

SUMMARY

This chapter has identified commodities as a distinct asset class and has described why the best way to get exposure to commodity prices is via the futures markets. It has described a commodity index as the best measure of the returns from the asset class. It has shown why historical returns have provided both inflation hedging and diversification benefits. It has described the economic factors which may lead to a continuation of these portfolio benefits from commodity index investment. It has described ways that an investor can gain exposure to commodity indexes, and discussed how this asset class can fit into an overall portfolio.

In closing, consider another quotation from Harry Markowitz, again from *Portfolio Selection*:

> "Only the clairvoyant could hope to predict with certainty. Clairvoyant analysts have no need for the techniques of this monograph."

Readers who are clairvoyant, who can see into the future, may not need the benefits of a commodity index, but for a financial analyst who cannot predict with certainty, who is not clairvoyant, a commodity index can improve the expected performance of a portfolio in a world where we are unsure what to expect.

CHAPTER 6

COMMODITIES—ACTIVE STRATEGIES FOR ENHANCED RETURN

Hilary Till and Joseph Eagleeye
Premia Capital Management, LLC

In this chapter, we note how a set of active commodity strategies could potentially add value to an institution's commodity allocation. However, we also emphasize the due care that must be taken in *risk management* and *implementation discipline*, given the "violence of the fluctuations which normally affect the prices of many ... commodities," as Keynes (1934) put it.

We take it as a given that a prudent investor should include commodities in their overall asset allocation mix. As PIMCO's Robert Greer noted in Chapter 5, the benefits of commodity indexes include positive correlation to inflation as well as positive correlation to *changes* in the rate of inflation. Commodity indexes can also potentially perform well during a number of adverse economic surprises that are harmful to investments in stocks and bonds.

In what follows, we will discuss the appropriate role of actively managed commodity strategies in an institutional portfolio. We will then outline the structural sources of return that are potentially available to an active commodity manager. Finally we will discuss some of the issues that an active manager needs to take into consideration when designing an investment process around these sources of return.

THE ROLE OF ACTIVELY-MANAGED COMMODITY STRATEGIES IN AN INSTITUTIONAL PORTFOLIO

We would argue that the role of active commodity strategies is as a *satellite* to an institution's *core* exposure to commodities, which in turn should be obtained through commodity index investments. With commodity indexes, an institutional investor obtains consistent exposure to the inherent returns of the asset class. This is important for institutional investors since the total risk of an institutional portfolio is managed through the diversification provided by balanced portfolios of uncorrelated assets. Another way of putting this is that under the institutional investment framework, one manages risk through the careful combination of offsetting beta risks.

In an actively managed commodity hedge fund, there is no guarantee that a manager will remain consistently long of commodities. As a matter of fact, it is a core risk-management principle for most hedge funds that total risk should be managed by neutralizing systematic risk through hedging. An idealized hedge fund is not supposed to deliver a consistent beta; it is supposed to either deliver pure alpha (if it is a relative-value fund) or well-timed beta exposures (if it is a global macro fund.)

If an institution's long-term asset allocation plan were designed around the expectation that its commodity allocation would provide protection against, say, an oil shock, the plan's purpose could be compromised if the institution invested exclusively in actively managed commodity programs. For example, prior to the first Gulf War, an active commodity program might have excluded long positions in oil since, at the time, the term structure of that futures market indicated surplus. If an institution's commodity exposure were solely in such a program, then that institution would have missed out on having an oil dislocation hedge just when this portfolio protection was needed the most.

THE BENEFITS AND LIMITATIONS OF ACTIVELY-MANAGED COMMODITY STRATEGIES

Once an institution has obtained its core commodity exposure through a commodity index investment, the next logical step is to include active commodity managers for further value-added. This is analogous to the evolving nature of institutional equity management whereby active management is being unbundled from passive index investments. A number of institutions are now getting core equity exposure through equity index funds, exchange-traded funds, and/or futures and then investing in long/short equity hedge funds for further value-added.

Benefits

To demonstrate the benefits of active commodity management, Akey of Cole Partners (2005) created a comprehensive database of known active commodity futures traders. These traders identified themselves as focusing on nonfinancial commodity markets. Akey then created an equally-weighted portfolio of both active and inactive programs from this database. By including inactive programs, the author attempted to limit survivorship bias.

Exhibit 6–1 shows the return and risk statistics for an equally-weighted portfolio of active commodity futures traders from January 1991 through November 2004.

These results suggest that an institution may be able to source skilled commodity managers who can achieve superior returns with acceptable risk.

Akey also provided evidence that the active manager returns were likely not related to commodity index exposure. Exhibit 6–2 shows how low the empirical correlations of the active portfolio were with various commodity indices. This is a reassuring property for an institutional investor since under the core-satellite

EXHIBIT   6–1

Active Commodity Futures Traders Returns (January 1991 through November 2004)

Compound Annual Return	Annualized Standard Deviation	Sharpe Ratio	Worst Draw-Down
20.99%	10.48%	1.63	−8.49%

Source: Excerpted from Akey (2005), Figure 19.

EXHIBIT   6–2

Correlation of Monthly Returns. Active Commodity Futures Traders vs. Passive Indices (January 1991 through November 2004)

	CRBR	DJAIG	Active Portfolio	GSCI	RICI	SPCI
CRBR	1.00					
DJAIG	0.82	1.00				
Active Portfolio	0.25	0.26	1.00			
GSCI	0.65	0.89	0.18	1.00		
RICI	0.72	0.90	0.25	0.92	1.00	
SPCI	0.81	0.91	0.22	0.87	0.82	1.00

Abbreviations:

CRBR: Commodities Research Bureau – Reuters Total Return Index;
DJAIG: Dow Jones – AIG Commodity Index;
GSCI   Goldman Sachs Commodity Index;
RICI: Rogers International Commodity Index; and
SPCI: Standard and Poor's Commodity Index.

Source: Akey (2005), Figure 22.

approach to portfolio management, an investor should be obtaining their core commodity exposure through cost-effective index products rather than through expensive active managers. The role of active managers is then to provide uncorrelated returns over those of the institution's commodity index investments.

Limitations

The main limitation of active commodity strategies is scalability, which arises from two sources. First, one can argue that *all* hedge fund strategies, which exploit inefficiencies, are by definition capacity constrained. If hedge funds are exploiting inefficiencies, this means that other investors are supplying those inefficiencies and unfortunately, we cannot all profit from exploiting inefficiencies since in that case, nobody would be supplying inefficiencies. In Till (2004), we argue that a plausible maximum size of the hedge fund industry is 6% of institutional (and high net worth) assets.

A second factor that limits the size of active commodity strategies is unique to the futures markets. Unlike investors in the securities markets, traders of futures contracts in certain markets may not exceed the speculative position limits (spec limits) set for those markets. Spec limits impose a cap on the size of the net position that speculators may hold overnight in a single contract month and in all contract months of a particular commodity. Often, this cap is even more restrictive in the spot month.

The Commodity Futures Trading Commission (CFTC) sets the spec limits for grains and cotton. The commodity exchanges, with the Commission's approval, set the limits for all other markets. The purpose of spec limits is to prevent a trader from amassing a large position that he/she could use to manipulate futures prices.

According to Gillman (2005), the Commission routinely reexamines the utility of spec limits in different markets. For example, in the 1990s, it approved exchange rules adopting "trader accountability exemptions," which give more flexibility to traders in the largest and most liquid markets. For many of these large traders, spec limits have proven less of a burden than one might expect. This is because the size of spec limits is tied closely to market liquidity, and many large traders carefully limit positions in illiquid markets or avoid these markets entirely.

In the future, however, active commodity futures trading strategies may face new capacity challenges. During times of commodity market stress, it is not unusual to read of proposals for futures exchanges to "tighten position limits on traders," as discussed in Verleger (2005). For example, in early 2005, "The Consumers Alliance for Affordable Natural Gas ... recommended that the CFTC report to Congress if the number of [natural gas] contracts a single entity can own results in a concentration that may distort the market," according to a news bulletin quoted by Verleger.

One way that active commodity managers can potentially increase the capacity of their strategies is to move their transactions off futures exchanges and over to the over-the-counter (OTC) swap markets. This may be occurring now. According to Lammey (2005), "because of the controversy over the impact and influence of hedge funds in the [energy] market, some sources report that hedge funds have been quietly ... [using] brokerage companies to ... [enter into] complex combinations of futures, options, and other derivatives." Further, "funds have found that trading via the brokerage firms provides greater liquidity than at the NYMEX [the energy futures exchange] and reduces the chance that they will find themselves accidentally taking delivery of actual crude oil or gas. Additionally ... brokerage firms often allow big funds to make trades with favorable financing terms and trade with more leverage than on an exchange."

If an active commodity manager uses private transactions to gain exposure to the commodity markets, then the manager's clients must be willing to assume the attendant credit risk of the OTC counterparties used in these transactions.

In summing up this section, we would say that while an examination of the universe of commodity futures traders reveals that there are skillful active commodity funds, in which an institutional investor can potentially invest, the commodity markets present unique capacity problems, which can be even more challenging than for hedge fund strategies that focus on the financial markets.

SOURCES OF STRUCTURAL RETURN

In this section, we discuss persistent sources of return in the commodity futures markets. A later section of the chapter will then discuss how to create an investment process around these sources of return.

The key to understanding why there should be structural returns in the commodity futures markets is to realize that futures markets are *not* zero-sum games. As noted in Di Tomasso and Till (2000), when one focuses solely on the narrow realm of commodity futures markets, it is obvious that for every winner there must be a loser. This simplifies away the fact that each commodity futures market is embedded within a wider scheme of profits, losses, and risks of its physical commodity market.

Commodity futures markets exist to facilitate the transfer of exceptionally expensive inventory risk. Moreover, commodity futures markets allow producers, merchandisers, and marketers the benefit of laying off inventory price risk at their timing and convenience. For this, commercial participants will tolerate paying a premium so long as this cost does not overwhelm the overall profit of their business enterprise, as discussed in Working (1948).

Further, Cootner (1967) documents price-pressure effects resulting from commercial hedging in a number of agricultural futures markets and notes that these effects are well known by commercial market participants. He concludes that the fact that these effects "persist in the face of such knowledge indicates that the risks involved in taking advantage of them outweigh the gain involved. This is further evidence that the trade does not act on the basis of expected values; that it is willing to pay premiums to avoid risk."

Hedge Pressure

In this subsection, we review both the hypothesis and evidence that there is a persistent return from taking a position on the other side of commercial hedge pressure.

In certain commodity futures markets, there tends to be an excess of commercial entities that are short hedgers. Therefore, in order to balance the market, investors must be willing to take up the slack on the long side of these markets. Also, in order to be persuaded to enter these markets, investors need a return for their risk-bearing. "In effect the hedgers offer ... [investors] an insurance premium for this service," as Bodie and Rosansky (1980) put it. In other words, investors can earn an "insurance premium" for being long on certain commodity futures contracts. (Greer provides a concrete example of investors earning an insurance premium in the cattle futures markets in Chapter 5.)

Hicks (1939) explains that "in all forward markets there is likely to be a tendency for hedgers to predominate on one side or the other over long periods. No forward market can do without the speculative element." Further, in some commodity futures markets, producers are in a more vulnerable position than consumers and so will be under more pressure to hedge than consumers. This leads to a "congenital weakness" on the demand side for some commodity futures contracts, which causes these contracts' futures prices to be downwardly biased relative to future spot prices, which in turn leads to generally positive returns for holding the futures contract.

Live cattle and gasoline are examples of two commodity futures markets where there appears to be a systematic positive return due to a "congenital weakness" on the demand side for hedging.

Live Cattle

Helmuth (1981) reports that the "amount of short hedging in the live cattle futures market is almost four times as large as the amount of long hedging. Long hedging as a percentage of open interest averages about 8% while short hedging averages over 30%. Thus, unlike grain futures, in live cattle futures there is no significant group of commercial long-hedgers who act as a buying force without significant regard to price level. There is very little long hedging because meat is not sold on long-term, fixed-price forward contracts."

Gasoline

Verleger (2005) explains that "the gasoline business has for years lacked a natural long to offset the natural short position of refiners and traders. ... The absence of natural longs is explained by the retail nature of retail gasoline sales. Consumers buy product in very modest amounts—50 gallons at most—at any one time. Consumers generally do not frequent the same supplier for all their purchases, and prices vary widely by location. The random feature of the purchase decision combined with the dispersion of retail prices makes it almost impossible for most buyers to hedge."[1]

The most convincing evidence of there being a systematic downward bias in the prices of live cattle and gasoline futures prices comes from directly examining their long-term returns. Nash and Shrayer of Morgan Stanley (2004) report that the annualized returns for live cattle and gasoline have been 11.0% and 18.6%, respectively over 20-year-plus timeframes. Both calculations include the interest income from fully collateralizing positions in these two futures markets. The horizon over which the live cattle returns were calculated was from April 1983 to April 2004. For gasoline, the horizon was from January 1985 to April 2004.

Grain Markets

For the grain markets, there have historically been seasonal times when commercial hedging tends to be long rather than short. Therefore, one might expect that in order to capture the gains from being on the other side of commercial hedge pressure, there are times when an investor's positioning needs to be from the short side rather than from the long side. In other words, when commercial hedgers are net long, we would expect that the corresponding futures price would have a

---

1. Verleger (2005) notes, though, that with increased investor participation in the commodity markets, the dynamics of the gasoline futures markets might change. That said, he notes that open interest in the summer gasoline futures contracts currently "only covers ten percent of demand."

tendency to be biased upwards, leading to systematic profits for an investor taking a short position in the contract. Conversely, when commercial hedgers are net short, we would expect the corresponding futures price would have a tendency to be biased downwards, leading to systematic profits for an investor taking a long position in the contract.

Bessembinder (1992) provided empirical evidence that this is the proper way to approach the grain markets. He obtained net hedging data from the CFTC's Commitment of Traders (COT) report. In this way, he could identify periods when hedgers were net long vs. net short. Using data from 1967 to 1989, he examined what the average returns were for 22 futures markets, conditioned on whether hedgers were net short or net long. Exhibit 6–3 summarizes his results for soybeans, wheat, and corn.

Exhibit 6–3 shows that when commercial hedgers were net short in soybeans, wheat, and corn that the futures prices for these commodities increased on average. Correspondingly, when commercial hedgers were net long in these markets, their futures prices decreased on average.

Maddala and Yoo (1990) confirmed the thrust of Bessembinder's study using both futures price and COT data from 1976 to 1984. The futures markets that they studied included wheat, corn, oats, soybeans, soybean oil, and soybean meal. The researchers calculated the monthly rate of return to both larger hedgers and large speculators as a whole. They found that "large hedgers consistently lose money on ... average ... [while] large speculators consistently make money on ... average."

In the case of the grain markets, it appears that "future prices are biased against both long and short hedgers," quoting Cootner (1967).

Spread Markets

Price pressure effects due to commercial hedging can also be detected in futures spreads. Certain commodity futures spreads represent processing margins. Examples include the gasoline crack spread, which is the differential between gasoline futures prices and crude oil futures prices, and the soybean crush spread, which is the differential between soybean product prices and soybean futures prices. There are times when commercial entities lock in processing margins via the futures

EXHIBIT 6–3

Mean returns (% per day×250) in Selected Futures Markets

	Conditional on net hedging	
	Short	Long
Soybeans	4.35%	−1.21%
Wheat	5.71%	−10.53%
Corn	16.25%	−19.96%

Source: Excerpted from Bessembinder (1992), Table 1.

markets, which appears to exert one-sided pressure on these spreads. Again, on average a commodity investor earns a return by taking the other side of these transactions. Girma and Paulson (1998) provide empirical evidence of this price–pressure effect for a number of petroleum futures spreads. For heating oil vs. crude oil futures spreads, the horizon of Girma and Paulson's study is over the period April 1983 through December 1994. For gasoline vs. crude oil futures spreads, the horizon is over the period December 1984 through December 1994.

Scarcity

Another source of return in the commodity futures markets results from buying commodities when they are scarce. This sounds as simple as saying that a source of return in the stock market results from buying equities when they are cheap. The complications arise when one needs to define the technical indicator for when commodities are scarce or when equities are cheap.

In the case of commodities, we will use a futures curve term structure to indicate whether a commodity is scarce or not. By *term structure*, we mean one should examine the relative price differences of a futures contract across delivery months. When a near-month contract is trading at a premium to more distant contracts, we say that a commodity futures curve is in "backwardation." Conversely, when a near-month contract is trading at a discount to more distant contracts, we say that the curve is in "contango."

Exhibit 6–4 illustrates the copper futures curve as of the end of March 2005. The graph shows the relative prices of 12 copper futures contracts of varying maturity. Note that at this time we can say that copper is in backwardation.

As explained in Till (October 2000), in a normal futures market (i.e., a market in *contango*), the maximum price difference between the front and back contracts tends to be determined by carrying charges, which include storage costs, insurance, and interest. Backwardation occurs when supplies of commodities are inadequate; therefore, market participants are willing to pay a premium to buy the immediately deliverable commodity. This is precisely the time an active commodity manager should be long a particular futures market: when scarcity is indicated. Since backwardation indicates scarcity, one is on the correct side of a potential price spike in the commodity by being long at that time.

Further, backwardation provides a signal that there is *not* an excess of commodity inventories. The markets abhor an excess of commodity inventories, according to Keynes (1934), because of the enormous expense of financing them. If such excess inventories come into existence, "the price of the goods continues to fall until either consumption increases or production falls off sufficiently to absorb them."

Keynes wrote that our "present economic arrangements make no normal provision for looking after surplus" commodity inventories; this is arguably still true in 2005. Regarding the petroleum complex, Rowland (1997) explains, "from wellheads around the globe to burner tips, the world's oil stocks tie up enormous amounts of oil and capital. The volume of oil has been estimated at

EXHIBIT 6-4

COMEX Copper Futures Curve as of 3/30/05. Price vs. Contract Maturity

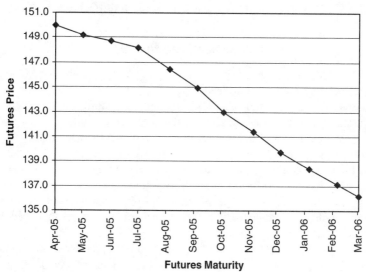

Data Source: Bloomberg.

some 7 to 8 billion barrels of inventory, which is the equivalent of over 100 days of global oil output or 2½ years of production from Saudi Arabia, the world's largest producer and exporter of crude oil. Even at today's low interest rates, annual financial carrying-costs tied up in holding these stocks amount to around $10 billion, which is more than the entire net income of the Royal Dutch/Shell Group, the largest private oil company in the world."

By establishing long exposure to commodities when scarcity is indicated, one would be attempting to avoid being on the wrong side of the "strong forces [that] are immediately brought into play to dissipate" surplus inventories, again quoting Keynes (1934).

A number of authors have confirmed that backwardation has historically provided an effective signal for profitably going long on certain commodities over lengthy timeframes. For example, Abken (1989) showed that going long on heating oil calendar spreads during the times of the year when heating oil tends to trade in backwardation had yielded statistically significant profits from January 1980 through December 1987. A calendar spread consists of taking offsetting positions during different delivery months of a particular futures contract. A long calendar spread consists of taking a long position in a near-month futures contract while simultaneously taking a short position in a deferred-month futures contract.

Humphreys and Shimko (1995) described a strategy whereby one invests in energy futures contracts according to which contracts are in backwardation and to what degree they are in backwardation. They find that such a strategy would have earned 20.3% per year in excess of T-bills from 1984 through 1994.

More recently Erb and Harvey (2005) showed how one could have histori-cally earned superior returns when investing in the Goldman Sachs Commodity Index (GSCI) by tactically investing in the GSCI only when its futures curve was in backwardation. Their study was over the period, July 1992 to May 2004.

Weather-Fear Premia

Another source of systematic returns in the futures markets are due to "weather premia." As discussed in Di Tomasso and Till (2000), a futures price will some-times embed a fear premium due to upcoming, meaningful weather events that can dramatically impact the supply or demand of a commodity.

In this class of trades, a futures price is systematically too high, reflecting the uncertainty of an upcoming weather event. We say the price is too high when an analysis of historical data shows that one can make statistically significant profits from being *short* on the commodity futures contract during the relevant time period. And further that the systematic profits from the strategy are suffi-ciently high that they compensate for the infrequent large losses that occur when the feared, extreme weather event does in fact occur.

Till (September 2000) provides examples of weather-fear premia strategies in the grain, tropical, and natural gas futures markets. Here, we provide an example from the coffee futures market.

The uncertainty of weather in Brazil appears to create a built-in weather pre-mium in coffee futures prices during certain times of the year. As Teweles and Jones (1987) note, "because of Brazil's significance as a producer, its susceptibility to frosts and droughts, and its April-to-August harvesting season, the June-July period is subject to volatile, uncertain price movements [in coffee futures prices]."

From 1980 to 2004 coffee futures prices have tended to decline coming into the Brazilian winter, consistent with the market getting comfortable with taking some weather premium out of the futures price. Accordingly, a historically prof-itable strategy has been to take a short position in coffee futures contracts before wintertime in Brazil.

Of note is that the exit date for this weather-premium strategy is *before* the onset of Brazilian winter.

The reason for exiting a short position before the start of winter is that when exceptionally "freezing temperatures … [do make] their way into the coffee-rich regions of Southern Brazil," the coffee price can explode, as described in Cordier (2005). Exhibit 6–5 illustrates the risk of taking a short position in coffee if such a position were held during the Southern Hemisphere winter: in 1994 consecutive bouts of extreme weather did occur.

Caveat on the Sources of Structural Return: Past Performance is No Guarantee of Future Success

One concern in identifying obscure strategies to monetize risk premia is that by their very identification, one will popularize these strategies to a sufficient degree that future returns may be dampened or even eliminated.

E X H I B I T   6–5

Coffee Futures Price (KCN94)

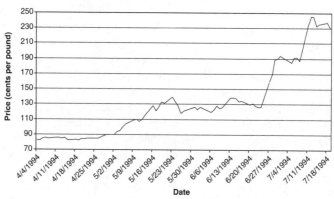

Data Source: Bloomberg.

For example, Siegel (2003) pointed out that "high-beta stocks beat low-beta stocks until William Sharpe discovered beta in 1964; [and] small stocks beat large ones until Banz and Reinganum discovered the size effect in 1979."

Further, Rosenberg et al. (1985) described how one could have earned abnormal returns in the stock market by buying stocks with a high ratio of book value of common equity per share to market price and selling stocks with a low book/price ratio. The authors' study was over the horizon January 1973 through September 1984. The authors said, "we felt that book/price ratio was an intriguing candidate for study. Since it had not been heavily described in the quantitative literature, it might possibly serve as an as-yet unspoiled instrument."

Fourteen years later, Cochrane (1999) wrote that "the size and *book/market* premia [in the equity markets] seem to have diminished substantially in recent years. If this is permanent, it suggests that these opportunities were simply overlooked." (Italics added.)

As a counter-example, one can also point to other market "inefficiencies" that have been published and yet continue to exist. For example, in 1939 J.R. Hicks developed the widely known "liquidity premium" hypothesis for bonds. In this hypothesis, Hicks (1939) notes that all things being equal, a lender would rather lend in short maturities since they are less volatile than longer-term maturity bonds. On the other hand, an entrepreneur would rather borrow in a long maturity in order to fix his/her costs and better plan for the future. In order to induce borrowers to lend long, they must be offered a "liquidity premium" to do so. The result is that bond yield curves tend to be upwardly sloping. Like the hedging pressure hypothesis for certain commodity futures contracts, the central idea behind the "liquidity premium" hypothesis is that commercial entities are willing to pay premiums from the profits of their ongoing businesses in order to hedge away key volatile price risks.

Hicks' identification that there is a liquidity premium in long-maturity bonds has not prevented the US yield curve from continuing to be persistently steep nor has it prevented both mutual funds *and* hedge funds from designing profitable trading strategies that monetize this premium.

Regarding weather-fear premia strategies, these risk premia could obviously be reduced if improvements in forecasting reduced weather uncertainty. Unfortunately, it does not appear that weather forecasting has improved sufficiently just yet to reduce the uncertainty surrounding key weather times.

While weather uncertainty should remain a fundamental factor in commodity trading, there is another way that these strategies can become obsolete. For decades the United States had been the dominant soybean producer. It is now the case that Latin American countries produce over 52% of the world's soybeans, according to Cronin (2003), which means that trading strategies that focus on US weather, no longer have the potency they once had in the past.

Also, to the extent that Vietnam becomes a more significant coffee producer, one may see coffee futures strategies that are timed around Brazilian weather events lose their potency as well.

In summing up this section, we would say that while a number of superior investment strategies have historically been quite fleeting, especially once they are popularized, one should add the following about the commodity strategies discussed here. We have discussed persistent sources of return in the commodity futures markets that were originally published between 1967 and 2000, and each of these strategies continues to exist in some form as of 2005.

A Note on Commodity Trading Advisors (CTAs) and Technical Trading Rules

Most traders who are known as Commodity Trading Advisors (CTAs) do not primarily trade natural-resource commodity futures contracts. Instead, they primarily trade financial futures contracts such as currency, interest rate, and equity futures contracts. CTAs are also known as "managed futures" traders. The dominant trading style employed by managed futures traders is medium-to-long-term systematic trend-following. Exhibit 6–6 shows that trend-following strategies in currencies, interest rates, and stocks have had the strongest statistical significance in explaining the returns of an index of managed futures traders.

This is not to say that trend-following strategies cannot be profitably employed in the commodity markets. If there are inadequate inventories for a commodity, only its price can respond to equilibrate supply and demand, given that in the short run, new supplies of physical commodities cannot be mined, grown, and/or drilled. When there is a supply/usage imbalance in a commodity market, the price trend may be persistent, which, in turn, systematic trend-following systems may be able to capture.

Researchers at Calyon Financial provide evidence that trend-following systems may be able to capture returns in the commodity futures markets. In Burghardt et al. (2004), the researchers create generic trend-following models

E X H I B I T   6–6

Regression of Managed Futures Returns on Passive Indices and Economic Variables (1996–2000)

	Coefficient	Standard Error	T-Statistic
Intercept	0.00	0.00	0.01
S&P 500	0.00	0.07	0.05
Lehman US	0.29	0.39	0.76
Change in Credit Spread	0.00	0.01	0.30
Change in Term Spread	0.00	0.00	0.18
CISDM/Interest Rates	**1.27**	**0.24**	**5.24**
CISDM/Currency	**1.37**	**0.25**	**5.48**
CISDM/Commodity	0.27	0.15	1.79
CISDM/Stock	**0.36**	**0.11**	**3.17**
R-Squared	0.70		

The CISDM indexes in this figure are based on passive strategies that replicate CTA strategies in Interest Rates, Currencies, Commodities, and Stocks.

Source: Center for International Securities and Derivatives Markets (CISDM) 2nd Annual Chicago Research Conference, 5/22/02, slide 48.

based on two popular systems, the "moving average/crossover" model and the "range breakout" model. "Each [model] defines a trend or price pattern by comparing a current market price or recent average price with a longer history of the price and buys or sells when the recent price measure is above or below the longer price measure."

While the Calyon research describes employing their technical models to the equity, fixed income, currency, *and* commodities futures markets, we will just focus on their results for the commodity sector. The commodity futures markets which are included in their simulations are as follows: crude oil, natural gas, sugar, heating oil, cotton, corn, coffee, soybeans, gold, and copper. Duncan (2005) cautions that if researchers partition out the commodity results from the overall Calyon study, then they need to emphasize that *unconstrained* results are being displayed. In practice, a managed futures program would include constraints on the sizing of commodity positions that take into consideration the liquidity of these markets.

The Calyon study sizes positions in individual futures markets according to their historical standard deviations in order to make sure that "each individual futures market would exhibit about the same amount of risk." Their reported returns include transaction costs but exclude other fees associated with investing in a futures program. They also exclude interest income. Finally, the researchers continuously resize the program's trading positions such that the portfolio would always be at a fixed size ($5 million.)

Exhibit 6–7 shows the yearly *simulated* returns of pursuing a 120/240-day moving-average crossover system solely in the commodity sector. The annual compounded returns over the period, 1995 to 2004, were 17.5%. In this system, one enters a long position in a commodity if its 120-day moving-average level is greater than its 240-day moving-average price level *plus* a buffer. Correspondingly,

EXHIBIT 6–7

Annual Returns Due to a Commodity-Only Technical Trading Strategy:
The Moving-Average Crossover System

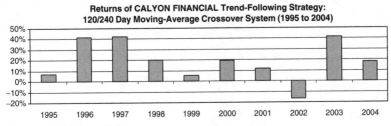

First quarter 2005 returns: 7.1%.
Calculations Based on Daily Data from Ryan Duncan, Calyon Financial, 4/1/05.

one enters a short position in a commodity if its 120-day moving-average level is
less than its 240-day moving-average price level *less* a buffer. Here, the 120-day
moving average is referred to as the fast-moving average, and the 240-day moving
average is called the slow-moving average. The buffer zone, in turn, is defined as
"two standard deviations of daily changes in the fast-moving average," write
Burghardt et al. (2004).

Exhibit 6–8 shows the yearly *simulated* returns of pursuing a 240-day range
breakout system again solely in the commodity sector. The annual compound
returns over the period, 1995 to 2004, were 11.3%. In this system, one enters a
long position in a commodity if its price is greater than the highest price over the
previous 240 days. Correspondingly, one enters a short position in a commodity
if its price is less than the lowest price of the previous 240 days.

EXHIBIT 6–8

Annual Returns Due to a Commodity-Only Technical Trading Strategy:
The Range Breakout System

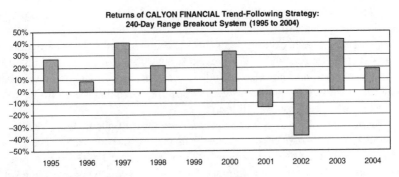

First quarter 2005 returns: 13.2%.
Calculations Based on Daily Data from Ryan Duncan, Calyon Financial, 4/1/05.

Again, Burghardt et al. (2004) emphasize that "commodity markets tend to be less liquid than financial markets. Many managers, to get around the constraint that illiquid commodities markets would place on their trading capacity, continue to expand by decreasing the weight that commodities play in their portfolio."

In summing up this section we would say that despite the promising results shown in the Calyon study, CTAs have tended to trade financial rather than natural-resource commodity markets because of the greater liquidity and capacity of the financial markets. The rest of this article will now focus on investing in the commodity futures markets based on identifiable fundamental factors.

CRUCIAL ELEMENTS OF AN INVESTMENT PROCESS

In this section, we will discuss the crucial elements of an investment process that takes advantage of the *fundamental* sources of return in the commodity futures markets. We will briefly discuss trade sizing, entry and exit rules, trade construction, portfolio construction, and risk management. We will finish up this section with an important caveat on solely relying on quantitative methods in futures trading.

Trade Sizing

The discovery of structural sources of return in the commodity futures market is only the first step in designing an investment program. For example, how should one determine how large each individual trading strategy should be? This section will discuss sizing trades based on their risk characteristics.

Sizing as a Function of Risk

Risk is "the currency of trading," notes Grant (2004). "Each trading account has ... a finite amount of this currency, and it is vital to manage portfolio affairs in such a way that respects this resource constraint."

Volatility   An initial way to respect this resource constraint is to size trades according to their recent volatility. One wishes to ensure that under normal conditions, a commodity position has not been sized so large that a trader cannot sustain the random fluctuations in profits and losses that would be expected to occur, even without an adverse event occurring.

Sizing a trade based on its volatility is especially important the longer the frequency of predictability. For example, if a trade's predictability is at quarterly intervals, the trade has to be sized to withstand the daily fluctuations in profits and losses.

(In one extreme example, Lettau and Ludvigson (2001) have found that equities are predictable at business-cycle frequencies, but that means that one cannot have a leveraged investment process to take advantage of this predictability.)

Worst-Case Loss   Using long-term data, one should also examine the worst performance of a commodity trade under similar circumstances in the past. In practice, such a measure will sometimes be larger than a measure based on recent
volatility. In that case, the trade size should be further scaled down to reflect the
worst-case loss.

Examining the worst-case outcomes can also serve another purpose. If the
loss on a particular commodity futures trade exceeds the historical worst case,
this can be an indication of a new regime that is not reflected in the data. This
would trigger an exit from a systematic trade since one no longer has a handle on
the worst-case scenario. This point will be further discussed below in the Entry
and Exit Rules section of this chapter.

Optimal Sizing

The equity markets have shaped the professional experiences of most financial
market participants. This can present a problem for a new participant to the
commodity markets. Unlike equities, most commodity price distributions are
positively skewed. This is because of the asymmetric nature of storage. If there is
too much of a commodity, some of it can be stored and the price can decline to
encourage the placement of the commodity. The existence of storage can dampen
the price decline because this is an additional lever with which to balance supply
and demand. On the other hand, if there is too little of a commodity, then that
means there are inadequate inventories and therefore the only lever available to
balance supply and demand is price, which must correspondingly increase. The
inability of "the market as a whole to carry negative inventories," as Deaton and
Laroque (1992) put it, "causes commodity markets to be prone to violent upward
price spikes."

Exhibit 6–9 and Exhibit 6–10 provide examples from the copper and corn
markets, which show how explosive commodity prices can be during times of low
inventories relative to consumption.

E X H I B I T   6–9

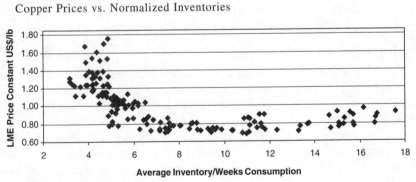

Copper Prices vs. Normalized Inventories

Average Inventory/Weeks Consumption

Souce: RBC Dominion Securities.

EXHIBIT 6–10

Corn Prices vs. Normalized Inventories

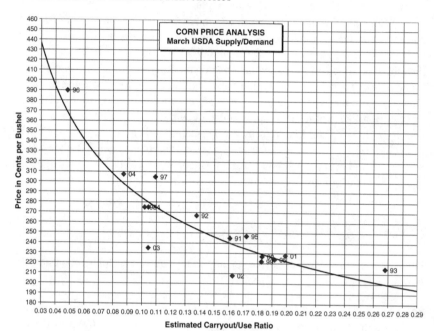

Source: Everett (2005).

Hooker of State Street Global Advisors (2004) confirms the positive skewness of a number of commodity return distributions. Exhibit 6–11 provides a summary of the skewness of a number of commodities as compared to US equities and bonds.

EXHIBIT 6–11

Distribution Moments: Skewness

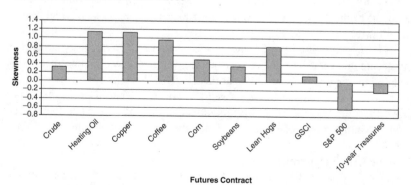

Source: Excerpted from Hooker (2004), Slide 11.

Walton (1991) notes that "the asymmetrical behavior of commodity stocks ... means that most price surprises are on the upside. Thus, it makes sense for investors generally to be long of commodities."

When constructing total-return commodity portfolios, one should take into consideration the asymmetric nature of commodity returns as follows. The risk budget allocated to individual *long* commodity positions needs to be much larger than the risk allocated to individual *short* commodity positions. Since commodity prices are positively skewed, long positions can have long-option-like payoff profiles, particularly during times of scarcity, while short positions can have short-option-like profiles if a supply shock occurs. By scaling up the investments that have long-option-like returns while scaling down the investments with short-option-like returns, a manager gets "paid disproportionately [when he/she is] ... right and the pain is limited when the manager is wrong," as two hedge fund managers put it in EuroHedge (2005).

Entry and Exit Rules

Fung and Hsieh (2003) note that an important source of alpha for systematic futures programs is superior entry/exit strategies.

Seasonal Strength and Weakness

In order to profit from commercial hedging pressure, Cootner (1967) provides historical examples of profitable entry and exit strategies in the grain futures markets. The author summarizes the results of studies that both he and others carried out, which use data that go as far back as 1921 and as recently as through 1966.

Cootner's (historically) profitable strategies are keyed off the following factors: (1) peaks and troughs in visible grain supplies, (2) peaks and troughs in hedging positions from data provided by the Commodity Exchange Authority, a predecessor organization to the CFTC, and (3) fixed calendar dates that line up on average with factors (1) and/or (2).

Similarly, Girma and Paulson (1998) write that "the gasoline crack spread seasonality seems to parallel the seasonality of the gasoline inventory levels." Also, the heating oil crack spread reaches peaks and troughs that parallel the heating oil inventory cycle.

Using reasoning from Cootner (1967), the turning points for price–pressure effects are on average around peak (trough) inventory levels because that is when hedging by commercials would be at their highest (lowest). Commercials do not generally take advantage of these well-known effects because "for hedgers to profit from the [futures price] bias requires that they be long when they already hold maximum inventories and short when they hold minimum inventories."

Positive Curve Dynamics

Another entry and exit signal is based on whether a futures curve for a commodity is in backwardation or not, as covered in the Scarcity section of this article.

Structural Break

As discussed in the Worst-Case Loss section of the article, if a loss on a particular commodity futures trade exceeds the historical worst case, this can be an indication of a break from past structural phenomena that had been detectable in historical data. In that case, a trader would exit a trade since one no longer has a handle on the magnitude of additional losses.

The following is an example of a structural break from the fall of 2003. Up until that point, soybean futures prices typically declined in the face of the US crop harvest. Further, the magnitude of the decline had been largely related to US summer weather conditions. From 1980 through 2002, the September-to-October decline in soybean prices could be related to the following three variables: (1) the change in soybean prices during the summer, which historically had been highly correlated with the change in Good-to-Excellent ratings, as provided by the US Department of Agriculture; (2) a government loan figure, which served as a proxy for US soybean inventories; and (3) a price ratio, which was highly correlated with farmers' decisions in choosing between planting corn or soybeans. This model had explained 81% of the variation in autumn soybean prices over the 23-period, 1980 to 2002. In the fall of 2003, this model predicted a drop in soybeans of about –50c. Instead, soybeans rallied over +60c from early September through early October.

From 1980 through 2002, the most that soybeans had rallied in the face of a new US crop harvest was +36c. So once soybeans had rallied to this level in 2003, one had an indication that new factors were in place that had not been the case in the past. By exiting the trade at +36c, one limited the ultimate losses from being short on soybeans in the face of an explosive rally.

According to Cronin (2003), massive Chinese import demand combined with unusually damaged US crops caused soybean prices to rally to encourage farmers in the Southern Hemisphere to increase the amount of soybean planting still possible at that time. As of early October 2003, Brazil had only planted 4% of its soybean acres, and as touched upon earlier in the Weather-Fear Premia section of the article, Latin American countries now produce a majority of the world's soybean crops. The new demand (from China) and supply (from Latin America) appeared to cause a structural break in historical soybean price dynamics.

The conclusion from this discussion is that a trading program will not experience the full brunt of a structural break if one exits a trading strategy after experiencing losses that are greater than have been the case in the past.

Trade Construction

As discussed in Till and Eagleeye (2004), one can have a correct commodity view, but how one constructs the trade to express this view can make a large difference in profitability. In the commodity futures markets, one can choose to implement trades through outright futures positions, spreads, and/or options. One can make this decision by examining which implementation has provided the best historical return-to-risk profile.

Futures spreads can sometimes be more analytically tractable than outright futures contracts. There is usually some economic boundary constraint that links related commodities, which typically (but not always) limits the risk in position-taking. Also, one hedges out a lot of first-order, exogenous risk by trading spreads. For example, with a heating-oil vs. crude-oil futures spread, each leg of the trade is equally affected by unpredictable OPEC shocks. Instead, what typically affects the spread is second-order risk factors like timing differences in inventory changes in the two commodities.

Portfolio Construction

Diversification

Uniquely among asset classes, commodities can offer uncorrelated investment opportunities across individual commodity markets. Moreover, energy-sector commodities are frequently *negatively* correlated to non-energy-sector commodities. This greatly aids in setting up dampened-risk portfolios. The reason for this negative correlation is due to the fact that an energy spike can dampen economic growth, which in turn, dampens demand for other less economically essential commodities, as noted in Till (2001).

Further, hedge fund manager Paul Touradji argues, "One of the best things about being a commodity manager is the natural internal diversification." "While even unrelated equities have a beta to the overall market, many commodities, such as sugar and aluminum, traditionally have no correlation at all," according to Teague (2004) in his interview with Touradji.

Exhibit 6–12 provides an example from the summer of 2000, which illustrates the portfolio effect on volatility of incrementally adding unrelated commodity strategies. This portfolio combined long, hedge-pressure trades with short, weather-fear premium trades.

EXHIBIT 6–12

Portfolio Effect of Combining Unrelated Commodity Strategies

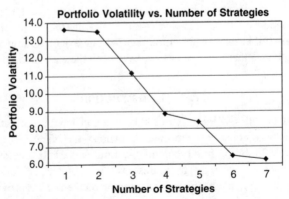

Source: Based on Till (Fall 2000), Exhibit 5.

Avoidance of Inadvertent Concentration Risk

In order to meet the goal of creating a diversified portfolio, a commodities portfolio manager needs to exercise due care in ensuring that each additional trade is in fact a risk diversifier rather than a risk amplifier. If two trades are in fact related, then one should consider them as part of the same strategy bucket and require them to share risk capital. If each trade is instead allocated full risk capital, then one may be inadvertently doubling up on risk.

Natural Gas and Corn   Recent correlations will not necessarily be a sufficient guide as to whether two seemingly unrelated trades are in fact separate trades. For example, one might expect the price of natural gas to be unrelated to the price of corn, but in July of 1999, these two markets became 85% correlated with each other. This is because both of these markets are highly sensitive to the outcome of July weather in the US Midwest. For natural gas, a heat wave can cause prices to rally in order to ration demand so that storage injections for peak winter demand will continue on schedule. For corn, a heat wave can be damaging to corn yields during the key pollination time, which in turn would cause corn prices to rally.

In July 1999, blistering hot weather did occur, which caused corn and natural gas futures prices to simultaneously rally, which in turn caused them to appear like the same trade.

If a commodity manager had included both corn and natural gas futures trades in his/her portfolio during July, then the portfolio would contain concentrated risk to the outcome of US Midwest weather.

Platinum and Copper   Chinese demand for commodities has become a relatively recent dominant factor in the commodity markets.

Exhibit 6–13 shows the importance of Chinese demand for a number of metals markets.

Note particularly that the Chinese share of recent growth in platinum demand is 90% while the share of growth for copper demand is 70%.

E X H I B I T   6–13

Chinese Metals Demand

	Percentage Share of World Demand	Percentage of Growth Contribution (1997-2002)
Platinum	**25%**	**90%**
Copper	**17%**	**70%**
Zinc	18%	59%
Aluminum	18%	57%
Nickel	8%	34%
Silver	4%	11%

Source: Excerpted from Smith (2004).

Exhibit 6–14 shows the time-varying correlation of changes in platinum and copper prices. During the first 6 months of 2004, the monthly changes in these two markets were +93% correlated while during the next 7 months, this correlation was only 17%.

E X H I B I T   6–14

Change in Platinum Prices vs. Change in Copper Prices. First Six Months of 2004

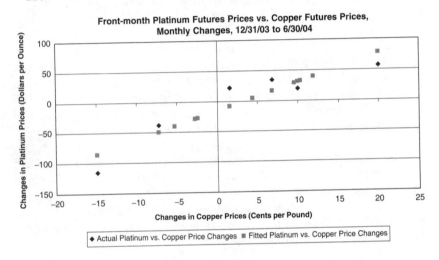

Change in Platinum Prices vs. Change in Copper Prices. Succeeding Seven Months

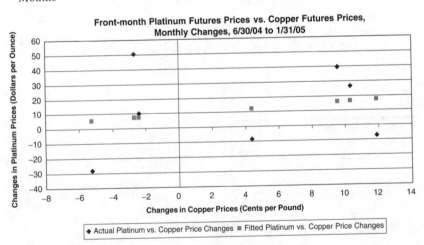

Data Source: Bloomberg.

In early 2005, if a commodity manager only examined the recent correlations of platinum and copper futures prices, then that manager would have missed the two markets' strong previous relationship, not to mention their common fundamental driver. These two trades need to share the same risk capital because in the event of a Chinese demand shock, there could be similar price responses by both metals contracts, as occurred during the last 2 weeks of April 2004. At that time, following reports of a more stringent official policy towards industrial loans in China, both copper and platinum prices declined precipitously, as shown in Exhibit 6–15.

Energy Spreads   When managing an absolute-return commodity program, one may want to limit the amount of "beta risk" that a portfolio has to a particular commodity.

Exhibit 6–16 illustrates an example from March 2005. At that time, an energy subportfolio consisted of petroleum-complex intramarket and intermarket spreads as well as natural gas futures contracts. The sensitivity of the portfolio's energy positions to front-month gasoline prices almost doubled from the original period of study, 12/1/04 to 2/22/05, as compared to a later timeframe, 2/22/05 to 3/22/05.

If a manager had intended that his/her actively-managed commodity portfolio should have limited exposure to the outright direction of commodity prices, then this doubling of exposure to the fortunes of front-month gasoline may have been unacceptable.

E X H I B I T   6–15

Platinum and Copper Prices during the Last Half of April 2004

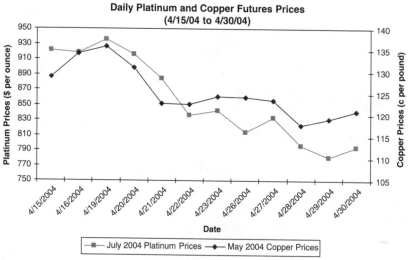

Data Source: Bloomberg.

Changing Sensitivity of a Portfolio to Gasoline Prices

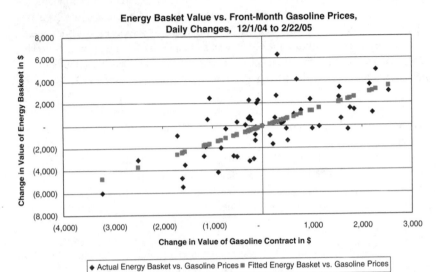

Beta = 1.4
R-squared = 46%

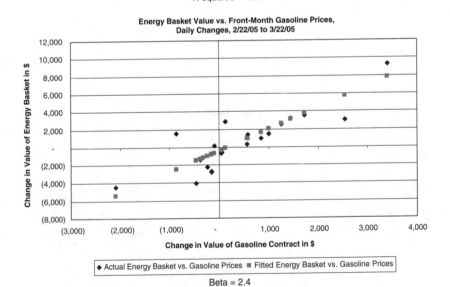

Beta = 2.4
R-squared = 76%

Data Source: Bloomberg.

Long-Option-Like Payoff Profile

A final consideration in combining trading strategies is to attempt to ensure that the portfolio will have a long-option-like payoff profile. Historically, futures products have been classified with managed futures programs and global macro hedge funds. The traditional investors for these products have historically expected a great deal of long optionality from them.

Confirming this point, Grant (2004) notes that global macro traders should have an additional objective besides a return threshold. He provides a benchmark objective for the "performance ratio," which is the ratio of average daily gains divided by average daily losses. Based on Grant's experience, a performance objective "in the range of 125% is entirely achievable ... [although some traders can exceed that], consistently achieving 200%+ in this regard."

The Optimal Sizing section of this article noted the importance of allocating a disproportionate amount of risk capital to individual long commodity positions, which tend to have positively skewed outcomes, relative to the amount of risk taken with individual short commodity positions, which correspondingly tend to have negatively-skewed outcomes. This trade construction methodology increases the chances of a portfolio having a long-option-like payoff profile over time.

Exhibit 6–17 shows a commodity futures-portfolio-return analysis from August of 2004, which shows how the portfolio would have performed from 1981 through 2003. This portfolio has the desired long-option-like payoff profile. A long-option-like payoff profile, in turn, is one where there are a small number of very large returns and a large number of moderately positive or slightly negative returns.

Exhibit 6–17 summarizes the historical returns of an actual portfolio whose individual strategies are summarized in Exhibit 6–18. Exhibit 6–18, in turn, will be further explained in the Example Risk Report section of this chapter.

E X H I B I T   6–17

Verification of (Historical) Long-Options-Like Profile

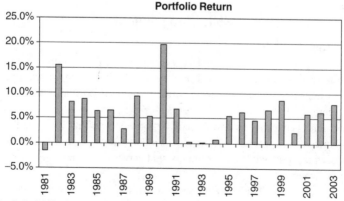

Source: Premia Capital Management, LLC.

E X H I B I T   6–18

Strategy-Level Analysis

8/11/2004

	Strategy	Value-At-Risk	Worst-Case Loss During Normal Times	Worst-Case Loss During Eventful Period
1	Gasoline Front-to-Back Spread	2.59%	–5.59%	–4.31%
2	Deferred Outright Gasoline	3.81%	–2.50%	–2.76%
3	Deferred Outright Natural Gas	0.67%	–0.15%	–0.29%
4	Deferred Eurodollar Futures	2.42%	–5.92%	–0.96%
5	Hog Spread	3.87%	–2.66%	–3.23%
6	Deferred Gasoline Spread	1.60%	–0.29%	–0.53%
7	Cattle Spread	1.62%	–0.50%	–1.34%
	Portfolio	**9.24%**	**–8.89%**	**–2.27%**

	Strategy	Incremental Contribution to Portfolio Value-at-Risk*	Incremental Contribution to Worst-Case Portfolio Event Risk*
1	**Gasoline Front-to-Back Spread**	**1.62%**	**0.64%**
2	**Deferred Outright Gasoline**	**2.93%**	**–0.72%**
3	Deferred Outright Natural Gas	0.52%	0.16%
4	**Deferred Eurodollar Futures**	**0.77%**	**–2.86%**
5	Hog Spread	1.18%	–0.29%
6	Deferred Gasoline Spread	1.33%	0.29%
7	Cattle Spread	0.25%	–0.32%

* A positive contribution means that the strategy adds to risk
while a negative contribution means the strategy reduces risk.

Notes
While under "normal" times, the gasoline spread position is less risky than the outright, during particular "eventful" times
the spread adds to risk while the outright reduces risk.

While under "normal" times, the Eurodollar futures position adds to risk, during particular "eventful" times this interest-rate
position reduces risk.

Source: Premia Capital Management, LLC.

Risk Management

Value-at-Risk

As noted in Till (2002), in the standard value-at-risk (VAR) approach, one calculates the portfolio's volatility based on recent volatilities and correlations of the portfolio's instruments. If a portfolio of instruments is normally distributed, one can calculate the 95% confidence interval for the portfolio's change in monthly value by multiplying the portfolio's recent monthly volatility by 2 (or 1.96, to be exact.) Now, this approach alone is obviously inadequate for a commodity portfolio, which consists of instruments that have a tendency towards extreme positive skewness.

As noted in the Trade Sizing section of this article, the measure is useful since one wants to ensure that under normal conditions, a commodity position (or portfolio) has not been sized sufficiently large that one cannot sustain the random fluctuations in profits and losses that might ensue.

For a more full representation of risk, one also needs to use VAR in concert with appropriate scenario tests.

Scenario Testing

In Till (2002), we recommend using long-term data to directly examine the worst performance of a commodity trade under similar circumstances in the past. In practice, such a measure will sometimes be larger than a VAR measure based on recent volatility.

Because a commodity investment is frequently intended to be a hedge for an institution's financial portfolio, a commodity manager should also examine the portfolio's sensitivity to a number of events based on historical data. If the commodity portfolio would do particularly poorly during times when the financial markets performed poorly, then this may be disappointing for a manager's clients.

Event Risk: Sharp Shock to Business Confidence   Although a commodity futures portfolio may contain no financial futures contracts, the portfolio could still have systematic risk to the stock market. For example, Bessembinder (1992) found that live cattle and platinum futures had statistically significant betas to the US stock market using data from 1967 to 1989.

A manager should therefore consider examining what the portfolio's performance would have been during the October 1987 stock market crash, the 1990 Gulf War, the fall 1998 bond debacle, and during the immediate aftermath of September 11, 2001. If the commodity portfolio would have done poorly during these events, then the manager may consider buying macro-portfolio insurance against these events, which is covered below.

Event Risk: Extreme Weather Outcomes   A key reason for the existence of commodity futures markets is because of the uncertainty surrounding weather and the need to hedge this uncertainty. We already noted in the Avoidance of Inadvertent Concentration Risk section how the outcome of US Midwest weather during July is a key influence on the prices of both corn and natural gas futures contracts.

Another example is during the month of February. This is a key time for determining the prices of both natural gas and heating oil prices. Throughout the US winter, utilities draw both commodities from storage in order to provide for heating demand. If there is extremely cold weather as one nears the end of winter, price will be the main variable which balances supply and demand, since inventories of natural gas and heating oil are approaching their seasonal lows at this time of year. In this case, their prices can both respond explosively to extremely cold weather.

What this means for the commodity manager is that one should consider examining how an energy portfolio would have performed during those rare times of extreme weather during the month of February.

Macro Portfolio Hedges

If losses would have exceeded a threshold amount during any of a program's event-risk scenarios, then a manager should consider implementing macro-portfolio hedges, which would do well during the relevant scenario.

Rajagopal (2004) notes that a commodity index investment provides "tail protection for fixed income." In other words, during those quarters where bonds had negative performance, commodities cumulatively performed well over the period 1992 to 2004. For a portfolio that has a long commodity bias, one can also state the converse: long fixed-income positions can provide event-risk protection for a commodity portfolio. This is illustrated in Exhibit 6–18.

Example Risk Report

Exhibit 6–18 provides an example strategy-level risk report, which shows the VAR and worst-case scenarios at both the strategy and portfolio level. (The events used in Exhibit 6–18's risk report were defined in the Event Risk: Sharp Shock to Business Confidence section of this article.) Note that a deferred long position in Eurodollar (short-term US interest-rate) futures contracts reduces the portfolio's risk to extreme financial events.

Caveat on the Crucial Elements of an Investment Process: An Investor's Risk Tolerance

Gehm (2004) lay down a challenge to financial-market writers. This author of the 1995 book, *Quantitative Trading and Money Management*, said that most financial literature is unrealistic. If financial articles were realistic, they would include both the joys and tears of trading. We will now provide a small window to that which Gehm references.

In discussing the crucial elements of an investment process, we have left out one vital aspect of trading, and that is a manager's *risk tolerance*. Vince (1992) states that monetizing market inefficiencies "requires more than an under-standing of money management concepts. It requires discipline to tolerate and endure emotional pain to a level that 19 out of 20 people cannot bear. ... Anyone who claims to be intrigued by the 'intellectual challenge of the markets' is not a trader. The markets are as intellectually challenging as a fistfight. ... Ultimately, trading is an exercise in self-mastery and endurance."

This chapter has thus far not emphasized the psychological discipline that is required to carry out successful futures trading, but this factor is just as crucial as finding structural sources of return and designing an appropriate risk management methodology around them.

Taleb (2001) explains why it is a challenge for a manager to follow a disci-plined investment process. He provides an example of a return-generating process that has annual returns in excess of T-bills of 15% with an annualized volatility of 10%. At first glance, one would think it should be trivial to carry out a trading strategy with such superior risk and return characteristics.

However, Taleb also notes that with such a return-generating process, there would only be a 54% chance of making money on any given day. If the investor felt the pain of loss say 2.5 times more acutely than the joy of a gain, then it could be potentially exhausting to carry out this superior investment strategy.

As a further example of the challenge of carrying out a disciplined invest-ment process, this chapter provided an example of a heating oil calendar spread that had been published in 1989. Of note is that this strategy has continued to work in some form during the past 15 years. Although this strategy has been demon-strably statistically significant, its maximum loss has been such that this loss could erase the previous year-and-a-half of the strategy's profits. The result is that if a manager experienced a loss of this magnitude, both the manager (and his/her investors) would need to be quite disciplined to continue this strategy.

CONCLUSION

Given how strong the case is for an indexed investment in commodities (both for inflation hedging and for diversification), one should be quite careful in recommending an actively managed commodity program. That said, skilled active managers may be able to provide incremental returns over an institution's core-indexed commodity exposure.

This chapter discussed persistent sources of return in the commodity futures markets, but we noted that this is insufficient for an actively managed commodity program to be successful. A successful futures program also requires extra care in risk management *and* exceptional discipline in implementation.

Acknowledgment.   The authors wish to express gratitude to Mr. Jerry Pascucci of Citigroup's Managed Futures department for support of Premia Capital's trading program.

BIBLIOGRAPHY

Abken, P., "An Analysis of Intra-Market Spreads in Heating Oil Futures," *Journal of Futures Markets*, September 1989, pp. 77-86.

Akey, R., "Commodities: A Case for Active Management," Working Paper, Cole Partners, 2/4/05.

Bessembinder, H., "Systematic Risk, Hedging Pressure, and Risk Premiums in Futures Markets," *The Review of Financial Studies,*" Vol 5, Number 4 (1992) pp. 637-667.

Bodie, Z., and V. Rosansky, "Risk and Return in Commodity Futures," *Financial Analysts Journal* (May-June 1980), pp. 27-39.

Burghardt, G., R. Duncan, and L. Liu, "What You Should Expect From Trend Following," *Calyon Financial Research Note*, 7/1/04.

Center for International Securities and Derivatives Markets (CISDM) 2nd Annual Chicago Research Conference, 5/22/02.

Cronin, W. (professional grain futures trader), private correspondence, 10/4/03.

Cochrane, J., "New Facts in Finance," *Economic Perspectives*, Federal Reserve Board of Chicago, Third Quarter, 1999.

Cootner, P., "Speculation and Hedging." *Food Research Institute Studies*, Supplement, 7, (1967), pp. 64-105.

Cordier, J., "My Best Trade," *Trader Monthly*, April/May 2005, p. 44.

Deaton, A., and G. Laroque, "On the Behavior of Commodity Prices," *Review of Economic Studies*, (1992) 59, pp. 1-23.

Duncan, R., Calyon Financial, private correspondence, 4/7/05.

Di Tomasso, J. and H. Till, "Active Commodity-Based Investing," *Journal of Alternative Investments*, Summer 2000, pp. 70-80.

Erb, C. and C. Harvey, "The Tactical and Strategic Value of Commodity Futures," Working Paper, Trust Company of the West and Duke University, 2/11/05.

EuroHedge Magazine, "Tried and Tested Team Aims to Squeeze a Bit More Juice," March 2005, pp. 22-23.

Everett, B., "FCStone Grain Recap," 3/18/05, p. 1.

Fung, W. and D. Hsieh, "The Risk in Hedge Fund Strategies: Alternative Alphas and Alternative Betas," a chapter in *The New Generation of Risk Management for Hedge Funds and Private Equity Investments*, Euromoney Books, London, 2003, pp. 72-87.

Gehm, F., "Risk Management in Hedge Fund of Funds Panel," Presentation at Chicago Professional Risk Managers' International Association (PRMIA) meeting, 12/16/04.

Gillman, P. (Chicago commodities law attorney), private correspondence, 4/4/05.

Girma, P. and A. Paulson, "Seasonality in Petroleum Futures Spreads," *Journal of Futures Markets*, August 1998, pp. 581-598.

Grant, K., *Trading Risk*, Wiley Trading, Hoboken, NJ, 2004.

Helmuth, J., "A Report on the Systematic Downward Bias in Live Cattle Futures Prices," *Journal of Futures Markets*, March 1981, pp. 347-358.

Hicks, J.R., *Value and Capital*, Oxford University Press, London, 1939.

Hooker, M., "Portfolio Risk Measures," State Street Global Advisors, Presentation at IQPC Conference on Portfolio Diversification with Commodity Assets, London, 5/26/04.

Humphreys, H.B., and D. Shimko, "Beating the JPMCI Energy Index," Working Paper, JP Morgan, August 1995.

Keynes, J., *A Treatise on Money*, Macmillan and Company Limited, London, 1934.

Lammey, A., "Investors Clamor for Stake in Bull Run in Stocks, Commodities," *Natural Gas Week*, 4/4/05, p. 19.

Lettau, M. and S. Ludvigson, "Consumption, Aggregate Wealth, and Expected Stock Returns." *The Journal of Finance*, June 2001, pp. 815-849.

Maddala, G.S., and J. Yoo, "Risk Premia and Price Volatility in Futures Markets," Center for the Study of Futures Markets, Columbia Business School, Working Paper Series CSFM #205 (July 1990).

Nash, D. and B. Shrayer, "Morgan Stanley Presentation," IQPC Conference on Portfolio Diversification with Commodity Assets, London, 5/27/04.

Rajagopal, M., "Examining the Financial Benefits of Commodities and Practical Issues of Implementation," Deutsche Bank, Presentation at Marcus Evans Conference on Investing in Commodities, London, 11/8/04.

Rosenberg, B., K. Reid, and R. Lanstein, "Persuasive Evidence of Market Inefficiency," *Journal of Portfolio Management*, Spring 1985, pp. 9-16.

Rowland, H., "How Much Oil Inventory is Enough?," Energy Intelligence Group, 1997.

Siegel, L., *Benchmarks and Investment Management*, Association for Investment Management and Research, Charlottesville, Va., 2003.

Smith, A., "Precious Thoughts," Mitsui Global Precious Metals, 4/29/04.

Taleb, N., *Fooled By Randomness*, Texere, New York, 2001.

Teague, S., "The Commodities 'Gladiator'," *Risk Magazine*, June 2004, p. 88.

Teweles, R. and F. Jones, *The Futures Game*, McGraw-Hill Book Company, New York, 1987.

Till, H., "Systematic Returns in Commodity Futures," *Commodities Now*, September 2000, pp. 75-79.

Till, H., "Trading Scarcity," *Futures* magazine, October 2000, pp. 48-50.

Till, H., "Passive Strategies in the Commodity Futures Markets," *Derivatives Quarterly*, Fall 2000, pp. 49-54.

Till, H., "Laughing in the Face of Diversity," *Risk & Reward*, February 2001, pp. 18-21.

Till, H., "Risk Management Lessons in Leveraged Commodity Futures Trading," *Commodities Now*, September 2002, pp. 84-87.

Till, H., "On the Role of Hedge Funds in Institutional Portfolios," *Journal of Alternative Investments*, Spring 2004, pp. 77-89.

Till, H. and J. Eagleeye, "How to Design a Commodity Futures Trading Program," a chapter in *Commodity Trading Advisors: Risk, Performance Analysis, and Selection* (Edited by Greg Gregoriou, Vassilios Karavas, Francois-Serge L'Habitant, and Fabrice Rouah), Wiley Finance, Hoboken, NJ, 2004, pp. 277-293.

Verleger, P., "Inflating the Commodity Bubble: Impact of Pension Fund Investment on Oil Prices," *The Petroleum Economics Monthly*, January 2005.

Vince, R., *The Mathematics of Money Management*, Wiley Finance, New York, 1992.

Walton, D., "Backwardation in Commodity Markets", Working Paper, Goldman Sachs, 5/28/91.

Working, H., "Theory of the Inverse Carrying Charge in Futures Markets," *Journal of Farm Economics*, February, 1948, pp. 1-28.

CHAPTER 7

GOLD AND INFLATION

James E. Burton, Jill Leyland, Katharine Pulvermacher
World Gold Council

INTRODUCTION

Two hundred and fifty years ago, in 1755, Dr Johnson published, in London, the first comprehensive dictionary of the English language. It cost 10 shillings—or half an English pound. Two ounces of gold—then worth £9.50—would have bought 17 copies. Today, for the cost of 2 ounces of gold, you could purchase from Amazon, or from leading booksellers, 17 copies of what is perhaps the nearest equivalent to Dr Johnson's dictionary today in the UK—the authoritative hardback Oxford English Dictionary. By contrast, £9.50 would not even buy you one dictionary.

In the Middle Ages an ounce of gold enabled a man to buy an acceptable, although not sumptuous, outfit of clothing, suitable perhaps for a clerk. At the time of American independence in 1776 the same would have been true and it remains the same in 2005, when the price of gold is around $430 per ounce and will buy an acceptable outfit for office wear.

These examples illustrate one of the most remarkable financial qualities of gold: its ability to hold its real value—and therefore act as an inflation hedge—over the centuries. This does not mean that it will be true for all goods and services since the relative prices of these vary. An ounce of gold would today buy more of some goods or services than it would in the past and less of others, but overall, gold's ability to hold its purchasing power over the very long term has been well documented for a range of countries.

In his seminal work, *The Golden Constant*, published in 1977, Jastram constructed indices of commodity prices, gold prices, and gold purchasing power from 1560 for Britain (England) and from 1800 to 1976 for the United States.[1] He found that gold tended to return to an historic rate of exchange (purchasing power parity) with other commodities. Harmston, updating the original analysis to 1997 and extending it to France, Germany, and Japan, found that Jastram's results were maintained in these three countries.[2] Exhibit 7–1 illustrates how the price of gold has tracked consumer price inflation in the United States over 2 centuries.

---

1. *The Golden Constant—The English and American Experience 1560–1976*, Roy W. Jastram, University of California, Berkeley, 1977.
2. *Gold as a Store of Value*, Stephen Harmston, World Gold Council research study no. 22, November 1998.

EXHIBIT 7–1

US: consumer price index and the price of gold (1800=1)

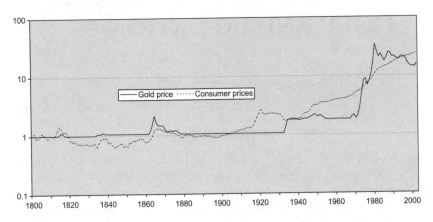

However, for much of this period, the monetary role of gold was dominant, reinforced by the existence of gold or bimetallic standards in a number of countries, particularly during the International Gold Standard that lasted from around 1870 to 1914. The role that gold has played as money for the better part of 2500 years is key to understanding why it has consistently displayed such a strong relationship with inflation. For today's investors, in a world where nonmonetary demand for gold has been dominant for decades, it is crucial to understand the grounds on which gold's role as an inflation hedge can be expected to continue. In the section that follows, we present the theoretical foundations for gold's role as an inflation hedge that are consistent with its role as a monetary asset, followed by a brief review of research focussing on a range of periods and countries since the transition from fixed to floating exchange rates in the early 1970s.

Throughout history in different cultures different commodities have been used as money, but, as Bernstein points out, "in modern times, nothing useful has ever functioned as money for very long... Gold... has always been useless for most practical purposes that call for metal, because it is so soft. With only [153,000] tonnes of it in existence, gold is also too scarce to have many uses. But gold has clear advantages as money compared to other kinds of useless substance that people have used for the purpose. Unlike cowrie shells, which were the main form of money for centuries in parts of Asia, gold is remarkably durable and does not easily fragment. Every single piece of gold, no matter how small or how large, is instantly recognisable everywhere as a receptacle of high value. Furthermore, every piece of gold is valued only by its weight and purity, attributes that are inconveniently applied to cattle."[3,4]

---

3. Bernstein, Peter L. (2000), *The Power of Gold: The History of an Obsession*, John Wiley & Sons, New York. p. 19.
4. GFMS Ltd. estimated that approximately 153,000 tonnes of gold had been mined by the end of 2004.

Bernstein is incorrect of course in that industrial applications for gold are actually quite varied, ranging from electronics and dentistry to less well-known applications in medicine via nanotechnology, with the totality of these accounting for around 12% of the demand for gold.

The monetary use of gold i.e., as a store of value and means of payment, is not to be confused with the International Gold Standard. A *de facto* gold standard existed in Britain from 1717 when Sir Isaac Newton, then Master of the Mint, overvalued gold by setting the official silver price of the gold guinea at 21 shillings, although it was only from 1816 that Britain was on a full legal gold standard. The International Gold Standard came about as other countries followed the lead set by what was at the time the world's dominant economic and military power.[5] Bordo and Rockoff provide a breakdown of the periods over which nine countries adhered to the gold standard during the 19th and early 20th centuries— see Table 7–1.[6] Countries that adhered faithfully to the gold standard rule generally benefited by being charged lower interest rates on long-term borrowing in the core capital markets, so that adhering to gold at that time was similar to a "Good Housekeeping Seal of Approval." Bordo and Rockoff emphasise however, that "adherence to the gold standard rule, although a simple and transparent test, implied a far more complex set of institutions and economic policies. Indeed, those countries that adhered to the gold standard rule generally had lower fiscal deficits, more stable money growth, and lower inflation rates than those that did not. But those countries that adhered to gold also paid a price for doing so because they gave up the flexibility to react to adverse supply shocks by following expansionary monetary policies and altering the exchange rate."[7]

Attempts to return to the gold standard after the First World War were badly mismanaged with a return to prewar parities in certain countries, despite the intervening inflation, the use of lower parities in others and the blocking of needed adjustment mechanisms. The fixed dollar–gold parity of US$20.67/troy ounce, which had remained unchanged through the war years and after, was suspended in 1933, but in 1934 the dollar was refixed at a new parity of US$35/troy ounce.

After the Second World War, the core of the Bretton Woods international monetary system that was established was that the dollar should be pegged to gold at the $35/troy ounce parity while other currencies should be defined in terms of the dollar with fixed but adjustable pegs. The Bretton Woods system helped to form what was, at least for western countries, probably the most successful period of economic history. Growth was high, and inflation, while higher than in the classical gold standard period, was relatively low and stable.

---

5. Cooper, Richard N. (1982), *The Gold Standard: Historical Facts and Future Prospects*, Brookings Papers on Economic Activity, No. 1, 1982, pp. 1–56.
6. Bordo, Michael D. and Hugh Rockoff (1996), *The Gold Standard as a "Good Housekeeping Seal of Approval"*, Journal of Economic History, Vol. 56, No. 2 (June), pp. 389–428.
7. Bordo and Rockoff (1996), ibid. p. 416.

T A B L E   7–1

A chronology of adherence to the gold standard for nine countries: circa 1870 to 1914[*]

Country	Period	Standard
Canada	1853–1914	Gold
Australia	1852–1915	Gold
United States	1792–1861	Bimetallic (*de facto* gold after 1834)
	1862–1878	Paper ("Greenbacks")
	1879–1917[a]	Gold
Italy	1862–1866	Bimetallic
	1866–1884	Paper
	1884–1894	Gold
	1894–1914	Paper
Spain	1868–1883	Silver
	1883–1914	Paper
Portugal	1854–1891	Gold
	1891–1914	Paper
Argentina	1867–1876	Gold
	1876–1883[b]	Paper
	1883–1885	Gold
	1885–1899	Paper
	1899–1914	Gold
Brazil	1857–1888	Paper
	1888–1889	Gold
	1889–1906	Paper
	1906–1914	Gold
Chile	1870–1878	Bimetallic
	1878–1895[c]	Paper
	1895–1898	Gold
	1898–1925	Paper

[*] Reproduced from Bordo and Rockoff (1996), p. 401.
[a] Gold Embargo 1917–1919, Standard not suspended.
[b] Failed attempt to restore convertibility in 1881.
[c] Failed attempt to restore convertibility in 1887.

Many developing countries too made rapid progress during that era. However, the $35/troy ounce fixed price became unrealistic over time, partly as a result of existing inflation and a surge in demand for gold as a result of the Vietnam War. The $35/troy ounce peg was replaced in 1968 by a two-tier system with a free private market, but with gold still exchanging hands officially at an official rate. When the United States finally abandoned the system in 1971, the last fixing price before the "gold window" was closed was $42.22/troy ounce, and to this day the United States officially values its gold holdings at that price.

In terms of the evolution of the world's monetary system, then, one can distinguish three key phases. During the first, commodities generally were used directly as money and more usually, this tended to be in the form of precious and base metals that were minted as coins. The value of the species was the value of the metal it contained, in the same way that a 1-ounce gold bullion coin today is worth one fine troy ounce of gold. A second phase gave rise to paper money that could be exchanged for a fixed amount of gold or silver—even today, so long after Britain abandoned any form of gold standard, Sterling bank notes carry the words, "I promise to pay the bearer on demand the sum of... pounds," although the bearer would, for his pains, presumably receive simply another bank note. This is the final phase, where money is backed by nothing other than the confidence that its holders place in the issuing bank: that they will be able to exchange cash for goods and to use money as a way to store their wealth, but which is dependent on the ability of that government to keep inflation under control, ensure that real interest rates do not descend into negative territory, and that the international purchasing power of the currency is maintained over the long term.

Under the gold standard, currency units were defined in terms of a given quantity of gold and were typically convertible into gold (and/or silver, in the case of a bimetallic system).[8] Given this constraint, growth of the money supply was equal to growth of the country's ownership of gold bullion stocks, which was partly dependent on the rate of growth of mine production itself but also on fluctuations in the nonmonetary demand for gold.[9] To the extent that specific episodes of inflation were caused by an increase in the money supply, and that such episodes fell within the period of history covered by the gold standard, it is surely tautological to claim that gold is a hedge against inflation: by definition, under that set of circumstances, it must be. What is of interest to contemporary investors seeking to protect the real value of their investments against the corrosion of inflation is the extent to which gold may still offer some protection against inflation, which may of course be caused by demand-side as well as supply-side pressures, and whether they would not simply be better off using financial products specifically designed for that purpose, such as inflation-linked bonds.

In what follows, we provide a brief review of studies of gold and inflation over a variety of periods since 1968 in order to evaluate whether gold has in fact continued to act as an inflation hedge since the breakdown of the Bretton Woods system.

Focusing on the period from March 1968 to February 1980 and using the IMF consumer price index of the industrialised nations, Kolluri (1981) finds that gold was a good inflation hedge, specifically, a 1% increase in anticipated inflation resulted in a 5% increase in the capital gain on gold. This relationship was stronger over the period from January 1974 to February 1980. Kolluri's first approach is to test a model proposed by Martin Feldstein, which suggests that a positive relation between the rate of inflation and the relative price of gold could be expected to exist in an economy where income tax rates are higher than capital gains tax rates. In this case, "because of unindexed taxes on capital income,

---

8. Sachs, Jeffrey D. and Felipe B. Larrain (1993), *Macroeconomics in the Global Economy*, Englewood Cliffs, New Jersey: Prentice Hall. See in particular Chapters 9–11 and 15 for a general background on money supply, fixed and flexible exchange rate regimes, and inflation.
9. See Cooper (1982), p. 13.

a higher expected rate of inflation raises the price of gold relative to the general price level, making gold an inflation hedge." (p. 14). However, Kolluri does not restrict the theoretical grounds for gold being an inflation hedge to Feldstein's model, pointing out that conventional macroeconomic theory suggests a liquidity effect on prices of financial assets in the short run—"an initial excess supply of money creates additional demand for assets including gold." Or "too much money chasing too few goods." Specifically, Kolluri tests for a positive relationship between the expected rate of inflation and the nominal rate of return on gold.[10]

In a more recent paper, Sjaastad and Scacciavillani test the relationship between changes in the gold price and "world inflation" between 1982 and 1990, finding that "gold continues to be a store of value as 'world' inflation increases the demand for gold; it is estimated that the real price of gold rises by between two-thirds and three-quarters of 1% in response to a one point increase in the world inflation rate."[11] The inflation variable in this case is the change in the natural logarithm of a weighted average of the European, US and Japanese price levels.

Taylor uses 80 years of US data ending in April 1996 and a range of statistical methods to test whether gold, silver, platinum and palladium acted as both short-run and long-run inflation hedges.[12] Noting that "it was not until the beginning of 1968 that the gold price was allowed to be determined by market forces," he concludes that all the precious metals could have been used as a long-run inflation hedge. The results with respect to the short-run are not as clear-cut, indicating that precious metals did offer "minor protection" against short-run movements in the inflation rate but that this hedging quality was concentrated around the second OPEC oil shock in 1979.

Levin *et al.* focus their analysis of gold as both a short-run and long-run inflation hedge on the period from January 1976 to December 1999.[13] Using cointegration regression techniques to test their model, they find a positive relationship between the nominal price of gold and the US retail price index.

Despite the abundance of empirical work that supports the notion that gold has continued to provide a good hedge against inflation since the breakdown of the Bretton Woods system, theories as to why this role has persisted are apparently as scarce as the yellow metal itself. Here we postulate both a supply side approach and a demand side analysis—that is, inflation caused by supply side factors as well as inflation caused by demand side factors. These approaches should be viewed as complementary rather than mutually exclusive. The first revolves around the idea that both the gold price and consumer price levels may move together because they are responding to a common underlying factor.

10. Kolluri, Bharat R. (1981), *Gold as a hedge against inflation: an empirical investigation*, Quarterly Review of Economics and Business, Vol. 21, No. 4 (Winter), pp. 13–24.

11. Sjaastad, Larry A. and Fabio Scacciavillani (1996), *The price of gold and the exchange rate*, Journal of International Money and Finance, Vol. 15, No. 6, pp. 879–897.

12. Taylor, Nicholas J. (1998), *Precious metals and inflation*, Applied Financial Economics, Vol. 8, pp. 201–210.

13. Levin, Eric J., Dipak Ghosh, Peter Macmillan and Robert E. Wright (2000), *Gold as an inflation hedge?* University of Stirling Working Paper, http://staff.stir.ac.uk/e.j.levin/gold.pdf.

On the gold side, investment demand tends to increase during periods of heightened uncertainty, given gold's traditional role as a "safe haven." On the inflation side, if the monetary authorities respond to pressures in the financial system by increasing liquidity, whether through the mechanism of reducing interest rates or increasing the money supply directly, this can be expected to lead to an increase in the rate of inflation albeit with an extended lag, as set out in the review of Kolluri's paper above. The demand side argument is allied to a more general case of increased demand for commodities in the face of supply constraints, such as we have been witnessing over the past couple of years with respect to oil and certain industrial metals. This impacts not just on the price of the commodities in question, but also on the price of other commodities that use the former as inputs in the production process. In the case of gold, this effect is then amplified because of the historical association between gold and inflation.

Gold's investment attributes are not confined to its role as a hedge against inflation. It can also provide investors with a "natural" hedge against dollar weakness and is a particularly effective diversifier with respect to equities (see Exhibit 7–7).

A dollar hedge

Gold's role as a hedge against dollar weakness has long been accepted and is easily demonstrated with respect to the trade-weighted dollar—see Exhibit 7–2.

Capie, Mills and Wood explore the extent of this relationship with respect to the DM/USD, Yen/USD, CHF/USD, GBP/USD, trade-weighted dollar, and trade-weighted pound between 1971 and 2002, finding that in the case of typical (modal) weekly changes in exchange rates, the gold price tends to overshoot.[14] In other words, in the face of a decline in the dollar exchange rate, the gold price in local currency would not decline by as much as the pure exchange rate calculation would suggest and in some cases would actually increase slightly. Capie, Mills and Wood provide two examples to illustrate this point:

> The first concerns a UK holder at the time that gold is $350 an oz and $1 = £0.67 so that gold is therefore £234.50 per oz. Suppose the dollar falls against the pound by the typical amount of 0.005, so that $1 = £0.665. Without a move in the dollar gold price the sterling price would fall to £232.75. But the gold price would, on average, rise to $350.9976 per oz and the new sterling price would be £233.41. This would still be slightly lower than the price to start with, but some of the loss would have been recuperated.

> The second example consists of a German holder at the time that gold is $350 an oz and $1 = DM2.00, making gold DM700.00 per oz. A typical fall in the dollar results in $1 = DM1.99. If the gold price remained unchanged in dollar terms then the new DM price would be DM696.50 per oz, but

---

14. Capie, Forest, Terence C. Mills and Geoffrey Wood (2004), *Gold as a Hedge against the US Dollar*, World Gold Council Research Study No. 30 (September).

EXHIBIT 7–2

Trade-weighted dollar and the gold price

Source: Global Insight.

since the dollar price rises, on average, to $300.9982 per oz, then the new DM price is DM 701.35. In this case the price in the target currency would have been higher than the price it started at.

Changes in the dollar exchange rate have been far from typical since the middle of 2002. Tests on the relationship between the log daily changes in the trade-weighted dollar and the log change in the gold price between January 2002 and mid-February 2005 reveal that, on average, a decline in the dollar of just over 1% resulted in a corresponding 1% increase in the dollar price of gold and that this accounted for just short of 30% of changes in the gold price over the period.[15]

This leads one to ask what other factors impact changes in the gold price. In the next section we review the current state of gold supply and demand and recent movements in the gold price.

SUPPLY, DEMAND AND GOLD PRICE MOVEMENTS

Gold is different to most commodities in that the stocks of above-ground gold dwarf annual mined output. The latter is around 2500 tonnes a year compared to 153,000 tonnes of above-ground stocks. Gold, as we have seen, does not corrode

---

15. Pulvermacher, K.M (2005), unpublished mimeograph.

or rust and is virtually indestructible. Much of the above-ground stock that exists is held in a form under which it could come back to the market when conditions are appropriate. It follows that the supply and demand dynamics of gold are more complex than those for most other commodity markets.

Gold supply and demand flows can be broken down as follows: [16]

On the demand side:

Jewelry accounts for around 70% of demand and just over half of all the gold that has ever been mined is held in this form.

Industrial and medical uses of gold account for a further 11% of annual demand and 12% of above-ground stocks.

Investment has made up 13% of annual demand on average since 2000. Sixteen percent of above-ground stocks are in private investor hands (as opposed to public sector investors such as central banks).

On the supply side:

Two-thirds of annual supply comes from "freshly mined" gold.

The balance is made up from central bank sales of gold (13%); gold scrap (20%, of which three-quarters comes from "recycled" jewelry and one-quarter from industrial scrap); and the remainder from net disinvestment.

Exhibit 7–3 shows a breakdown of above-ground stocks at the end of 2004 and of supply and demand flows over the last five years.

Jewelry

Asia and the Middle East account for around 60% of the jewelry market (Exhibit 7–4). Caratage here ranges from 18 through 21 carat in Saudi Arabia and the Gulf to 22 carat in India and right up to 24 carat (pure gold) in China.

Traditionally jewelry in these countries is sold by weight and priced according to the current price of gold in the international market plus a relatively small mark-up—often around 30% although it can be even less in some countries. It is common in Asia and the Middle East for gold jewelry to be sold back either in exchange for a new piece or for cash. This, together with its other characteristics, means that this market is very sensitive to price volatility, although less so to the price level. When prices rise, customers hang back from purchasing or purchase by trading in an existing piece they own thus sharply reducing the consumption of new gold. They may also sell pieces for cash to make a profit. Buying of new gold will resume once prices are perceived to have stabilised, whether this is at a lower or higher level. Clearly a higher level of prices will make gold less afford-able and will thus depress buying but it also makes it more desirable. Most stud-ies of this market suggest that the elasticity with respect to the price level is less

---

16. Annual gold supply and demand are published in the GFMS Gold Survey—see www.gfms.co.uk. The percentages reported here are based on five year averages from 2000 to 2004.

EXHIBIT 7-3

Breakdown of above-ground stocks of supply of and demand for gold

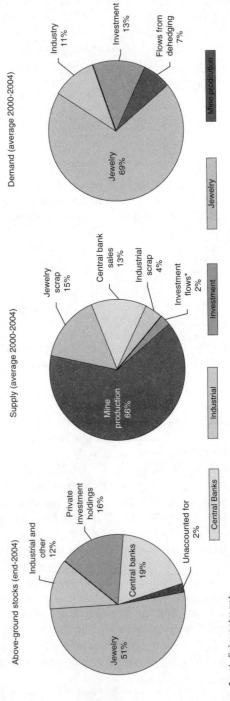

Above-ground stocks (end-2004)

Industrial and other 12%

Private investment holdings 16%

Central banks 19%

Unaccounted for 2%

Jewelry 51%

Supply (average 2000-2004)

Jewelry scrap 15%

Central bank sales 13%

Industrial scrap 4%

Investment flows* 2%

Mine production 66%

Demand (average 2000-2004)

Industry 11%

Investment 13%

Flows from dehedging 7%

Jewelry 69%

Mine production

Jewelry

Investment

Industrial

Central Banks

* net disinvestment

Source: GFMS Ltd.

E X H I B I T   7–4

Gold demand for jewelry, tonnes

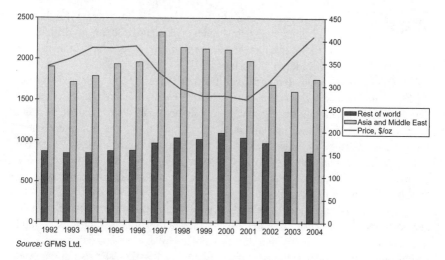

Source: GFMS Ltd.

than 1, but the reaction to price volatility means that this component of demand can at times be volatile and the rising price of the last few years was a major contributor to the fall in demand from 2000 to 2003.

Industrial and Medical Use

Over half of industrial and dental demand (around 7% of total demand) comes from the use of gold in electronic components due to its high thermal and electrical conductivity and its outstanding resistance to corrosion. The share of electronics in total gold demand has grown over the past decade but its extent also fluctuates according to economic conditions and demand for electronic goods.

Medical applications include the use of gold wires in heart transplants and stents to support weak blood vessels. Its best-known use, however, is in dentistry. This currently accounts for just less than 2% of gold demand and is stable.

Gold is also used in a number of other industrial and decorative purposes such as gold plating and coating and in gold thread (such as *jari* in India). Other applications take advantages of gold's reflectivity of heat and lasers and its optical properties. Overall these uses of gold account for 2% to 3% of total demand.

Investment

Investment in this section is defined as the purchase of gold bullion in the form of bars and coins. In the final section of this chapter, we will see that gold investment vehicles extend far beyond this definition although ultimately, investors seeking ownership of a real asset may prefer vehicles that are solidly backed by physical gold to those that simply provide price exposure.

Analysts usually draw a distinction between retail investment (purchases by individuals) and institutional investment (purchases by investment funds and other corporate entities such as pension funds). In practice it can be difficult to distinguish between these two categories particularly given that some private investors may have considerable holdings.

Annual investment demand over the last 5 years has averaged around $5.4 billion annually and accounted for around 13% of demand, but flows can be very variable and in some categories there has been net disinvestment in some years (Exhibit 7–5). Retail investment is particularly important in Japan (where investment can surge in times of economic or financial concern), India, Vietnam (where gold tael bars are used to buy property), Turkey (where gold coins are popular and are sometimes used to purchase goods and services) and, at times, in the USA and some European countries.

Institutional investment has traditionally been difficult to measure directly and, with the exception of exchange traded funds and similar vehicles, is implied as a residual from the supply and demand table. This is frequently dominated by hedge funds and similar vehicles and can be highly volatile. The rise in the gold price in 2003 saw a substantial inflow of such investment, some—but not all—of which was sold back in the middle of 2004 before turning positive again towards the end of the year.

E X H I B I T   7–5

Investment by category, 2000–2004, tonnes

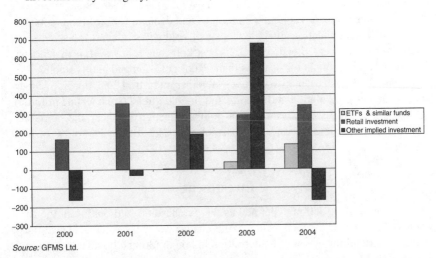

Source: GFMS Ltd.

Mine Output and Hedging

Gold mining occurs in a number of countries worldwide—GFMS identify over 60 in their annual survey and there are a number of additional countries with some smaller production. South Africa remains the largest producer of mined gold but its output is on a downward trend and in 2004 it accounted for only 14% of global output. The USA and Australia vie for second place, but increasingly gold is mined in developing countries, primarily those classified by the World Bank as low income or lower middle income. For a number of these it makes a substantial contribution to exports. Overwhelmingly output today comes from formal, modern mines, both underground and open pit, but some gold is still mined by alluvial panning or small-scale mines.

After a period when it was on a rising trend, gold production has been broadly stable for the last few years (it fell in 2004, although this was primarily due to temporary factors). The fall in the price in the late 1990s—see below—caused a number of companies to cut back on exploration. While this started to recover from 2003, the time lags implicit in bringing a new mine into operation mean that most analysts expect output to remain flat or even decline over the next few years.

A peculiarity of the gold market is the impact of forward sales and other derivative operations—normally referred to as hedging—by mining companies. The existence of large above-ground stocks of gold which are owned by institutions and others who have no immediate use for them and are therefore willing to lend them for a short period—primarily central banks, but also some other institutional holders—means that gold can be borrowed. The lending market is small relative to the size of those stocks which means that central banks and other holders are willing to lend gold to trusted counterparties at low rates of interest (particularly also as this means they can dispense with storage costs for the period of the loan).

The basic forward selling mechanism works (in its "plain vanilla" form) as follows. A mining company decides to sell a certain quantity of the gold it will produce at a future time—say 1 year ahead—forward in order to ensure price certainty. It arranges this transaction with a bullion bank.[17] The bank therefore has a commitment to buy gold in 1 year's time on its books. To offset this, it borrows the same amount of gold from a central bank (or other large holder) for 1 year. This gold is then immediately sold into the market and the bank can invest the proceeds. In 1 year's time the bank receives the gold from the mining company, pays the company from the invested proceeds and uses the gold to repay the central bank. Thus the amount of gold in question reaches the market not when it is mined but at the time the transaction is made—in other words the sale is "accelerated."

This whole transaction is made attractive to the bullion bank and the mining company by the low interest rate paid to the central bank. This enables the

---

17. A bank that deals in gold and other precious metals. A list of members of the London Bullion Market Association is available on www.lbma.org.uk

bullion bank to receive more interest from investing the cash from the sold gold than it will pay out. It can thus offer attractive terms to the mining company who will therefore normally be paid a premium for its gold above the spot price at the time the transaction is initiated. Thus gold, unlike other metals, is nearly always in contango (forward price higher than spot price).

The description above refers to a simple transaction. In practice options and other, more complex, derivative instruments can also be used. Nevertheless the important issue for the gold market as a whole is that when a forward sale takes place an equivalent amount of gold is placed on the market at that time rather than when it is mined making the quantity of gold sold into the market greater than it would otherwise be. When the gold is actually mined it is used to repay the loan to the central bank and is therefore not available to the market, thus reducing the amount sold.

Therefore, if the overall amount of hedging is rising—i.e., mining companies as a whole are entering into more forward sale contracts than they are redeeming—the amount of gold supplied to the market rises, tending to depress the price. When the opposite happens the overall amount of gold available to the market is reduced. These trends, as we will see shortly, can sometimes have an important impact on the gold market.

Scrap

As is the case with most metals, the gold that satisfies demand each year comes both from mine production—accounting for around two-thirds—and from the recycling of metal that has been mined in previous years. In fact this secondary supply forms a smaller proportion of total supply flows than is the case with some metals, for example aluminium and lead. Scrap supplies account for around 19% of total supply. The majority of scrap comes from recycled jewelry with lesser amounts from industrial (notably electronics) uses and, at times, from investment products. As explained in the section on jewelry, scrap supplies tend to rise in times of rising prices, when there is an incentive for the owner to cash in a profit. Scrap supplies also rise in times of economic distress. They reached a peak in 1998 during the Asian crisis.

Central Bank Selling

Central banks can buy and sell gold but they have been net sellers since 1989. The fact that gold is no one's liability, and therefore holds its value in a crisis, and its beneficial diversification properties are among the reasons that most central banks still hold gold even though it is no longer part of the formal international monetary system. Since 1999 gold sales by 15 European central banks—the main sellers of gold since for historical reasons some of them hold large stocks—have been controlled by the Central Bank Gold Agreement that limits the collective quantity of gold they place on the market. The initial agreement covered the 5 years from 1999 to 2004 and proved very successful—it was renewed for a further 5 years in 2004. Signatories to the agreement account for around 45% of official gold stocks. Around four-fifths of central bank holdings are either covered by the agreement or are owned by declared nonsellers, most notably the United States.

PRICE MOVEMENTS OVER THE LAST DECADE

For a period in the mid-1990s the gold price (in dollar terms) was reasonably stable, fluctuating mainly between $350 and $400 per ounce. This changed from 1996. The last years of the 1990s provided almost a "perfect storm" scenario for gold with both external circumstances and developments in the gold market combining to produce a sharp fall in the price (Exhibit 7–6).

The late 1990s were a period of rapid economic growth in the world economy with low inflation, a strong dollar and booming stock markets. Adverse events, such as the Asian crisis and the collapse of Long Term Capital Management, seemed to have little impact on the world economy as a whole. Everything seemed to be going well, the USA was apparently undergoing a productivity miracle and the dot.com boom crowned the whole affair. There seemed little need for a defensive or safe-haven asset such as gold.

Meanwhile more gold was coming on to the market both from mining companies and, in certain years, from central banks. Gold production had grown in the mid-1990s, due largely to technological advances which made the treatment of lower grade ores more economic. This was accentuated by growth in forward selling (hedging)—before the early 1990s this had been only very limited—and this, as described above, resulted in yet more gold coming on to the market. As

E X H I B I T   7–6

Gold prices, $/oz, monthly average

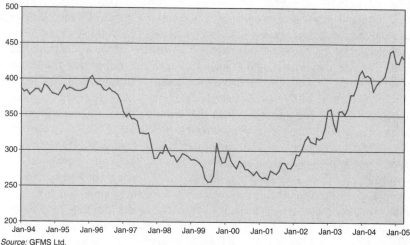

Source: GFMS Ltd.

the price started to fall there was additional incentive for many companies to hedge, thus bringing yet more gold on to the market. Meanwhile a small number of high profile central bank sales raised fears of a tidal wave of central bank selling. Speculators, believing that the price was likely to fall further, also entered into forward selling contracts with bullion banks; these sales were also offset by the bullion banks borrowing gold from central banks and selling this immediately into the market in the same way as they treated forward sales from mining companies.

Meanwhile mining companies, faced with the inevitable consequence of a falling price, reduced the amount they were able to give the World Gold Council to promote gold so that promotion was reduced. The falling price stimulated demand to a certain extent but, as explained above, jewelry, the main element of demand, is not very responsive to changes in the price level; with less promotion demand was not sufficiently strong to stop the fall in the price while the price fall itself, while making gold more affordable, also made it less desirable.

The situation came to a head in 1999 following a surprise announcement by the UK government of plans to sell half its gold holding against a background of possible substantial sales by both Switzerland and the IMF (the latter in order to help fund debt relief to heavily indebted poor countries). The price fell further reaching a low of $252 per ounce in July 1999. To restore order to the market, and following the publication of evidence that the fall in the price was causing substantial harm to some of the world's poorest countries who were gold producers, the first Central Bank Gold Agreement (CBGA) was announced in September 1999 in order to regulate the amount of central bank gold coming on to the market and to make central bank selling plans transparent. At the same time IMF sales plans were dropped in favour of funding debt relief via a revaluation of the Fund's gold.

The CBGA was successful in restoring order and confidence to the market although the immediate price spike it produced was followed by renewed downward drift in the dollar (although not the euro) price as the US currency strengthened further. The wave of hedging by gold mining companies ended, and was reversed thus reducing supply to the market. The fall in world stock markets in 2000 suggested that the economic euphoria of the late 1990s was ending. From April 2001 the gold price started to rise again against a background of a slowing world economy. The increase in geopolitical tension following 9/11, and the fall in the dollar from 2002, increased investor interest. Increased gold promotion started to boost buying which rose from 2003 in value terms, although the rise in the price restrained the volume of gold bought until 2004.

The gold price remained on a rising trend in 2003 and 2004. However in the latter 2 years this was stimulated above all by the weakening dollar—in euro terms the price fluctuated around a flat trend. Nevertheless confidence had now returned to the market. 2003 saw substantial investment buying—although some of this was from short-term speculative holders who were to sell in 2004—while the launch of gold Exchange Traded Funds (see section 4) stimulated a quantity of new buying. Finally, by the end of 2004 jewelry buyers in Asia and the

Middle East had become acclimatised to a higher gold price and buying remained brisk even with a price in excess of $400 per ounce. The strengthening of the dollar in the first part of 2005 saw the gold price ease somewhat, but it averaged $427 per ounce in the first quarter—a substantial rise from the low of $252 in July 1999.

This extensive review of gold supply and demand and recent price movements provides insight into a third crucial investment attribute of returns on gold: a consistent lack of correlation with returns on equities in the world's major capital markets, as can be seen in Exhibit 7–7.

While gold is not unique among commodities in offering excellent diversification properties, the large extent of above ground stocks, coupled with the diverse sources of demand, set it apart. The price drivers of gold are not the same as other commodities and help to underpin its lack of correlation with mainstream assets. Demand drivers include factors such as income changes in high consumption countries (India, China, Middle East), but geopolitical tension and macroeconomic factors such as uncertainty about inflation, the international purchasing power of the US dollar, evidence that others are investing or disinvesting, that influence investment (monetary) demand are generally believed to be key price drivers. Research shows it maintains its diversification properties at times of economic stress. Gold, in contrast to other diversifiers, keeps its low correlation attributes and there is evidence that correlations tend to fall during these periods.

Increasing convergence among mainstream asset classes has led investors to consider nontraditional alternative investment vehicles as a way of stabilising

EXHIBIT   7–7

Correlation of weekly returns: equity indices and gold (USD)

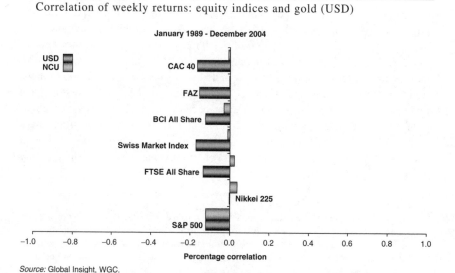

Source: Global Insight, WGC.

and enhancing portfolio performance. Investors today face a wider choice than ever—from hedge and private equity funds to timber and fine art. Compared with other alternative asset classes, gold bullion offers very high diversification benefits while at the same time being low-risk, highly liquid and inexpensive to hold and manage.

Investors have a wide range of methods to choose from when it comes to taking a position in gold, and although some investors may choose to take delivery of their gold, this is in fact relatively rare. In this final section, we review a range of investment methods, starting with the oldest and probably best-known.

The first gold coins were struck by King Croesus in Lydia during his reign between 560 and 547 BC. Gold coins have continued as legal tender since that time. Today, bullion coins such as Krugerrands and small bars offer private investors an attractive way of investing in relatively small amounts of gold. Investors can choose from a wide range of gold bullion coins issued by governments across the world. These coins are legal tender in their country of origin for their face value, rather than for their gold content.

For investment purposes, the market value of bullion coins is determined by the value of their fine gold content, plus a premium or mark-up that varies between coins and dealers. The premium tends to be higher for smaller denominations. Bullion coins range in size from 1/20 oz to 1000 g, although the most common weights (in troy ounces of fine gold content) are 1/20, 1/10, 1/4, 1/2, and 1 oz.

Gold bars can be bought in a variety of weights and sizes, ranging from as little as one gram to 400 troy ounces (the size of the internationally traded London Good Delivery bar). Small bars are defined as those weighing 1000 g or less.

The bullion banks offer large-scale investors two facilities for holding gold in accounts. In the first case, the gold is held in an allocated or segregated account. Specific bars, which are numbered and identified by hallmark, weight and fineness, are allocated to each particular investor, who typically pays the custodian for storage and insurance. In the second case, investors can hold gold in an unallocated account which functions in much the same way as a currency deposit account. They do not have specific bars assigned to them but can of course take delivery of their gold should they wish to do so—usually within 2 working days. Traditionally, one advantage of unallocated accounts has been that investors have not been charged for storage and insurance, because the bank reserves the right to lease the gold out. As a general rule, bullion banks do not deal in quantities under 1,000 ounces—their customers are institutional investors, private banks acting on behalf of their clients, central banks, and gold market participants wishing to buy or borrow large quantities of gold.[18]

---

18. Retail versions of gold accounts are available to investors in a range of countries—for more information about this, see www.gold.org/value/invest/howbuy/metal_accounts.html. In some countries, gold accounts effectively take the form of certificates that are issued by individual banks and confirm ownership on the client while the bank holds the metal on their behalf—see www.gold.org/value/invest/howbuy/gold-certs.html for further information.

The most recent innovation in investment in physical gold has been the advent of gold exchange traded funds, which currently trade in Australia, South Africa, the United Kingdom and the United States. Although the specific structure of these products differs from one jurisdiction to another, the underlying principle is the same. Each security is backed by physical gold held by a custodian in an allocated account. Small increments may be held in unallocated form. These instruments trade in exactly the same way as securities and are designed to track the gold price as closely as possible, in the same way that exchange-traded funds such as SPDRs track an underlying index—the S&P 500 in that case.

Gold derivatives, such as futures, options and structured products provide investors seeking exposure to gold price fluctuations but not direct ownership of the underlying asset, with a further method of investment. The largest volumes of gold futures are traded on the Comex division of the New York Mercantile Exchange and the Tokyo Commodities Exchange although a number of other exchanges, including the Chicago Board of Trade are also active in this market.

Institutional investors dominate the market for structured products. Typically, this type of vehicle—sometimes referred to as a gold-linked bond or structured note—provides investors with some combination of exposure to gold price fluctuations, a yield and principal protection. This combination of features is achieved by allocating part of the sum invested to purchasing either put or call options (depending on whether the product is designed for gold "bulls" or "bears"). The balance is invested in traditional fixed-income products to generate the yield. These notes can be tailored to provide capital protection and a varying degree of participation in any price appreciation or depreciation over their term, depending on market conditions and investor preferences.

Gold-oriented funds provide investors with a final means to gain exposure to the gold-mining sector. These funds typically invest in gold mining companies although some may also include gold itself, structured products and derivatives. Thus they provide exposure to the commercial fortunes of the mining companies they invest in, and hence to their commercial risks, as well as the gold itself and for this reason are not viewed as a "pure" play on gold.

CONCLUSION

In the 2500 years that gold has fulfilled a monetary role, it has proved an asset worthy of the trust that investors have placed in it over the long term, providing shelter from the unforeseen and the unforeseeable.

CHAPTER 8

REAL ESTATE AS AN INVESTMENT: OVERVIEW OF ALTERNATIVE VEHICLES

Merrie S. Frankel
Moody's Investors Service

John S. Lippmann
Eurohypo AG

ALTERNATIVES FOR REAL ESTATE INVESTMENT: FINANCIAL AND OWNERSHIP STRUCTURES

Real estate investment opportunities have evolved throughout the years to the point where there is a form of investment to suit each investor's needs in the private and public sectors. The basis of this text is to show that the risk-return paradigm determines the availability and choice of equity and debt capital in both the public and private markets. The financial structure can magnify and mitigate both risk and return. The primary ownership structures that will be discussed in this chapter consist of:

- Direct Ownership—Individual, Tenancy in Common

- Partnerships—Limited partnerships

- Corporations—REITs

- Group Forms of Ownership/Hybrid interests—Mezzanine funds, Joint Ventures, Syndications

Structuring real estate equity and debt investments is a means to divide a transaction into elementary economic tranches consisting of debt and equity investments:

- Landowner (unsubordinated)

- First mortgage

- Second mortgage, third mortgage

- Equity

- Mezzanine equity

Very often, the sum of the parts is greater than the whole. The purpose of such division is to raise more money, or raise money at lower overall cost, by arbitraging appetites of different classes of investors. The sources of equity financing are:

- Owner/developer—personal resources such as friends, family, and business associates

- Land owner—seller financing, contribution, option, lease

- Institutional investors such as pension funds and opportunity funds

- Public companies—equity REITs and operating companies

- Third party investors—Syndication to third parties through banks and investment vehicles; Joint Ventures; and Mezzanine funds.

The next chapter will discuss in detail the four quadrants (public debt, public equity, private debt, and private equity), real estate as an asset class and the ways to gain exposure to real estate returns through the four quadrants. The goal in this chapter is to provide an overview of the panoply of potential equity and debt investments, and to show that real estate returns have matched or exceeded the returns from the other asset classes such as bonds and stocks and provide an uncorrelated alternative investment.

Without knowing the basics, it is difficult to make wise investment decisions. To understand the equity and debt vehicles available, it is helpful to compare real estate finance to corporate finance:

Corporate finance	Real estate finance
• Common stock	• Equity
• Preferred stock	• First mortgage
• Unsecured debt	• Second mortgage
• Hybrid equity/debt securities	• Hybrid equity/debt (aka
○ Convertible bonds	"Mezzanine Financing")
○ Convertible preferred	○ Preferred equity
	○ Preferred debt

This chapter will explore the "what" and the "why" of real estate.
What are the characteristics of real estate?

- Industry is highly fragmented with few barriers to entry

- Each property is a unique, individual business enterprise

- Investment, operation, and management requires technical and financial training

- Long-term, illiquid nature of private real estate ownership does not allow for instantaneous, trading-like solutions due to market inefficiencies

- Competition is constant and continuous; neither real estate nor capital markets are ever in equilibrium for sustained periods

- Illiquid nature of private real estate ownership does not allow owner to change financial structure (leverage) quickly/without cost

- Industry lacked transparency as compared to financial markets and other business models until advent of securitized vehicles like REITs and CMBS

- Transactions may be complex and costly to execute and require third-party expertise

- May provide tax benefits not available in alternative investments

Why invest in real estate?

- Risk vs. return has historically been attractive
- An array of structures exists to match risk and return profiles
- Cash flow from property operation provides return on investment that grows with the economy
- Proceeds of property sales provides return of investment and price appreciation
- Lower volatility than equity securities
- Diversification of an overall portfolio
- Matching of liabilities
- Tax benefits
- Inflation hedge

Exhibit 8–1, Exhibit 8–2, and Exhibit 8–3 show that real estate, as represented by the public (National Association of Real Estate Investment Trusts—NAREIT) and private (National Council of Real Estate Investment Fiduciaries—NACREIF) indices, are an inflation hedge. These graphs indicate a variety of conclusions. Over the past 10 years, both the NACREIF Index and the dividend yields of the NAREIT Index have annual returns that supercede the CPI by an average of 8.5% and 4.5%, respectively. Annual returns of the NAREIT Index equities have been more volatile, with returns ranging from +27.4% to −25.4%, but have an average annual return of 5.8%. Although the price of publicly traded REITs (NAREIT) clearly dipped in the late 1990s, their total return and cumulative return (>400%) surpasses the other indices and measures.

The NCREIF index is considered the bellwether indicators of changes in the US private equity commercial real estate markets. (More discussion of this index can be found in Chapter 9.) Calculations are based on quarterly returns of individual properties before deduction of asset management fees. Each property's return is weighted by its market value. Income and capital appreciation changes are also calculated.

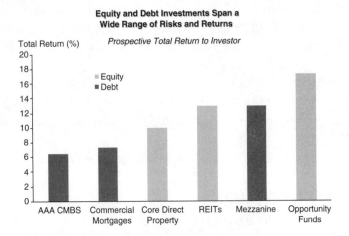

Equity and Debt Investments Span a Wide Range of Risks and Returns

Private Structures: Direct Ownership in Equity or Debt

Real estate equity represents ownership of a property, a participation in the operating and financial risks of property ownership of a share in the profits and losses of property operation and proceeds of any property sale. Real estate equity competes with investment in equity securities, mutual funds, venture capital, and variable annuities.

EXHIBIT 8–1

Historical Annual Total Returns for NACREIF, NAREIT, CPI, BBB Industrials, S&P

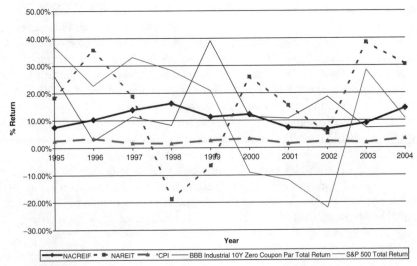

Source: NACREIF, NAREIT, CPI—US Dept. of Labor/Bureau of Labor Statistics, Bloomberg.

EXHIBIT 8-2

Comparative Returns for NACREIF, NAREIT (Yield and Price Components), CPI

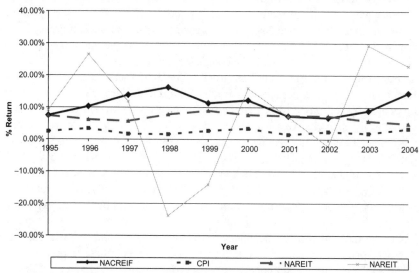

Source: NACREIF, NAREIT, CPI—US Dept. of Labor/Bureau of Labor Statistics.

EXHIBIT 8-3

Ten-Year Total Returns NACREIF, NAREIT, CPI and BBB Industrials

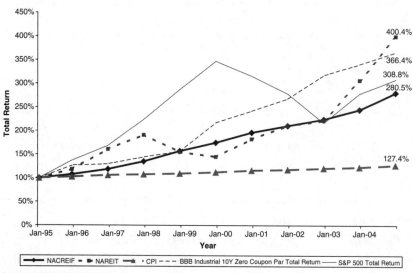

Source: NACREIF, NAREIT, CPI—US Dept. of Labor/Bureau of Labor Statistics, Bloomberg.

Real estate debt or mortgage capital is money loaned to an owner, developer or investor in exchange for a promise to repay principal (the amount borrowed) together with a specified return (interest) for the use of the funds for a specified period of time. Real estate loans are categorized by the term. Short-term loans access the "money markets" for planning through construction stages or until permanent, long-term financing is completed. Long-term or permanent loans, accessing the "capital markets," are used for operation and management states. Real estate loans are either recourse or nonrecourse to the borrower and secured or unsecured by the property. A loan can be either self-amortizing over the entire period of the loan or have a balloon payment in 5, 10, or 15 years, at which point the remainder of the loan is due. Prepayment provisions in commercial (not residential) loans include lock-out provisions whereby a borrower may not pay off the loan for a number of years without a yield-maintenance or defeasance penalty that is the difference between the interest rate and often the current Treasury rate present valued. The primary purpose of this penalty is to thwart borrowers paying off loans in declining interest rate environments and, thus, denying the institutional lenders of their interest payment stream. Real estate debt competes with alternative fixed rate and variable rate investments in Treasury securities; corporate, high-yield, and emerging market bonds; asset-backed securities, and fixed annuities.

Private ownership structures include owning property individually, by tenancy in common, and through partnerships. Individual ownership may consist of a fee simple complete interest in the land and accompanying building, an interest in the land solely, or a leasehold interest in the building alone. Tenancy in common, terminology that dates to medieval times, involves owning the property with another person where you have an undivided interest in the whole, but acquire the other person's interest upon their demise. Partnerships consist of a means to own an interest in a property or portfolio with other people.

Real estate refers to land and the improvements thereon. Property rights include the right to possession, use, quiet enjoyment, and sale. Value of real estate-total return buyer(s) are willing to pay for the flow of benefits associated with the property rights.

Terminology:

- "Fee Simple"—ownership of all of the property rights.
- Leasehold interest—interest in a specific property right(s) for a defined period of time.
- Estate for Years—up to 99 years in duration for investments such as a ground lease, improvements lease, or master lease of ground and improvements.
- Life Estate—lasts until the death of the owner of the leasehold
- Reversion—property rights revert to grantor at future time
- Remainder—future interest of a third party in specific property rights
- Leasehold—interest in a specific property right for a defined period of time, whether it be a leased fee interest—right to receive contracted rent payments or the leasehold estate—use and occupancy of the real estate.

Public Structures: Real Estate Investment Trusts (REITS) and Commercial Mortgage Backed Securities (CMBS)

Securitization

Securitization is the process of creating a synthetic, tradable security whose performance seeks to mirror the performance of the underlying assets. The advent of the real estate securitization market in the 1980s has transformed real estate from an exclusively private market to a market where private and public coexist— from illiquid to liquid. However, the trading of real estate in the public securities markets sometimes is disconnected from property market fundamentals, thus, creating short-term arbitrage opportunities. An example of such an environment is the softness in the early 2000s of the multifamily, office and industrial real estate markets, but the positive returns of the multifamily, office and industrial REITs. Securitized real estate, whether in an equity format (REIT) or debt format (CMBS) possesses the following characteristics—liquidity, security (hard asset underlying paper), diversification, competitive rates of return, low-return correlation with other asset classes, lower correlation (beta) than other asset classes, and provides a hedge against inflation.

The Morgan Stanley REIT Index (RMS) has a beta of substantially less than 1, i.e., from 5/31/95 through 5/31/05 it is 0.024 with a standard deviation of error of 3.89, a correlation of 0.07 and a beta of 0.08. This low beta suggests low correlation with the S&P 500 and low volatility.

What are the positive results of securitization? Increased transparency has led to better decision making and the real estate capital markets are capable of pricing a wide array of risks due to improved liquidity and investment alternatives. The challenge in upcoming years may be that low interest rates have been driving many investment, operating, and financing strategies. Real estate values are at all-time highs with lagging improvement to the underlying real estate fundamentals. Thus, increases in interest rates could derail the market improvements to the point where liquidity would be impacted due to the withdrawal of equity, mezzanine capital, or mortgage debt from the marketplace. However, real estate executives believe that even if capital flows decrease to real estate equity and debt markets, they would remain adequate to supply required liquidity as real estate has become cycle-tested.[1]

Real Estate Investment Trusts

REITs consist of both equity and mortgage REITs. We will focus on equity REITs here. Suffice it to say that mortgage REITs invest in or provide mortgages. An equity REIT is a corporation (trust) that owns real estate and passes its income and losses through to its investors without the entity incurring income tax. It is a "mutual fund" for individual real estate assets, allowing real estate companies to access the public markets. To qualify as a REIT, an entity must have at least

---

1. Emerging Trends in Real Estate 2005, ULI and PriceWaterhouseCoopers, pp. 3–13.

100 shareholders, and 75% of a REIT's assets must be invested in cash, government securities, and real estate. Regarding income:

- 75% of a REIT's income must be from real estate sources—rents, reimbursements, etc.

- 90% of taxable income must be distributed to shareholders as dividends

REITs have performed better than other equity markets during the early 2000s due to:

- Hard assets with an easily comprehendible business premise

- Investors willing to accept a lower return from real estate while they wait for the stock market to become more stable

- Cash flow protected by underlying leases

- High dividends, averaging 7% historically

- Low leverage—averaging 40% of capitalization

- High interest coverage—at least 2 to 1 typically

- Trade at approximately net asset value (NAV)

- Addition of REITs to S&P indices has helped to broaden investor base; however, there is concern that the "momentum" and "yield" investors may rotate to the next "new" sector as corporate earnings increase.

REITs traded for a substantial discount to NAV in 1998 and 2000, after trading at premiums to NAVs in 1996 and 1997, when many went public. A similar capital market environment in 2003 and 2004 led many real estate companies to go public during that period. (Please refer to Exhibit 8–4 and Exhibit 8–5 for the size of the IPO and secondary markets and Exhibit 8-6 and Exhibit 8-7 for the growth.)

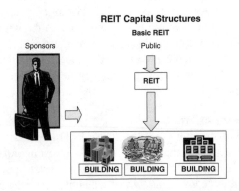

REIT Capital Structures

The first of the modern REITs to go public was Kimco Realty Corporation in 1991. An Umbrella Partnership REIT or UPREIT was first used in the 1992 Taubman Centers IPO. In the typical UPREIT (per NAREIT), the partners of the Existing Partnerships and a newly-formed REIT become partners is a new

EXHIBIT 8-4

REIT IPOs

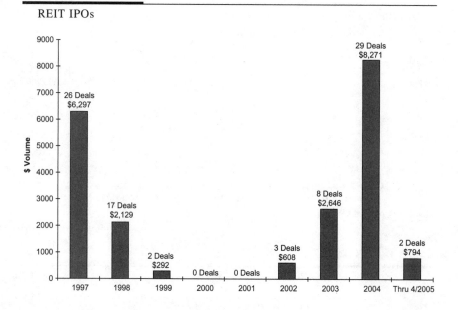

EXHIBIT 8-5

REIT Secondary Offering Market

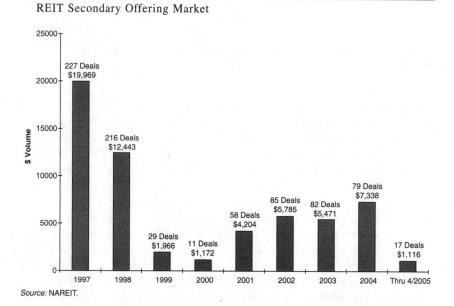

Source: NAREIT.

E X H I B I T   8–6

Growth of REIT Equity Capitalization

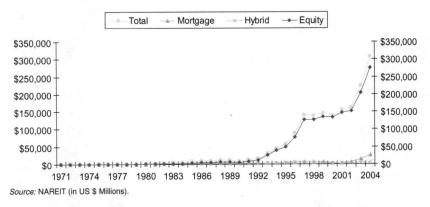

Source: NAREIT (in US $ Millions).

E X H I B I T   8–7

Growth in Number of REITs

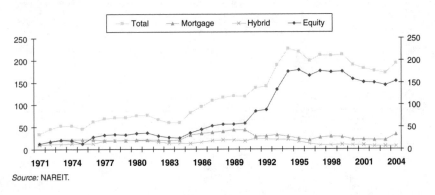

Source: NAREIT.

partnership termed the Operating Partnership. For their respective interests in the Operating Partnership ("Units"), the partners contribute the properties from the Existing Partnership and the REIT contributes the cash proceeds from its public offering. The REIT typically is the general partner and the majority owner of the Operating Partnership Units. After a period of time (often one year), the partners may enjoy the same liquidity of the REIT shareholders by tendering their Units for either cash or REIT shares (at the option of the REIT or Operating Partnership). This conversion may result in the partners incuring the tax deferred at the UPREITs formation. The Unit holders may tender their Units over a period of time, thereby spreading out such tax. In addition, when a partner holds the Units until death, the estate tax rules provide that the beneficiaries may tender the Units for cash or REIT shares without paying income taxes. Using the UPREIT structure defers and eliminates serious tax liabilities for owners of "low tax basis" properties and it allows REITs to use UPREIT equity interests as currency in tax-deferred acquisitions. Operating partnership units (OP units) held by the UPREIT and by other partners of the OP are separate securities from those of the REIT itself.

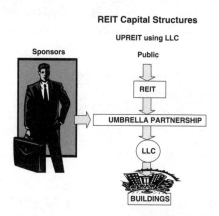

REIT Capital Structures

UPREIT using LLC

Whereas in an UPREIT newly-admitted partners to the existing OP acquire interests in all the properties associated with the UPREIT, DownREIT owners only have an interest in the specific properties in the DownREIT. A DownREIT is structured much like an UPREIT, but the REIT owns and operates properties other than its interest is a controlled partnership that owns and operates separate properties. A DownREIT is like a JV agreement with institutional investors such as pension funds who select the REIT for its property type and expertise to run a portfolio with them of specific properties, without the investor purchasing the REIT stock itself.

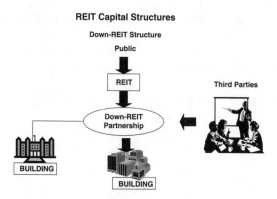

REIT Capital Structures

Down-REIT Structure

REITs, generally being public vehicles, can access the public markets like C-corps by issuing unsecured debt and preferred stock. (There are private REITs as well.) As a result of the tech debacle in the early 2000s, REIT issuances were generally oversold as institutional investors took a flight to quality. For example, REITs issued $11 billion of unsecured corporate debt in 2003 versus $16 billion in 2004. Proceeds from these issuances were utilized to pay down lines of credit, mortgage debt, acquisitions and other corporate purposes. Generally, investors tend to prefer REITs with larger equity bases, liquidity or "niche" plays, high return-on-equity and value-added models, and long-term cash flow growth potential.

Commercial Mortgage Backed Securities (CMBS)

CMBS adapted the securitization technology from residential mortgages and asset-backed securities that evolved in the 1980s. CMBS characteristics include:

- Multiple tranches
  - o Fixed and/or floating-rate
  - o Interest only (IO)
- Prioritized payments: Senior gets paid before mezzanine; subordinate before the mezzanine (the "waterfall")
- Loan servicer collects payments from individual borrowers and forwards to
- Trustee who remits principal and interest to bond investors
- Special servicer handles defaults and loan workouts

CMBS has been used to dispose of loans acquired by the US government in the process of liquidating the failed savings and loans institutions (S&Ls) by the Resolution Trust Corporation (RTC) in the early 1990s; to restructure lender balance sheets by disposing of real estate estates, transform mortgages into bonds; and for liquidity. Beginning in 1995, the conduits have become the primary source of product for CMBS deals. Whereas the risk in residential mortgage-backed securities transactions is mostly from prepayment since most residential loans in the US are prepayable at any time without penalty, the risk in CMBS is mostly from credit, as many loans have penalties, lockout periods, and/or yield maintenance requirements that deter prepayment. The tranche structure allows investors to choose their tolerable risk level.

Senior Bonds Have Highest Priority Claim on Cash Flows

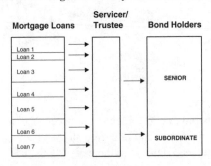

The subordinate bonds have the "first loss" exposure to risk.

Who The Players Are

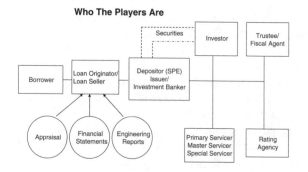

The CMBS market has grown from a $4.8 billion market in 1990 ($3.4 billion US and $1.4 billion foreign) to a $136 billion worldwide market in 2004 ($93 billion US and $43 billion foreign including Europe US $28.7 billion, Japan US $10 billion, ex-Japan Asia US $2.6 billion, and Canada US $2 billion).[2] Suppliers of product to the CMBS engine most recently consisted of: Banks and thrifts 61%, investment banks 27%, finance mortgage companies 7%, and insurance companies 5%.[3]

Who buys CMBS?

- Public institutional fixed income securities investors

- Private real estate high yield investors

- Varies by class, by rating, by structure

Why buy CMBS?

- Yield advantage (relative value investing)

- Asset allocation (satisfy allocation to real estate debt)

- Non-correlated risks to other asset-backed securities such as residential mortgage-backed securities (RMBS), asset-backed securities (such as automobile, credit card and other securitized structures)

CMBS spreads have tightened more than ABS spreads generally over the past 4.5 years due to increased money flow toward real estate.

Purchasers consist of: insurance companies 29%; banks 27%; investment advisors and money managers 22%; government-sponsored entities (GSEs) 13%; and opportunity funds, finance companies, and pension funds 9%.[4]

---

2. Moody's Investors Service, Special Comment "2004 Review and 2005 Outlook: US CMBS," January 27, 2005.
3. Moody's Investors Service.
4. Moody's Investors Service.

Private Real Estate Hybrid Structures: Mezzanine Equity, Joint Ventures, Mortgage Syndications

A variety of structures share risk, responsibility, and return among passive investors and active participants in real estate. Direct equity investments and joint ventures are available with many sources—individuals, pension funds, opportunity funds—for all product types. These investments may utilize third-party financing for 65% to 80% of the asset value with a 1- to 5-year term and with a defined exit strategy. Typically the passive equity investor contributes the majority (approximately 90–95%) of the capital required with the real estate partner contributing the balance. The operating partner's returns are subordinated to the passive equity investor's receipt of: (1) a current cash-on-cash return; and (2) a cumulative return (based upon a look-back internal rate of return (IRR) of 15% to 20%). The operating partner handles the day-to-day operations and is paid market-rate management fees, which increases his return on investment.

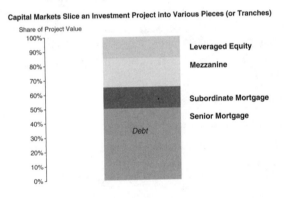

Capital Markets Slice an Investment Project into Various Pieces (or Tranches)

Mezzanine Financing

Mezzanine financing can be considered a debt, equity or hybrid debt/equity investment position. It is subordinate to the first mortgage financing and any other debt financing encumbering the property, but is senior to the property owner's equity investment. Consequently, it is less secure than the first mortgage or any other debt financing, but ranks more secure than the property owner's interest. Key terms in Mezzanine Financing:

- Pay Rate: minimum current return paid to lender; may be fixed or floating rate

- Accrual Rate: Preferred return due lender before any cash flow is distributed to sponsor; may be paid currently or accrued during loan term

- Subordination: Priority of the lenders right to take action against the collateral or borrower; usually, the higher the leverage, the deeper the subordination

The advantage to mezzanine investments are a higher cash return than available from traditional real estate equity investments with an investment structure that insulates investors from declines in value and cash flow due to the subordinate equity position, a shorter investment horizon, and matched to current market conditions. Typically the mezzanine investor has performed due diligence on the property and would be comfortable assuming the equity owner's position. The negatives are that the mezzanine investor has limited control of the asset and limited liquidity.

The mezzanine market is a niche market whose investors are opportunity funds, investment banks, and commercial banks who are attracted to its high-risk-adjusted rates of return.

Types of Mezzanine investments:

- Stabilized—existing property with current cash flow coverage for return on mezzanine investment

- Value added—existing property with moderate to substantial lease-up and/or releasing risk; generally requires cosmetic rehabilitation

- Development-to-be-built property with substantial development, construction, and lease-up risk

- Stabilized mortgage pool—purchase of nonrated tranche of commercial mortgage-backed securities

Risks of Mezzanine investing include:

- Financial risk

- Quality of underwriting

- Management control

- Exit strategy and timing

- Quality of asset management

- Real estate risks-development, construction, operation, etc.

- Agency risk

- Increased market risk relative to senior debt

- Illiquidity risks

An example of a mezzanine debt transaction is senior debt of 75%, mezzanine loan of 15%, sponsor equity of 10%. Sponsor equity usually includes full deferral of fees. The profit participation by the mezzanine lender is a significant part of the return. Pricing is often 9% to 12% preferred return plus 40% to 60% of net profits from property operation and sale.

Joint Ventures

Joint ventures are utilized in both the public and private markets with the purpose of acquiring a distinct property or portfolio. REITs are increasingly joint venturing with pension funds in structures whereby the REIT supplies either equity of 10% to 25% or contributes properties equaling that amount and the JV partner contributes 75% to 90% of equity. The term is generally 3 to 5 years with a call option whereby prior to the 3rd or 5th year the REIT or partner may acquire the property(ies) for cash sufficient to provide the JV partner with a certain IRR (e.g., 15%). The REIT or private owner receives acquisition, leasing, management, and disposition fees for their expertise with this property type.

The pension fund partner and REIT each receives a fixed return on invested capital with the balance distributed, or equivalent to the percentage of their respective investment. Upon sale, each will receive a return of investment capital plus 9% IRR, additional proceeds to an 18% IRR divided 75% pension fund and 25% REIT, and then additional proceeds above the 18% IRR in a negotiated split such as 60% to the pension fund and 40% to the REIT.

Mortgage Syndication Market

Overview: Although real estate assets frequently find attractive leverage from the long-term, fixed-rate loans that the securities markets provide, through either the mortgage-backed bond market at the asset level or the corporate bond market at the company level, lending to real estate via these securities may expose debt investors to inflation-related risks. To avoid these risks, many debt providers lend in the syndicated debt market. Uses for syndicated loans are:

- Property and portfolio acquisitions
- Construction/repositioning
- Stabilized asset and portfolios
- Corporate working capital
- M&A/LBOs/MBOs
- Mezzanine and B-notes

Major investors in the syndicated debt market are banks and other financial institutions that rely on LIBOR as a source of funding and use LIBOR as the base rate for their loans. Syndicated and other floating-rate debt transforms risk from a lender's inflation-related risks to interest rate risk, i.e., the ability of the under-lying real estate to service the debt in a rising interest rate environment.

Syndicated loan borrowers consist of:

- Middle market developers
- Pension fund advisors
- Opportunity funds
- Wealthy families
- Public REITs and real estate operating companies (REOCs)

Hedging: Many borrowers either elect or are required to hedge their expo-sure to rising rates in a separate transaction as a condition of the syndicated loan. It should be noted that although a borrower may have a hedge to protect against rising rates (where he/she pays fixed and receives floating), the syndicated debt remains a floating-rate instrument.

Although hedging a floating-rate instrument may result in the borrower incurring the additional costs of a swap, collar or cap, borrowers are drawn to this financing source for many reasons, including the following: (1) syndicated debt providers are typically able to structure debt to account for uneven cashflows of a property that is being developed, redeveloped, or is not stabilized; (2) the lead agent typically acts as the servicer in a securitized transaction, ensuring that the borrower will be able to work directly with the original debt provider throughout the loan's term; and (3) the debt is typically more flexible, in terms of prepayment and restructuring, than securitized debt. Additionally, if the borrower perceives that interest rates are decreasing, the borrower may be able to benefit from decreasing rates by either floating down to a lower rate or benefiting from the value of an "in-the-money swap." If the loan were funded in the CMBS markets, the borrower may well be subject to the costs of defeasance or yield maintenance to refinance at a lower rate. Whatever a borrower's reason for choosing syndicated debt to lever its investment in real estate, syndicated debt can be employed in all phases of the real estate lifecycle, from initial development through stabilization. Moreover, syndicated debt is typically available to a wide variety of established owners/operators of real estate, who range from local middle-market players to advisors of pension funds and public REITs.

Role of Lead Lender: As the name implies, syndicated debt is sold to financial institutions by the lender who originates and actively services the loan. This lead lender, called the administrative agent, is the primary point of contact with investors, who participate, i.e., buy a portion of the loan from the administrative agent. The administrative agent typically charges an underwriting or arrangement fee to the borrower and increases the return on investment by capturing a portion of these up-front fees before the balance is paid to participants or by tranching the loan similar to the way a CMBS issue is tranched. These retained fees or increased yield on the portion of the loan retained by the Administrative Agent are the reward for successfully negotiating the winning term sheet and documents, making a commitment to fund the loan irrespective of the ability to actually place portions with participants (frequently called "underwriting risk" or "syndication risk"), servicing the loan, and working with third parties to complete reports that mitigate basic real estate risks associated with lender liability and which may be required by law, e.g., appraisals, environmental reviews, and engineering reports. In addition, the administrative agent may skim a portion of the margin that the borrower pays on drawn funds.

Undrawn Funds: To ensure that investors are compensated for funds set aside for the borrower but not actually drawn, as may be the case with a delayed draw-term loan or revolving credit facility, syndicated loans frequently charge fees on the undrawn amount. These fees typically take the form of either "unused fees" or "facility fees." Unused fees, as the name implies, are simply fees, not a spread over LIBOR, that are charged on undrawn, but available funds. A facility fee is charged over the entire commitment and functions much in the same way, except that it must be added to the stated margin on the loan to determine the true cost of drawn funds to the borrower.

Underwriting Analysis: Whether an investor's intention is to hold the debt as an asset or repackage the risk for sale (via a collateralized debt obligation/CDO or credit default swap/CDS), the credit analysis of the underlying real estate remains the same: understand the risks of achieving the projected future cash flows, ensure that there are sufficient mitigants to those risks, and demonstrate that the projected cash flow is adequate to service the debt and to support repayment (via refinancing or sale) in the future.

At the basis of property financing is land, which, in its raw form, has difficulty attracting syndicated debt due to the lack of cash flow usually associated with it. Although raw land may produce some crop (or function as a car park), which can generate cash, that land use is not the typical residential or commercial use focused on in this section. For the purpose of evaluating traditional syndicated debt, lending against land, in the absence of proper and adequate zoning, sponsorship, equity and approved plans for future development presents risks to the development lenders that are difficult to mitigate because zoning is based on local laws and usually controlled by municipal boards, not the borrower or lender. It would not be prudent to lend to a sponsor that had never before participated in real estate development and had no track record on which to base an investment decision.

The sponsor's amount and form of equity that is to be invested in collateral must be evaluated, as must its liquidity and access to capital. The amount of invested equity will be important as it relates to the amount of debt needed. Simply stated, if the amount of debt needed is greater than the amount of debt that the project can support, there is a disconnect in the project's capitalization. In addition to the amount of equity invested in a project, the form of that equity is also important. Will the borrower fund its equity prior to the debt funding, or will the debt facility fund on a pro-rata basis with the debt? Will the equity be comprised of all cash or will it take the form of the "appreciated value" of contributed land or a "deferred developer's fee," in which, as the name implies, the developer exchanges his cash fee for a portion of the project's equity? These and other related issues about the equity must be addressed prior to lending on not only construction projects but also all real estate transactions. Obviously, the greater the hard cash contribution to the project, the easier it is to assess a project's true loan to cost; the underwriting can thus be more conservative.

The basic evaluation of a real estate holding company's credit is very similar to the evaluation of a single asset's, with the exception that the various property data must be aggregated and evaluated as a whole. In both analyses, it is important to consider not only the ability of the properties to attract and maintain tenants, but also the tenants' ability to pay the contract rent. In multifamily residential properties, a property's ability to attract and maintain tenants is primarily a function of the asset's location, quality, amenities, security, etc., relative to competitive projects in the area. Combined with a market's particular economic environment, prevailing rents, average expenses (including taxes), the amount of competing supply (both currently and planned), and the credit quality of the tenants, the surety of the cash flow can be estimated. For commercial properties, the analysis is similar, although gauging the quality of a commercial tenant is often more difficult than the quality of an individual or family. In addition to an evaluation of the macro factors affecting their businesses going forward, commercial tenants' credit can be gauged by their historical cash flow, size and projected growth plans. Coverage and leverage can sometimes be used to gauge a commercial tenants' credit quality in the same way that a residential landlord would require a tenant to list his/her income, debt obligations, and so on.

In addition to the evaluation of specific tenants, investors should examine any significant concentrations in the collateral. To avoid exposure to any one tenant and the exposure to the market when that tenant's lease expires, investors in real estate syndicated loans may benefit from a diversified tenant roster with a laddered lease expiration schedule. Multi-tenant properties spread risk over a number of tenants as leasing risk is distributed also across time, mitigating the exposure to short-term demand fluctuations in the real estate market. Lease structure, which can dictate the functions for rent, e.g., as a percentage of sales in a retail property or for property operating expenses to be reimbursed by tenants, should be understood, as it may contribute significantly to true variables that determine the operating cashflow of a building. Furthermore, the careful examination of a lease's structure may reveal early termination or extension provisions, which can materially alter a property's ability to generate the cashflow.

By examining these issues, an accurate understanding of the future cashflows can be developed. While developing these projections, risks can be identified and capital can be structured to provide the borrower with adequate flexibility and the lenders with adequate protections. Typical structural enhancements include resource to a credit-worthy entity, holdbacks for leasing costs, reappraisal rights by the lenders, interest-rate hedging requirements, and earn-out provisions that entitle the borrower to more proceeds as the project's operating cashflow improves over the term. Reporting and compliance issues are also important for a debt investor to keep track of a borrower's cashflow and operating metrics. Based on these metrics, lenders will determine the borrower's compliance with minimum performance standards on which the financing was structured and priced. A borrower's failure to comply with debt covenants can force the borrower to find replacement financing in order to preserve his/her equity investment. Alternatively, the existing group of debt investors may amend or waive certain requirements of the original loan documents to restructure the debt.

HISTORICAL RETURNS AND DRIVERS OF RETURNS

REIT Performance Versus Other Public Securities Markets*

	REITs	DJIA	NASDAQ	NCREIF	RUSSELL 2000
2004	30.4%	3.2%	8.6%	14.5%	18.3%
2003	38.5%	25.3%	50.0%	9.0%	47.3%
2002	5.2%	−6.8%	−31.5%	6.7%	−20.5%
2001	15.5%	−7.1%	−21.1%	7.3%	2.5%
2000	25.9%	−6.2%	−39.3%	12.2%	−3.0%
1999	−6.5%	25.2%	85.6%	11.4%	21.3%
1998	−8.8%	18.0%	40.1%	16.2%	−2.4%

Source: NAREIT.
* Indices from NAREIT website data at www.NAREIT.org and NACREIF at www.NACREIF.com

The liquidity of publicly-traded REIT securities decreases the correlation of real estate returns relative to the returns of privately-held real estate (as shown by the comparative returns of the NAREIT and NACREIF indexes over the past 10 years in the first section of this chapter). In recent years, this increased liquidity has lead to the NAREIT index outperforming the NACREIF index by a significant margin. Furthermore, publicly-traded REITs have a lower volatility than the broader market, as evidenced by the low beta and correlation of the Morgan Stanley REIT index (RMS) to the S&P 500.

Due to the greater acceptance of not only REIT equity securities, but REIT bonds, there has been a growing convergence in the spreads and yields on REIT bonds versus industrial bonds and Treasuries as seen in Exhibit 8–8 and Exhibit 8–9. Thus, REIT securities and bonds are becoming viable alternative investments to stocks and bonds, albeit with greater returns.

GLOBAL VERSUS US REAL ESTATE: DIFFERENCES AND SIMILARITIES

The real estate capital markets are firmly interlinked with the global capital markets. US owners and developers are increasingly implementing global, cross-border strategies as are foreign investors. Due to its vast size and diversity, the global commercial real estate market is difficult to quantify. It is estimated that the size of the investable universe of institutional-quality properties, i.e., global commercial real estate market, is approximately US$14 trillion at year-end (see Exhibit 8–10)[5]:

Although globalization appears counter to the local owner/developer business model, it provides a platform to acquire assets in markets where ownership is fragmented and resources for new development are limited. US real estate firms are increasingly venturing abroad as the transparency of financial and business practices are improving worldwide and public market models are increasingly being adopted. For investors seeking inflation protection, it makes sense to invest worldwide, as increased globalization ties inflation rates more closely in different countries (see Exhibit 8–11).

The global public real estate market is undergoing a transformation in countries throughout Asia, Europe, and Latin America as REIT-like vehicles similar to US REITs and Australian listed-property trusts (LPTs) proliferate.[6] Hong Kong, Japan, Korea, Malaysia, Singapore, Taiwan, Brazil, Mexico, Belgium, France, Italy, Luxembourg, Netherlands, Spain, and Canada already have REIT-like vehicles. Germany and the United Kingdom are currently considering such vehicles. Although the legal and tax features of the various REIT vehicles vary widely by country, the common thread is the desire to provide investors, particularly smaller institutions and individuals, access to real estate instruments.

---

5. Conner and Liang, Prudential Real Estate Investors, "Global REITs: A New Platform of Ownership," January 2005.
6. Conner and Liang, Prudential Real Estate Investors, "Global REITs: A New Platform of Ownership," January 2005.

EXHIBIT 8–8

Spreads Between REIT Bonds/10-Year Treasury and Industrial
Bonds/10-Year Treasury

Source: Bloomberg.

EXHIBIT 8–9

Yield on REIT Bonds Versus Industrial Bonds Versus 10-Year Treasury

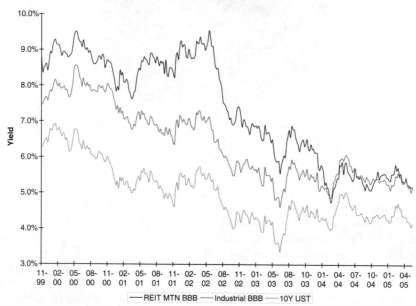

Source: Bloomberg.

EXHIBIT 8–10

Regional Distribution of Global Commercial Real Estate (at YE 2004)

Region	Real Estate ($US billion)	Regional Distribution (%)
North America	$ 5,334.7	37.8%
Europe	5,287.6	37.5%
Asia-Pacific	3,084.9	21.8%
Latin America	406.0	2.9%
Total	$ 14,113.2	100.0%

EXHIBIT 8–11

Global Real Estate Universe

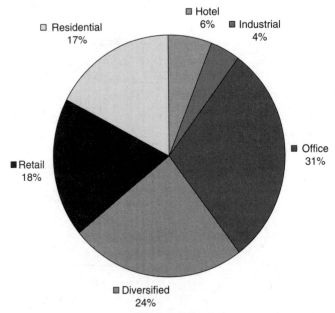

Source: UBS Warburg, AMP/Henderson Global Investors, PCA, NAREIT.

The typical characteristics include a relatively high, stable cash yield that: (1) passes directly through the entity to the shareholders exempt from corporate taxes,[7] and (2) represents a substantial share of the capital gains and income from the real estate assets owned and/or managed by the company or fund.

---

7. EPRA/NAREIT; Bloomberg, Prudential Real Estate Investors. An exception is Hong Kong REITs, which are not tax transparent.

EXHIBIT 8–12

Correlation of Listed Property Shares with Global Bonds and Stocks

	Listed Property	Global Gov t Bonds	Global Stocks
Listed Property	1.00		
Global Gov t Bonds	0.35	1.00	
Global Stocks	0.69	0.23	1.00

Source: S&P/Citigroup BMI World Property Index; MSCI World Index and Merrill Lynch Global Government Bond Index; Bloomberg; Prudential Real Estate Investors data from January 1990 to December 2004.

EXHIBIT 8–13

Real Estate Universe: Principal Real Estate Markets

	% World Underlying Real Estate	Underlying Real Estate (US$bn)	Listed Real Estate (US$bn)	Real Estate as % of Stock Market	% Underlying Real Estate Listed
United States	43%	2,525	295	1%	12%
Continental Europe	26%	1,500	50	1%	3%
Japan	12%	705	58	2%	8%
Hong Kong/ China	9%	540	68	7%	13%
United Kingdom	8%	490	80	2%	16%
Australia	2%	100	45	9%	45%
Total	100%	5,860	596	3%	10%

Source: Prudential Real Estate Investors, Principal Real Estate Investors, Principal Real Estate Investors, AMP Henderson, UBS.

Listed property shares provide investors portfolio diversification as well as low correlations with government bonds and equities. Over 10 years, listed property indices have provided a 10.7% return versus global government bonds at 7.1% and global equities at 8.5%.[8] The correlation between global listed property/REITs and global bonds and stock has been low, which indicates that listed property shares provide an attractive yield complement to bonds and global stocks in a diversified portfolio (see Exhibit 8–12).

---

8. S&P/Citigroup BMI World Property Index, Bloomberg, MSCI World Index, Merrill Lynch Global Government Bond Index at December 2004.

E X H I B I T   8–14

Listed Property Equity Market Capitalization by Region

Region	Real Estate ($US billion)	Regional Distribution (%)
North America	$ 266.0	49.6%
Asia-Pacific	169.2	31.5%
Europe	101.1	18.9%
Total	$ 536.3	100.0%

Source: S&P/Citigroup BMI World Property Index; Prudential Real Estate Investors at YE 2004.

It should be noted that the equity market capitalization is not directly comparable to the aggregate market value estimates in Exhibit 8–10, since the listed property sector represents a small fraction of the total commercial property universe seen in Exhibit 8–13 and Exhibit 8–14.

There is a net flow of global investment capital into the US real estate market due to a dearth of domestic investment opportunities in many foreign countries, higher rates of return in the US, and the size and stability of the US market. The fundamental performance characteristics of the underlying assets—stability, attractive yields, consistent appreciation, and low correlation to other asset classes—remain appealing to both domestic and foreign investors desiring a diversified portfolio.

CHAPTER 9

IMPLEMENTING A REAL ESTATE ALLOCATION

Susan Hudson-Wilson, Margaret Harbaugh
Property & Portfolio Research, Inc.

INTRODUCTION

A previous chapter talks about the asset class returns and inflation hedging characteristics of real estate. This chapter examines, in more detail, the asset class itself and the many ways to gain exposure to real estate returns.

To say that one has, or wishes to, invest in real estate, is to say very little. Real estate is a multidimensional "asset"—in fact given its debt-equity hybrid nature, one wonders whether it is an asset, *per se*, or a collection of distinguishable assets. In any event it is conventional to describe it as the asset class known as "real estate." In this chapter we will endeavor to slice the asset up into its component parts and to describe a bit about how each component can, or cannot, be accessed by institutions and individual investors. Real estate investing has come a long way in the last 20 years in terms of its accessibility to institutional and retail investors, but it is not universally accessible even today. We organize the discussion around the four quadrants, or sectors, of the real estate investment universe–public equity, public debt, private equity and private debt.

First, within each of these sectors we look at property-type coverage, geographic coverage, strategies available, and suitability for investors. Next we delve into the ways in which an investor might actually execute the investment of an allocation to each quadrant and pursue some of the specific strategies within each sector. Real estate is a very large part of the overall economy and investible universe, yet the options available to investors are less than what one might think or desire. Access to real estate investments continues to be limited. However new ideas are being worked on as these pages are being written and the newest thinking along with the issues around it will be presented.

Finally we present the topic of performance measurement and, again, find less than perhaps is desired in terms of the sophistication of practice in this all-important area. As a hopeful note however, we describe the ground-breaking work that is being done in the United Kingdom and is now spreading to other European countries thanks to a very creative and persistent group of data collectors and performance attribution experts based in London.

Throughout the chapter we mention foreign real estate investment options, but in no way are they treated exhaustively herein.

REAL ESTATE IS A MULTI-DIMENSIONAL "ASSET"

The term "real estate" is overly broad and covers a diverse set of choices. This is different than is the case for the stock equity asset (which concentrates on publicly traded companies), the private equity market (focus on nonpublic companies), the fixed income market (focus on corporate and governmental debt markets, both public and private) and the private placement market (focus on private corporate debt oriented transactions).[1] The expression "real estate" covers publicly-traded real estate markets consisting of equity-oriented real estate investment trusts (REITs), homebuilding companies, mortgage REITs and traditional C-corporations, or real estate operating companies (REOC), which focus on real estate. Also in the realm of real estate equity are nonpublicly-traded REITS—a rapidly emerging investment option, and all other forms of private equity—commingled funds, separate accounts, one-off individual transactions, joint ventures, investments in operator entities, and self-directed/self-managed individual investments. Even more broadly, and unusually, the term "real estate" includes debt-oriented investments and strategies such as commercial mortgage-backed securities, private mortgages, and on the residential side (not a focus of this chapter) GNMA and FNMA securities comprised of large pools of multifamily and single family mortgages. Thus real estate is somewhat less readily tractable to the novice investor as "real estate" can encompass a wide range of approaches to the market. Again, to say "I am invested in real estate" is to say very little.

We simplify the way we think about real estate by creating categories or quadrants defined as public equity, private equity, public debt, and private debt. The capital wheel presented in Exhibit 9–1 shows how the US investible universe is allocated across these sectors or quadrants. It is interesting to note that while the bulk of US commercial and multifamily real estate is held by investors of one type and another, this is far less true in Europe and in Asia where the transition from user-owners to investor-owners is less advanced. This creates the situation where even though the Euro-zone is nearly as large, in terms of population and GDP, as the US, the real estate investment opportunity set is far smaller (see Exhibit 9–2 and Exhibit 9–3). The same is true for Asia.

Within these four capital market sectors is a set of subinvestment classes concerning the choice of property type, the choice of geography and the choice of strategy—with strategy encompassing the stage of development, the investment objective, the use of diversification as a risk mitigant, the use of leverage, and the use of market timing. In general we confine our discussion to the property types of office, industrial, apartment, and retail as these are the largest pieces and the

---

1. For further information on real estate as it relates to these and other asset classes, see Bodie (2003).

EXHIBIT 9–1

Real Estate Investible Universe by Quadrant

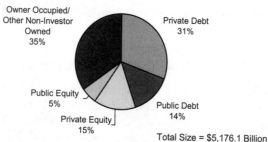

Owner Occupied/
Other Non-Investor
Owned
35%

Private Debt
31%

Public Equity
5%

Private Equity
15%

Public Debt
14%

Total Size = $5,176.1 Billion

Source: Property & Portfolio Research Inc.

EXHIBIT 9–2

Potential Investible Universe: Europe vs. US

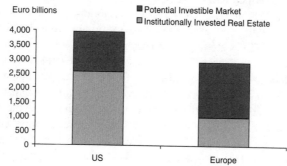

Euro billions

■ Potential Investible Market
□ Institutionally Invested Real Estate

Source: Hordijk and Ahlqvist; Property & Portfolio Research Inc.

EXHIBIT 9–3

Limited Institutional Ownership in Europe

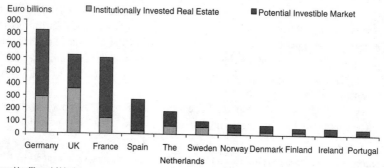

Euro billions

□ Institutionally Invested Real Estate   ■ Potential Investible Market

Germany   UK   France   Spain   The Netherlands   Sweden   Norway   Denmark   Finland   Ireland   Portugal

Source: Hordijk and Ahlqvist.

most driven by real estate market fundamentals and capital markets. Performance of other sectors such as hotels and triple net-leased assets is more driven by either operating skills and/or by the credit of the tenants. Below we go into each quadrant and describe the subclasses including a discussion of valuation practices.

Publicly-Traded Real Estate Equity

This market is among the better defined and encompasses $281.9 billion of capitalized value as of December 2004, traded in well-known public equity markets such as the New York Stock Exchange, the American Stock Exchange and in global stock exchanges. The largest companies traded are listed below along with a brief description of the purview of each firm (Exhibit 9–4).

Most public real estate companies are structured as REITs, or as REOCs. The REOC is a normally-structured corporate entity that simply specializes in buying and operating real estate assets. The REOC is not entitled to the federally tax-exempt status of the REIT, but neither is it subject to the rules on distributions and asset sales to which REITs are held. A REIT, interestingly, is not a trust but rather it is a tax election. Essentially a REIT acts as a perpetual ownership vehicle of one or more buildings. In exchange for the exemption from all federal taxation at the REIT level, REITs are required to pay out at least 90% of all accrual-based accounting earnings (holders of REIT shares must pay federal taxes on dividends, just like holders of nonREIT securities).[2] Some REITs pay out more than is required in order to defend their dividend levels and yields. In the past there were considerable restrictions on a REIT's ability to sell buildings, but these rules have been relaxed and REITs now are pretty much allowed to run their portfolios without concern for impairing their tax-exempt status through sales activities.

Some argue that the tax exemption comes at too high a price—that the pay-out requirement is too high for an asset as capital intensive as is real estate. The high payouts impede the REIT's ability to retain earnings to protect against significant capital expenditure requirements. This lack of available capital may impair the integrity of the assets over long periods of time. As well, the lack of retained earnings means that the REITs must sell assets or go to the capital markets for more cash when they see advantageous buying opportunities in the hard asset marketplace or when they wish to rebalance their portfolios. Given this, some former REITs have de-REITed themselves, although the number of these transitions has been small. In the early 1990s, Brookfield Properties Corporation (BPO) converted from a REIT to a REOC in order to divest itself of residential properties in favor of high-growth office markets and take advantage of operating losses as a tax shelter.

REITs come in all property type and geographic "flavors" with good coverage across the US real estate investment universe. That said, as is clear from

---

2. A primer to REIT investing is provided online by NAREIT at www.investinreits.com. Block (2002) offers more information.

E X H I B I T 9-4

Largest Public Equity Real Estate Investment Trusts

Company	Ticker Symbol	Equity Market Capitalization ($M)	Percent of REIT Universe	Property Sector	Property Subsector	Website
Simon Property Group. Inc.	SPG	13,391.0	4.6967	Retail	Regional Malls	www.shopsimon.com
Equity Office Properties Trust	EOP	12,139.9	4.2579	Industrial/Office	Office	www.equityoffice.com
Equity Residential	EQR	9,024.6	3.1653	Residential	Apartments	www.eqr.com
Vornado Realty Trust	VNO	8,706.9	3.0538	Diversified		www.vno.com
General Growth Properties, Inc.	GGP	7,457.7	2.6157	Retail	Regional Malls	www.generalgrowth.com
Public Storage, Inc.	PSA	7,327.2	2.5699	Self Storage		www.publicstorage.com
ProLogis Trust	PLD	6,822.7	2.3930	Industrial/Office	Industrial	www.prologis.com
Archstone-Smith Trust	ASN	6,814.6	2.3901	Residential	Apartments	www.archstonesmith.com
Plum Creek Timber Company, Inc.	PCL	6,544.6	2.2954	Specialty		www.plumcreek.com
Boston Properties, Inc.	BXP	6,518.9	2.2864	Industrial/Office	Office	www.bostonproperties.com
Kimco Realty Corporation	KIM	5,994.5	2.1025	Retail	Shopping Centers	www.kimcorealty.com
Host Marriott Corporation	HMT	5,744.6	2.0148	Lodging/Resorts		www.hostmarriott.com

Equity market capitalization does not include operating partnership units or preferred stock.

Source: NAREIT.

Exhibit 9–5, the distribution of the REIT universe differs somewhat from the distribution of the true real estate market universe. Thus REITs, as a group, cannot be regarded as a perfect replica or index of the overall real estate investible universe. Hess and Liang (2004) provide an overview of the holdings of public REITs by property type. REITs are what they are, allocated due to historic accident and not in accordance with any plan. This is just as well, since REITs only comprise 5.4% of the overall real estate investible universe, it would be a surprise if at any time the REIT universe did perfectly replicate the larger real estate investment universe. Thus, when investors take a position in a REIT index such as the MSCI US REIT Index (RMS, at www.msci.com/reit) or the National Association of Real Estate Investment Trusts (NAREIT) index (www.nareit.com/library/domestic/overview.com) they should not imagine that they have "bought" the larger real estate market. They have bought a smaller and idio-syncratic index. Whether that "skewed" index is a better or a worse portfolio of real estate holdings is an empirical question whose answer can change through time.

A similar problem of a lack of synchronicity holds between the private equity investment universe and the most commonly used indexes for that quadrant, this is discussed further below.

REITS generally do use leverage at the entity level, introducing additional volatility to the cash flows (which are otherwise quite stable). Volatility is a consideration in REIT investing, although the level of leverage is generally quite low, as the analyst community has always frowned on any excessive use. While the use of leverage is one source of volatility in the cash flows, a more important source of value volatility is introduced by the simple fact that REITs trade in the public equities markets along with all of the other stocks in the stock markets. As many are aware, capital shifts are not always orderly and rationally grounded! A small sector like the REIT sector, comprising 2.4% of the overall capitalization of the US stock equity market (measured against the Wilshire 5000), can be whipsawed by relatively large flows into and out of the real estate sector. Some of these flows are driven by investors' expectations for real estate but many of them are driven by investors' expectations for other sectors' relative performance, and the REITs are caught in the rush. Conner and Falzon (2004) discuss frameworks for understanding REITs' heightened volatility relative to the private

E X H I B I T   9–5

(a) REIT Universe by Property Type; (b) Real Estate Investible Universe

Source: SNL Data Source.   *Source:* Property & Portfolio Research Inc.

markets, and Glascock et al. (2004) examine how REITs' performance was affected by the stock market decline of October 1997. This volatility of overall performance relative to the volatility of the performance of the underlying hard assets must be recognized and accepted by investors if they are to be suited to REIT investing.

Most REITs hew to a pretty conservative line of investment strategy within their portfolio. Generally REIT operators are seeking good growth in operating income (measured a variety of ways) and commensurate growth in value, plus a little alpha. A good track record of growth in earnings ought, over time, to be accompanied by an improving multiple, thus boosting the investment performance of the portfolio to the investor. REIT operators are challenged to develop a portfolio strategy that produces the desired steady growth in income and to explain to the analyst and investor community how that challenge will continue to be met. This approach to strategy is sensible and appropriate to the characteristics of the underlying real estate. In past years (especially during the "dot com" era) there was a tendency to cast REITs (and for REITs to cast themselves) as high-growth investments; fortunately this "pitch" has been all but silenced.

REITs are subject to considerable public disclosure requirements. Many REITs were created from formerly privately-operated real estate companies and so had structures and management policies that were not entirely consistent with best practice, especially in light of the new Sarbanes–Oxley standards. The best REITs and the right-minded REITs have accepted the challenge of "cleaning up their acts" and so governance, compensation, and board structures are enormously improved over past practice. That said, there are still laggards, even among some REITs that are fairly new to the public market, which heightens the need for investor due diligence. In general REITs have significantly "profession-alized" and the difference is welcome.

Valuation in the public equity market is straightforward. The market tells you what the share price is. Now the market can be wrong, and as the real estate sector is pretty small, the market is frequently wrong, but there is opportunity in these misjudgments.

Privately-Traded Real Estate Equity

The size of the US private real estate equity market is difficult to assess as there are so many ways to invest in real estate privately and there are some types of real estate, such as marinas, golf courses, senior housing, hospitals, and the like that some are included as a part of the investible universe and others are not. For purposes of this chapter only the traditional categories of office, retail, apartment, and warehouse are included. Best estimates are that the unleveraged value of this sector is $762.7 billion, compromising 14.7% of the real estate capital market wheel.

Private real estate equity is allocated across the key property types as shown in Exhibit 9–6. Since there is no investible index of private equity there is no

EXHIBIT 9-6

(a) Private Equity by Property Type; (b) Real Estate Investible Universe

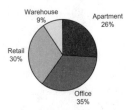

Source: NCREIF.   Source: Property & Portfolio Research Inc.

potential investment with which to compare the allocations. This then is one issue facing investors, right off the bat; private real estate equity is highly idiosyncratic and very difficult to access by smaller institutional investors and by mere mortals.

The key property types considered as "core" or baseline for inclusion in a well-designed real estate portfolio are: office, retail, apartment, and warehouse. These assets can be further divided into categories such as: suburban office, strip center retail, mall retail, lifestyle center retail, pad retail, community center retail, townhouse apartments, high-rise apartments, major warehouse, secondary warehouse, manufacturing warehouse, and office showroom, as examples. The geographic distinctions are nearly as rich with primary, secondary and tertiary urban areas, central business district, suburban, ex-urban and resort locations. Each of these property types and locations and each combination thereof have different risks, returns, and drivers as manifest in the correlation matrix in Exhibit 9–7. For example, a commonly used index of real estate performance[3] shows an 88% correlation between office and industrial performance since 1978 (as measured by total return). Yet within those sectors, there is only a 59% correlation between CBD office and industrial R&D space, and indeed, only a 59% correlation between CBD and suburban office space. Clearly there are opportunities to increase returns by wisely choosing investment markets, submarkets, property type, and subclass.

Layer on to this mélange the various stages of, and ways to participate in, development—from land banking, land development, presales, infrastructure development, merchant building, construction, leasing, operations, and sale—and there are lots of ways to play and lots of risk profiles to assume within this quadrant! Many more than is the case for public equity where this variety of development activity is far less in evidence.

Plus there are many ways to finance portfolio creation and expansion in the private equity world. Typically an investment manager will execute a capital raise either from a community of friends and family, family offices, endowments and foundations, or large institutions such as pension funds and insurance companies

---

3. The NCREIF Property Index, to be discussed in full below, is published by the National Council of Real Estate Investment Fiduciaries (www.ncreif.com).

EXHIBIT 9-7

Correlations among NCREIF Property Types

	Apartment	Garden-type Projects	High-rise Elevator Projects	Low-rise Projects	Hotel	Industrial	Research and Development	Flex Space	Warehouse	Office	CBD	Suburban	Retail	Community Center	Neighborhood Center	Power Center	Regional Center	Super-Regional Center	Single-Tenant
Apartment	**1.00**																		
Garden-type Projects	0.87	1.00																	
High-rise Elevator Projects	0.79	0.67	1.00																
Low-rise Projects	0.43	0.45	0.21	1.00															
Hotel	**0.32**	0.35	0.45	0.36	**1.00**														
Industrial	**0.68**	0.66	0.81	0.10	0.34	**1.00**													
Research and Development	0.56	0.60	0.84	0.13	0.43	0.87	1.00												
Flex Space	0.64	0.67	0.66	(0.19)	0.31	0.76	0.70	1.00											
Warehouse	0.66	0.62	0.77	0.12	0.27	0.97	0.74	0.66	1.00										
Office	**0.60**	0.69	0.82	0.15	0.40	0.88	0.77	0.72	0.84	**1.00**									
CBD	0.44	0.69	0.79	0.00	0.31	0.69	0.59	0.72	0.67	0.89	1.00								
Suburban	0.62	0.65	0.81	0.25	0.44	0.86	0.77	0.68	0.82	0.89	0.59	1.00							
Retail	**0.38**	**0.39**	**0.42**	**0.06**	**0.06**	**0.55**	**0.38**	**0.38**	**0.56**	**0.45**	**0.38**	**0.39**	**1.00**						
Community Center	0.41	0.53	0.49	(0.21)	0.08	0.59	0.43	0.52	0.57	0.46	0.32	0.48	0.87	1.00					
Neighborhood Center	0.47	0.58	0.50	(0.19)	0.14	0.67	0.50	0.47	0.68	0.68	0.57	0.62	0.70	0.65	1.00				
Power Center	0.02	0.09	(0.14)	(0.22)	(0.02)	(0.25)	(0.26)	(0.35)	(0.17)	(0.24)	(0.15)	(0.28)	0.55	0.47	0.35	1.00			
Regional Center	0.45	0.51	0.39	0.10	0.13	0.55	0.40	0.40	0.57	0.54	0.62	0.43	0.85	0.73	0.74	0.56	1.00		
Super-Regional Center	0.34	0.18	0.30	(0.21)	0.01	0.42	0.28	0.23	0.44	0.35	0.45	0.23	0.94	0.77	0.56	0.53	0.69	1.00	
Single-Tenant	0.73	0.71	0.60	(0.17)	0.35	0.94	0.79	0.72	0.91	0.93	0.78	0.87	0.68	0.66	0.75	0.05	0.70	0.59	1.00

Source: NCREIF.

and will execute the investment plan using that capital combined with a little, or a lot, of leverage. Again, this is very different from the experience of the public market vehicles where leverage is generally moderate, and strategies are generally conservative.

Strategies can also be set around ideas like investing in assets or investing in operating entities, investing for cashflow or investing for IRRs and multiples, and investing domestically and/or investing transglobally. See Chen and Hobbs (2003) for analysis of the varying risks of global real estate.

As far as the rules under which the investments will be made and the relationships among the parties will be governed—"whatever" is the rule. The private market dictates what structures, fees, governance, and rules for the allocation of proceeds will be employed. The terms of engagement are privately negotiated among the parties, each of whom has different levels of market knowledge and different senses of urgency and priority.

Given all of this is there a way to organize the wide range of possibilities into broad categories? Yes, there are three main categories of strategy within private equity and they are: core, value added, and opportunistic. Each will be described below.

Core. This strategy seeks stable returns derived from stable cash flows. Most REITs also follow a variant of this model. There is room for moderate leverage, there is room for moderate development as a way to acquire assets at cost and there is room to invest moderately in nonprimary markets and property types. However, notice the use of the word "moderate." Core strategies are generally executed within very large portfolios of $1 billion and much more. These strategies consciously seek to use the math of portfolio theory to mitigate risk and to select and adjust allocations to markets. These portfolios employ mathematical techniques to take advantage of the differences in behavior across markets and property types evident in the correlation matrix above. Core strategies typically assume a long-term place in an investors' portfolio and so are generally operated as perpetuities.

Value added. As the name implies these strategies call for the investor to bring some expertise to the real estate. The operators of these strategies are looking to acquire assets with a physical issue or defect, a capital structure problem and/or a management/leasing deficit. These assets generally have "hair" on them as they say in the business. In some cases the value add is simply the discovery of a miss-priced asset, an opportunity the large but inefficient real estate capital markets have missed. While these miss-pricings certainly do exist, it would be tough to build a whole portfolio around such a thesis.

More typically the investor raises a pool of capital, again from the same sources listed above and buys, often using leverage and generally at a higher level than is true for a core strategy, seeking problem assets. Then they go to work. Each asset will require some effort, beyond the usual management and leasing activities. As an asset is repositioned into a core asset with stabilized cashflows and values, the investor is likely to want to sell it to a core investor. There are cases where a value-added investor decides that they want to keep the stable portfolio they have created, but this is rare and rarely appropriate. Thus a value-added strategy, unlike a core strategy, is a finite life concept. Picking the right start date and setting in advance the absolute sell date is a troublesome aspect of these finite strategies. As a result usually such strategies come with an end date and rights to extend the life of the strategy several times.

Value-added strategies generally do not use portfolio allocation tools to mitigate market and property type exposure risk. These strategies tend to be defined by geography and/or property type and are associated with a kind of expertise. For example the investor might be experienced at converting apartments to condominiums or racetracks to large-scale mixed-use properties. The premise might be as simple as buying from undercapitalized owners of office buildings or hotels and then doing the necessary deferred maintenance, leasing them up and flipping them.

Opportunistic. This strategy is value added writ large and often involves very large transactions that only the really big players with access and sophisticated expertise can consider. Here there is generally lots of hair, in the form of complex and constraining capital structures, private corporate ownership where the corporation would like to release the value to the balance sheet, foreign assets with government involvement, infrastructure projects, purchases of whole banks in order to get at the bad loan portfolio, etc. In recent times these transactions often come from Europe, where real estate is rapidly being privatized (recall Exhibit 9–3) and moved off corporate balance sheets and out of public control, and from Asia, where bad loan portfolios are seriously impeding the growth of financial institutions and nations themselves.

Leverage is typically used and at quite a high level. The capital structure around these deals is generally very complex. The risks in terms of environmental concerns, currency, market turnarounds, and tenant exposure are usually high. And the expected returns are commensurately high. (Of course, actual returns may or may not cooperate.) These investment strategies are hard to access and hard to execute and are generally genuinely risky as well.

These strategies do not use portfolio risk-management techniques except insofar as there are usually multiple deals within the portfolio cutting across multiple locations (including countries) and property types. The idea here is to get access, close the deal, do the complex work that needs to be done and "get gone!" These are pure plays; no one expects to hold these assets for very long.

A "new" strategy that might be called "capital surfing" has emerged over the past 3 to 5 years in which the investor simply stays one step in front of the capital flows, which have been strong and are getting stronger. Is this a true opportunistic strategy? We think so. This strategy prefers assets that will be acceptable to the type of capital that is coming into the market—be it individual capital, the German banks, or the REITs. This strategy requires smart thinking about what to buy, where to buy it and how much truly is too much to pay. As long as the musical chairs continue, this strategy works well and can be a fast way to earn a high IRR with little actual asset level work required.

Valuation is a definite problem in the private equity quadrant. Since the market is by definition private, transaction and carrying values do not have to be disclosed to anyone except the investors themselves and sometimes, depending upon the rules of engagement, not even to them. Investors work hard to discover transaction values. There is a new firm, Real Capital Analytics, which works to discover and then sell this precious information. Even when one is an "insider" to a private portfolio, at best the valuation is "known" when the asset is acquired and then as it is marked to market (if it is marked to market) annually or even less frequently. Appraisers conduct the research to assign an interim value to an asset and while, over time, these valuation exercises have certainly improved, there is no guarantee that they are correct. Unfortunately in the private market, unlike in the public market, there are infrequent chances to revisit what may be an incorrect valuation. Thus until an asset is sold, the investor really does not know what its value is. For the closed-end portfolios of value-added and opportunistic strategies, the question of interim valuation is much less of an issue as your capital is locked up until the fund is liquidated in any event. As well, assets in such portfolios are even more difficult to value given their complexity and risk profiles.

Valuations can also be subject to selection bias, a distortion resulting from the fact that those properties changing hands may not be indicative of the underlying market. Fisher et al. (2003) observed that a property can be transacted, and thus valued, only when both buyer and seller agree on a price. In cyclic downturns, valuations may remain comparatively high due to selection bias, as buyers' offer prices drop while sellers' asking prices do not, leading to fewer transactions. Heckman (1979) sets out a procedure for correcting selection bias, which is an issue for any investor or manager attempting to outperform a benchmark like the National Council of Real Estate Investment Fiduciaries (NCREIF) property index.

These valuation problems are an issue for all strategies, but more so for any strategy that is "open ended" allowing for new investments and withdrawals through time. There is a very large mutual fund company that, as of early 2005, was preparing to launch a significant new private REIT that will allow for quarterly additions and withdrawals. It will be interesting to see how they provide investors with comfort that the valuation process will be fair and true. If this firm is able to successfully "crack this nut" individual investors' access to private real estate will improve dramatically. This is an experiment to watch closely.

Privately-Traded Real Estate Debt

Included in this quadrant are commercial and multifamily mortgages. This sector comprises the largest part of the real estate capital wheel although it is giving ground to the public real estate debt quadrant as will be discussed in the next section. This sector is exactly as it would appear to be—comprised of loans backed by real estate collateral. These loans are almost always nonrecourse to the borrower (a unique feature of real estate lending) and so the lender is highly motivated to be sure that they understand the performance attributes of the collateral. Loans can be fixed or floating rate and can include various other features like cashflow participation, shared appreciation, etc. The only constraint is the imagination of the borrowers and lenders. Again these are privately negotiated transactions, so the rules of engagement are subject to the competitive environment and the needs of each party.

Traditionally private debt has been the purview of the insurance companies and the banks, but these days the field has opened considerably and anyone who puts out a shingle can try to get in the game. Again a significant driver of this shift is the advent of the public debt quadrant. Whereas once private debt issuers had to hold those investments on their own balance sheets, now there is an active secondary market for individual mortgages and pools of mortgages. Even with this greater "democratization" of the commercial and multifamily mortgage world the spreads over Treasuries historically have been wide as shown in Exhibit 9–8. This is a signal that the market may not quite understand how to price the risk of a mortgage. This too shall pass, as the market will figure it out!

It is apparent from Exhibit 9–9, showing commercial mortgage delinquencies, that a change has occurred in this sector. The last recession, through the early 1990s, was characterized by very low delinquencies, especially as compared with the performance through the prior recession. The research predicting

EXHIBIT   9–8

Commercial Mortgage Pool Spreads to 10-Year Treasuries

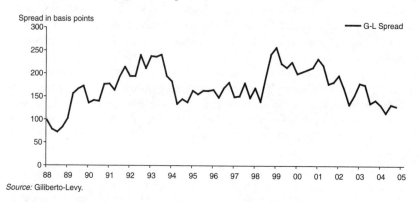

Source: Giliberto-Levy.

EXHIBIT   9–9

ACLI Commercial Mortgage Delinquency

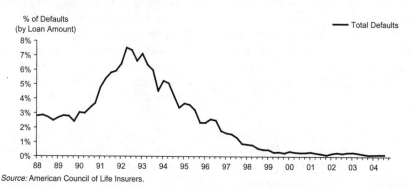

Source: American Council of Life Insurers.

delinquencies and losses is radically improved (see Pappadopoulos and Chen (2002) for a systematic methodology to model market-, property type-, and loan-specific default risk) and so the underwriting has improved and the performance results are better by far.

Following the real estate debt debacle of the cycle of the late 1980s and the difficulties with the corporate loan portfolio in the recent cycle, global banking and other nationally-regulated lending institutions and their regulators have determined that standards to guide reserve requirements are necessary. The publication *International Convergence of Capital Measurement and Capital Standards: a Revised Framework*, commonly known as the Basel II accords, will in the future guide how much of a reserve will be needed for each type of loan across a lenders' entire portfolio, including the real estate portfolio. There is no resolution at this time to the reserves that will be required for the real estate portfolio vs. the other lines of lending. The outcome of the deliberations will make a huge difference to the flow of debt capital to the real estate sector.[4] If one line's reserves are increased relative to another line's, then the lending institution will inevitably prefer to lend more through the "cheaper" line, in terms of reserve requirements, and less through the more "expensive" line. So whether the reserve requirements for real estate are ultimately increased or decreased is less important than how the *relative* reserve requirements, across lines, are set. If real estate were to become relatively "cheap" then you could expect to see a great unleashing of mortgage capital to the real estate sector. This might cause underwriting standards, which have been excellent, to falter and for the performance of this quadrant to suffer, or the opposite could occur. This uncertainty, likely to last for many more years, creates some unease in this quadrant (and in the public debt quadrant as well as the results will spill over). This may explain why spreads remain higher than many believe are justified, given the performance track record through the last cycle.

Mortgages are underwritten on all property types in all geographic locations. Most individual mortgages are larger than most individual investors could invest in. Originations and holdings of private mortgages are limited to large players, but again the advent of the public real estate debt sector (see below) begins to open this investment arena to individuals as well.

Strategies in this sector are somewhat limited. Debt is debt and the only issues are how much interest-rate risk and collateral risk (market, property type, tenant, and operator) one takes. Still the idea is that the lender will get all or at least a portion of their principal back either through repayment of the loan, or in the event of a default, through a sale of the asset itself. Lending on real estate (assuming no environmental or other liability) is not like lending on a corporation whose business model is based an idea and some people—at the end of the day

---

4. Case (2003) provides full details of the Basel II Accord in a white paper at www.federalreserve.gov. The Real Estate Roundtable (www.rer.org) is an industry group monitoring and commenting on its effects for the real estate debt markets.

there is almost always some value to the real estate collateral. Even an asset whose value has been impaired can often be rehabilitated either by the market cycle or by dint of effort by the operator.

Publicly-Traded Real Estate Debt

Through the fire of the troublesome real estate and economic cycle of the late 1980s emerged, helped along by government policy, a new industry—commercial mortgage-backed securities (CMBS). A CMBS is a security, backed by the cash flows from one or a pool of mortgages.[5] The security is "tranched" so that each holder of a piece of the security has a known piece of the hierarchy of rights to the cashflows and risks associated with the underlying collateral. These securities are exactly analogous to securitized corporate debt. The market's development was motivated by the large volume of impaired real estate mortgages held on the books of many lending institutions when the real estate markets crashed in the late 1980s. With the help of the Resolution Trust Agency, a quasi-governmental agency, lenders were able to sell their mortgages to securitizers who were then able to sell the pooled loans into the greater market, thus staunching the losses. The advent of the CMBS market has truly democratized the real estate debt investment sector to the benefit of borrowers everywhere. Borrowers and investors in other countries (where debt is generally less used and tends to be recourse to the borrower) are looking hungrily at the emergence of this new market.

Once the purview of the large banks and insurance companies, the US debt market is now open to conduit lenders—lenders who originate loans and, working with rating agencies, form securities and sell them, sometimes retaining a piece of the security on their books and sometimes just capturing an origination and securitization fee along the way. This new market is steadily eating away at the former dominance of the private debt market and now has topped $547.8 billion in size, comprising 11% of the capital wheel. In 1995 the CMBS market size was just $88.4 billion, 5% of the real estate investment universe. Expect to see this magnitude and share continue to grow.

The market is growing because the idea makes sense. Real estate mortgages are being "deoligopolized," creating greater efficiency and transparency in the process. Each multifamily and commercial mortgage is large and so the market of lenders has been constrained. However the securitization process creates instruments that are far more fractional and sized to fit the investment parameters of more capital sources, including individual investors. Also the process of securitization allows for the pooling of risk across more loans and for segmenting the return/risk hierarchy enabling each investor to participate in the portion of the capital hierarchy with which they feel most comfortable. Whole mortgages

---

5. An excellent introduction to commercial mortgage backed securities can be found in Esaki et al. (2003).

require the investor to "buy into" the entire hierarchy. Borrowers love CMBS as rates are reduced as a result of the new competitive pressures. Smaller investors love CMBS as a heretofore-inaccessible investment is suddenly more accessible (Exhibit 9–10).

Exhibit 9–11 presents CMBS spreads since the advent of the market. Although spreads have come in as information, modeling and so underwriting have improved, they have still been wide to comparable corporates. Again this is a learning curve issue. The rating agencies have erred on the side of conservatism as they have built databases enabling a more accurate prediction of performance. We expect that spreads will narrow as market experiences are documented.

The array of strategies in the public debt market is, as is true for the whole loan market, somewhat narrow. Nonetheless there are some extremes. Traditional fixed income investors have discovered that they can buy and hold the AAA tranche and receive performance that slightly outperforms the comparable corporate security with no additional risk (so far). Many have figured this out and as the

E X H I B I T   9–10

ACLI Mortgages by Property Type

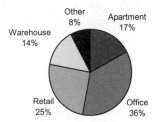

Source: Giliberto-Levy Market Monitor.

E X H I B I T   9–11

CMBS Spreads to 10-Year Treasuries

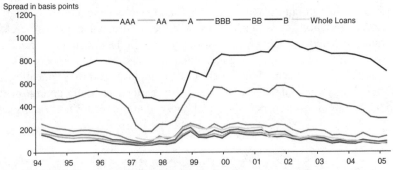

Source: J.P. Morgan; Lehman Brothers; Property & Portfolio Research Inc.

rest of the fixed income world catches on you can expect to see spreads across similar credits equalize. At the other end of the spectrum are the players in the unrated part of the security, where spreads are very wide. As good news about performance trickles in, these spreads will come in and nice gains have been and will be received (on top of nice yields along the way). Again, barring a disaster in the performance of the underlying collateral, this spread compression activity should continue until the relative wideness across the corporate and real estate sectors is competed away.

MANY WAYS TO EXECUTE

In this section we again use the organizing principle of public equity, private equity, private debt, and public debt to describe the key ways in which an investor might participate in the real estate sector. Unfortunately, in some cases the answer will be, "not easily" and in some cases, for some investors, the answer is "not at all." Real estate is still somewhat underdeveloped in terms of its accessibility.

Publicly-Traded Real Estate Equity

First, call your stockbroker. Individual REITs are publicly traded and mutual funds with REITs as their primary or only bet are available as are exchange-traded funds that offer indexes of the real estate securities market. The mutual funds and ETFs hold portfolios comprised of individual REITs and REOCs. The ETFs are traded as if they were individual stocks and so are available at very low fee levels and, as always, money managers will be happy to create individualized portfolios for larger investors.

For the individual investors it is probably best to either really study the market and pick individual REITS as one would pick any other stock, or invest in the many funds in the marketplace. Investing in individual securities is as easy in REIT-land as it is for the general stock market. "Buy 'em, hold 'em, trade 'em." Going through one of the many discount brokerage firms can reduce fees. As publicly traded instruments, REIT shares can and often do trade at a price other than the underlying net asset value (NAV) of the properties the REIT holds. Clayton and MacKinnon (2002) have explored the behavior of REIT pricing during the 1990s. While REITs traded at a premium to NAV through most of the 1990s, by late 1998 they were generally priced at a discount. In addition to the larger capital market effects on pricing, REIT-specific characteristics can drive prices above or below NAV as well. For example, a premium on REIT shares can reflect investor confidence in the REIT management's ability to improve earnings, while Clayton and MacKinnon observed a significant liquidity discount for thinly traded REITs.

The funds offered to individual investors are sponsored by generalist money management firms and by specialist firms. Some of the funds are essentially indexes of the REIT marketplace, others are "ex-dex" funds where they try to avoid the losers rather than pick the winners and others are real "picker" funds where specific bets are made by the portfolio manager. Obviously track record will be important in considering any of these offerings and track records should be readily available although they may be short. The managers' investment process and management expertise must also be considered.

The institutional investor has a wider range of investment possibilities in the public equity arena. Obviously they can invest in anything available to the individual, but as well they can set up separate accounts or participate in pooled funds with institutionally focused REIT specialists. There are firms that do not offer their stock selection expertise to the individual investor market. Institutions can participate in pooled strategies along with other institutions or can design a specific strategy to be executed by the manager.

Of course institutions can also hire the expertise to pick and trade REIT securities within their own operations; they do not need to hire an outside manager. Exactly as individuals can execute their own strategy, so can the institution.

With the explosion of hedge funds in the general investment market it is no surprise that there is a mini-explosion of such offerings in the REIT world as well. These strategies are characterized as long-short approaches and/or as event driven. They are generally only available to institutions or to qualified individual investors. Such strategies are usually closed-end in structure, so once you are in, you are in until the manager lets you out. Small secondary markets form on occasion, allowing for some relief from ownership, but the secondary trades tend to be offered by opportunistic investors looking for steep discounts to actual value. These strategies do not have deep track records, so the strength of the manager in other investment areas is the critical factor in thinking about placing a bet.

Fees for basic index strategies are quite market driven, asset value-based, and easily compared across vendors. Fees for the more selective and more institutional strategies are more likely to be individually negotiated and are likely to include a performance-based component as well as an asset-based management component.

Privately-Traded Real Estate Equity

In the realm of private real estate equity there is a wide gulf between what is available to the individual investor and what is available to the institutional investor. Within the institutional investor segment there is another wide gulf between what the small institution can do and what the very largest institutions can do, and with whom.

The individual has very little available to them in the private equity quadrant, although there are some hopeful signs for the future. Currently if you are a member of the TIAA-CREF pension system you have access, through your 401K, to an excellent core private equity strategy. Or, if Principal Capital Investment Management manages your employer's 401K offering you too may have the option of investing in a very nice, large, core portfolio. Both have long track records that can be easily examined by eligible investors. If you do not have access to one of these, you are basically out of luck.

As this is written in 2005, Fidelity Investments is planning to seed and ultimately offer to the general public a core private equity strategy. However the offering is dependent upon Fidelity solving two problems—one is how to conduct a valuation process that allows the investing public to have confidence in the values at which they enter and exit the fund over time and the second is how to ensure Fidelity itself against the risk of a "run on the fund." In the case of Principal and TIAA-CREF they are conducting quarterly valuations that seem to have made enough investors comfortable, as evidenced by a good flow of funds into the offerings, and they have addressed the "run on the fund" risk by self-insuring. Or, to put it less kindly, by hoping it will not ever be an issue! If it were to become an issue they would essentially slow down withdrawals and impose a set of rules on withdrawals that would seriously undermine the notion of liquidity. Fidelity is hoping to solve the problem rather than hope for the best. If they do solve the problem, others will not be far behind and we could expect to see a blossoming of private real estate equity offerings aimed at individual investors.

In the meantime there is another alternative, although not a very appealing one. It is the private REIT (or as they are called, nonpublicly-traded REITs). The saying in the industry is that such offerings are not so much "bought" as they are "sold" by aggressive and very well commissioned brokers. Institutions would not touch these offerings ever; the reason they are selling to individuals is because the individuals have no private market alternative. These offerings carry heavy loads about which the individual investor is often (temporarily) blissfully unaware.

In addition there are always a handful of private partnerships in the marketplace. These are only for qualified investors and should be very carefully scrutinized before making an investment. Finally, the individual investor can always strike out on his own and buy and operate individual buildings. Many families have created great wealth by doing exactly this, but it is not for the inexperienced or risk-adverse investor. In addition one must devote tremendous time to the acquisition and operational processes. The amount of specific risk in the real estate portfolio would rise radically when pursuing this approach.

While the individual investor can approach the private equity market in any of the ways presented above, the institutional investor can generally pursue one of two tracks, depending on the size of their allocation to real estate.

An institution with less than $1 billion to invest in private real estate equity will generally seek to diversify across strategies and managers. Of course the investor is then responsible for ensuring that when the allocations are viewed as a portfolio, the portfolio corresponds to their preferred risk and return profile for the real estate allocation.

Any investor looking to use multiple managers and strategies will need to evaluate a lot of different managers and investment ideas. Some of the considerations in doing this well are:

Manager track record *in the strategy being considered,*

Stability of employment within the manager's firm,

Incentives offered to the key employees,

Quality of the strategy being proposed,

Specificity of the strategy (or "trust me"),

Time horizon/liquidity of the investment (closed or open end),

Amount of additional capital to be raised and deployed (what if the planned amount is not raised, can/should the strategy go forward?),

Like-mindedness of the other investors,

Risk and return profile of the strategy, and

Fee structure relative to the goals of the strategy.

Geltner (2003) discusses using property-level attribution analysis to evaluate real estate managers' performance.

Generally an investor with $1 billion or less to place will prefer commingled strategy executions over separate account executions, simply because the size of each individual real estate investment tends to be large and a key to risk mitigation is to keep one's specific risk down by spreading one's capital over a larger number of investments. With the use of commingled executions one gives up control over the details of the operations. The investor using commingled structures (which can be insurance company separate accounts, private REITs, or partnerships) signs on to a set of negotiated rules governing strategy, fees, investor priorities to cash flows and gains (and losses...) and ultimately exit and possible manager termination. In fund offerings that are oversubscribed the investor will find that they have very little clout, as the terms of the arrangement are set. With emerging managers or more esoteric strategies the investor's voice at the negotiating table will be more effective.

A larger institution can of course invest in a similar fashion as the smaller institution but also has another spectrum of execution available to them. They can use separate accounts, direct investments, and joint ventures. Separate account investing is essentially the process whereby an investment manager or advisor works closely with the investor to specify a strategy and a process by which that strategy will be executed on behalf of the investor, by the advisor. The advisor will be paid a fee that is privately negotiated, and could have many facets (base, asset management, performance, disposition, and financing fees are all fair game in the negotiation). The advisor will be subject to a termination clause. The investor and the advisor will set the decision-making processes—for acquisitions, management and leasing, and dispositions and financings. The investor might design a process called "discretion in a box" in which the advisor is free to act without explicit approvals as long as the actions are "preapproved" by being within what is contemplated in the box. Alternatively, and tediously, the advisor might have to come to the investor with every decision above a certain dollar threshold.

Separate account executions are generally the province of very large institutions with high levels of internal staffing. The setting of the overarching strategy, the design of the component strategies, the selection of managers to execute, the negotiations of the arrangements with those managers, the monitoring of the assets themselves and the managers' actions all require a heavy commitment of time and real estate expertise.

An extreme way to execute is to execute directly using the institution's staff exclusively with no third-party advisor involvement. The staff is all employed within the investor's entity and the real estate is bought, managed, leased, developed, and sold directly by the investor. Typically such an approach will employ local third-party managers for leasing and property management and will use outside counsel and brokers to transact. Given the complexity of each real estate transaction and the complexity of getting the strategy figured out, this approach seems too extreme to become more prevalent and in fact is limited to the largest investors. Generally an institution has enough high value-added obligations concerning portfolio management, strategy design and manager selection and monitoring without taking on the lower value-added parts of the execution task.

A variant on the use of advisors for a large institutional investor would be to enter into joint ventures with real estate operators. These operators might be privately-held companies or might be in the public market. The institution can negotiate either a pure asset-level relationship or can become an investor in the entity level as well, or exclusively. There is really no substantive difference between an investment manager and an operator. A JV can be structured exactly as would a separate account. Some would argue that operators have greater depth and commitment to a particular aspect of the broad field of real estate investing, but many investment advisory firms are also deep and committed to a particular dimension of real estate. Again it goes to the experience of the people whether they are advisors or operators.

Fee structures for core strategies are generally asset-based (basis points × net or gross asset value) but often include a performance dimension as well. For example, an offering might carry a base asset management fee of 75 basis points plus a percentage of cashflow. As the risk of the strategy increases, through value-added to opportunistic, the fee structures strive to tie vendor rewards to the performance of the strategy. There are many variations on fees and there are no perfect structures. There are times when vendors are paid disproportionately well relative to their performance (for example in a down market when the structure is tilted towards asset-based and transaction-based fees) and other times when the investor is excessively rewarded (for example with the same fee structure, but in a raging bull market).

Privately-Traded Real Estate Debt

The only ways to participate in the quadrant are to be:

Big and do it directly, or

Big and set up a coinvestment program with a large originator.

An investor who does not meet these profiles is not going to obtain access to a piece of this quadrant of real estate. One minor exception to this would be for

EXHIBIT   9–12

Mortgage and Equity REIT Performance, 1971 to 2004

	Mortgage REITs	Equity REITs
Average Annual Total Return	7.8%	13.4%
Risk	27.1%	16.0%
Return per Unit of Risk	0.29%	0.84%

Source: NAREIT.

any size investor to go to the public equity market and purchase shares of mortgage REITs; but, seriously, how oxymoronic is that? Mortgage REITs do exist (a handful of them) but why remains a mystery. Some researchers find that mortgage REITs and equity REITs are substitutable asset classes—one is as good as the other—see Lee and Chiang (2004). Yet comparing performance indexes published by NAREIT shows that mortgage REITs have underperformed equity REITs since 1971 by a country mile. So while they are called *mortgage* REITs and they do contain mortgages, they perform like equity REITs (only worse) so do not really solve the private (or public) real estate debt investment riddle (Exhibit 9–12).

Fees for large investors to set up a coinvestment program would be reasonable (around 50 basis points) but the difficulty will be in getting a large player to want to invest your money. Generally anyone you would want to invest with is already working very hard to get their own capital deployed in an ever more competitive lending environment.

Fortunately this is less of a problem as we now have the public debt quadrant.

Publicly-Traded Real Estate Debt

While this field of investment is rapidly emerging it is still not as openly accessible as is the public equity market. Large investors of course can invest directly via an investment bank either when securities are issued or/and in the secondary market. Such investors are going to be buying individual securities however; few pooled options are available, apart from collateralized debt obligations (CDOs— pools of existing CMBS issues). A handful of investment managers periodically raise a pool of capital and create a commingled fund. These are offered to institutions first and to individuals almost never. There are a few mutual funds open to the general public that invest in CMBS along with, typically, other real estate securities such as REITs and preferred shares of real estate companies. These funds are new, so track records are difficult to assess.

The top-rated tranches of CMBS securities are widely available through investment banks and as noted previously, many fixed income portfolios now routinely include them. These are quite liquid and so are fairly easy to price and mark to market.

The really interesting unrated tranches are very small and closely held by a small group of very sophisticated CMBS players. This market is really controlled by these investors who hold the securities for their own accounts and only occasionally offer them to other institutions or to the public. The spreads on these investments, while reduced from past peak levels, are still very attractive.

The best way for a large or mid-sized institution to take a position in this quadrant is to coinvest with an existing B-piece player, who will have the infrastructure and relationships already set up. Fees will likely be a combination of asset- and performance-based. There are not many specialist advisors so the pickings are quite slim and an investor may or may not be able to get one's attention.

The bad news is that this very attractive real estate quadrant is not generally accessible to investors, but the good news is that this is changing as the size of the quadrant grows along with the transformation of how commercial and multifamily mortgage debt is originated and held in the US and in the rest of the world. There is more to come for this quadrant; count on it.

PERFORMANCE MEASUREMENT REQUIREMENTS AND CONSTRAINTS

Performance measurement starts with an index against which to compare the outcome of a particular strategy. In real estate indices are not as straightforward as they are for some other asset types. In real estate there are coverage shortfalls, valuation or mark to market shortfalls and frequency of measurement shortfalls. All this plus great difficulty with the notion that a proper benchmark should be investible! With the exception of the public equity quadrant the latter criteria for an acceptable benchmark is simply not going to be met. That said, there are one or more indices that may be used to greater or lesser effect to measure the performance of "the market" for each of the quadrants of the real estate investment universe. There is no index that measures the weighted performance of the entire real estate investment universe except those created by research firms to be used in high-level asset allocation work. Each quadrant will be discussed.

Publicly-Traded Real Estate Equity

This is the easy quadrant. The industry's trade organization, the National Association of Real Estate Investment Trusts (NAREIT at www.NAREIT.org) tracks individual securities and publishes very good indices of performance within the REIT universe. Of course these indices only cover real estate companies that are structured as REITs and so one has to go further a field to obtain an index of all real estate companies, REITs and REOCs. MSCI produces an index, the RMS, and Wilshire produces an index, the RESI. Both cover REITS and the Wilshire RESI includes other real estate companies structured as REOCs.

Using these indices, which are marked to market daily using the prices at which actual real estate securities trade, it is quite straightforward to see whether a particular strategy is out- or underperforming the market as defined by the index. Of course remember, as discussed before, there is no necessary correspondence between the property type and geographic coverage of an index and the true underlying real estate investment universe.

Privately-Traded Real Estate Equity

Now the measurement problem grows muddy. The best-known and most-used index to measure the performance of investments in the private equity quadrant is the National Council of Real Estate Investment Fiduciaries (NCREIF at www.NCREIF.org) index. NCREIF is a trade organization supported by fees collected from its member organizations. The members are predominantly real estate investment advisory firms, with a sprinkling of pension fund and other owner members. So, right off the bat we have a situation where the sponsorship that controls the rules of submission may have a bias. Each member of NCREIF submits to the organization a set of data on each property within the member's portfolio that meets NCREIF's criteria for inclusion in the index. Over time NCREIF has broadened the criteria in an effort to enlarge the coverage of the index, for example they collect leveraged properties and then "delever" them for inclusion in the unlevered database. The contribution process is voluntary; there is no "policing" of the contributions. Members submit a set of information on the income produced quarterly by the property and on the appraised value of the property (the value will be the transaction value if the asset is newly in the manager's portfolio). NCREIF generates and sells a basic set of indexes that is comprised of total, regional, and property type amalgamations of whatever assets were contributed to the pool in each quarter. The contents of the pool can and do change as a function of members joining and leaving membership, members buying and selling properties and, perhaps, members wrongly submitting or not submitting specific properties to the data collection effort. Again this latter area is a source of potential bias that is impossible to assess.

The staff of NCREIF is sensitive to these issues and work hard to create "side indices" that are perhaps more indicative of the behavior of the true real estate investment universe. All of these efforts are gratefully received, but must be regarded still as second-best to the idea of a true index comprised of the vast majority of privately-held real estate. The size of the NCREIF pool is $145.4 billion as compared with an estimate of the size of the overall private equity quadrant of $762.7 billion. Given this magnitude of gap it is hard to be overly reliant on the NCREIF indexes; yet people are. Many institutional investors rely heavily on the index to measure their own and their managers' performances. Managers are frequently compensated based on the degree of out- or underperformance relative to the overall index or one of the subindexes.

Private research companies do what they can to reweight the components of the NCREIF database in an effort to "jerry-rig" a more appropriate measurement reflective of true market and property type weights. In addition, firms derive time series of returns to try to expand the coverage of NCREIF information, but all of this is in lieu of the real numbers and is therefore second-best.

Why is it that the private market quadrant is so underserved by an index? The reason is the lack of motivation for submitting data to the NCREIF index. In the absence of a public market where the necessary data can be readily collected, with or without the owners' consent, the private markets must motivate owners to submit their information completely and in a timely fashion. Given that a voluntary membership organization, focused on the pension fund money management industry, is currently the key to the creation of an all-encompassing index to measure private equity market performance, there is virtually no hope of achieving the promise of such an index. NCREIF is what it is, and is serving its members well. It is not however serving the larger real estate investment community as well as might be desired. They are not to blame however; they were never constituted to serve the larger master.

It is interesting to note that in the United Kingdom there is a privately owned firm called the Investment Property Databank (IPD at www.IPDIndex.uk.co) that has succeeded in serving the larger investment community. IPD collects data, just like NCREIF (only they collect in far greater detail), on the performance of each property in a portfolio. Additionally they collect all of the relevant information on the other holdings of the portfolio, like portfolio-level cash and leverage. Around 85% of all private equity in the UK is included in the indices that are produced from this collection effort. The data that is collected is policed for completeness and accuracy. So why is IPD so successful at collecting this information? Because IPD is *not* a voluntary industry group, it is an independent profit-making company in the primary business of offering performance attribution services to the investment community. IPD charges fees (significant fees) to report to the investor exactly how their portfolio performed and why, relative to a truer investment universe. IPD provides a valuable service and so investors are pleased to participate and even to pay well for the privilege. IPD has expanded the model to other European and Asian countries and is trying to gain a toehold in America. The business model is sound and produces a good for the industry from a service to individual investors.

One might ask, why not use the better public real estate equity quadrant index to measure performance in the less well-measured private equity quadrant? Several researchers have investigated the relationship between the private and public real estate equity quadrants; Giliberto and Mengden (1996), Pagliari et al. (2003), and Gyourko (2004) have all found that when the public market pricing volatility is removed from the public market returns and when the private market pricing is lagged forward to the same timing as the public market pricing, and both datasets are reweighted to reflect one another's weights in various property types, there is *no* meaningful difference between the performance of the public and private real estate markets. This is fertile ground for the creation of a truer reflection of the performance of both the public market's underlying real estate and the private market's real estate. This research highlights that the differences in the composition of the public and private markets matters and that the appraisal oriented valuation process that characterizes the private markets are major sources of performance-measurement error.

While the NCREIF index and the NAREIT index measure fairly straightforward core-dominated investment strategies, there is a large and growing allocation to the opportunistic investment strategy–for which there is no publicly-available index. There is, however one private consulting firm that has begun to measure and track the performance of the universe (assuming 100% voluntary compliance with a data submission request) of opportunity funds (see Hahn, 2005). This is promising work, although the audience for its use is restricted to clients of the consultant.

Over time, research on the relationships between the public and private equity markets, plus better data-collection models will gradually improve the currently suboptimal state of affairs, especially in the private equity market. In the interim, be careful.

Privately-Traded Real Estate Debt

Well, if measurement in the private equity quadrant was difficult, the private debt quadrant presents even greater difficulty. There are two sources of benchmarks for this quadrant–a modeled time series called the Giliberto–Levy Commercial Mortgage Performance Index (G–L Index, available through www.ppr.info) and a private industry index (only available to select industry participants). The latter index suffers from all of the problems cited for the NCREIF index, as the industry group followed the NCREIF model (the index is governed by a voluntary, nonprofit organization) in setting the rules of collection and compliance. The $188-billion G–L index is the industry standard even though it suffers from the fact that it is a modeled time series, based on the very large database assembled by the American Council of Life Insurers (ACLI). The database is large, and this is good, but the mortgages in it must be marked to market by the analytic process and not through market forces. Also, only fixed-rate mortgages originated and held by life insurance companies are included in the database. The development of the public debt market will greatly improve our understanding of how the marketplace prices mortgages and this improved knowledge and experience will feed back into the modeled indexes, improving their accuracy and timeliness. Again, however, the really good solution would be to have an independent collector of *all* commercial and multi-family mortgages and then to look to the public markets for timely pricing metrics.

Publicly Traded Real Estate Debt

The public securitized mortgage market is new and so data collection has only just begun, but is off to a promising start. The Commercial Mortgage Securitization Association (CMSA at www.cmbs.org) and Lehman Brothers (at www.lehman-live.com) have engaged in good work seeking to measure the performance of the overall securitized market. The only real issue concerns the marking to market of the lower tranches as they trade less frequently. The higher tranches are well understood and their values are frequently documented. While the use of such indices applied to the private mortgage market might be fairly straightforward, the only caution concerns the reality that the mix of underlying collateral possibly differs between the two markets, thus creating a gap in the coverage.

SUMMARY

Real estate is not real estate is not real estate. Once the onion is peeled a very diverse world of behaviors and access is revealed. The "asset class" we call real estate combines debt and equity traded in public and private markets. The segmented market is also characterized by very different points of accessibility to institutions, large and small, and to individuals. It is getting better; greater accessibility to the quadrants is coming through the emergence of viable public trading and valuation arenas and through the cleverness of the investment management community.

Within the quadrants is another layer of onion peels concerning property types, geographies and strategies. Each quadrant is characterized by a nonuniverse-replicating allocation of collateral across the true market distribution. And there is no overarching index encompassing all of each of the quadrants to aid in our thinking about this broad asset "class."

Given the different trading markets and the historically closed investment communities of some of the private investment areas it is no surprise that valuation practices and so accuracies and frequencies are all over the map. Again however, there is good news as the growth of public markets and other forms of investment democratization have created opportunities to study values in one quadrant and apply the learning to values in another. After all, at the end of the day it all comes down to the property!

Indices are difficult with only partial coverage, poor valuation standards, and uneven participation by data contributors. There is some "best practice" in other parts of the world to which the US would be wise to attend in its efforts to improve the art of performance measurement. Assuming of course that the dominant players do want performance measurement to improve. Investibility remains and will remain an almost intractable problem, especially for the private market sectors of the real estate markets.

Access to real estate investments is limited as well. The very largest institutions can get what they want, but any investor falling below a very high $1 billion threshold for their allocation to real estate will be confronted by a lack of access. Medium-sized institutions can invest in the public debt and equity markets and in the private equity markets, but access to the private debt market is very difficult. Small institutions can easily participate in public equity and probably can get access to the private equity market and the high credit public debt market but the private debt and unrated public debt markets are off limits. As well their choices of managers and governance will be limited. The mere mortal is really confounded by the market place! Only through mutual funds and exchange-traded funds can they access much more than public real estate equity and the very dangerous strategy of direct investment. Again, there is more coming for the individual. In the interim individuals must be very cautious about investing in the very high-load nonpublicly-traded REITs.

Real estate is a great asset class, offering strategies grounded in very stable cashflows derived from physical assets whose values rarely ever diminish to tragic levels, and whose values, even if temporarily impaired, tend to recover at least partially with time and effort. It is no wonder that there are increased interest and capital flows to real estate; the problem for now is access.

REFERENCES

Block, R. *Investing in REITs: Real Estate Investment Trusts* (2nd Edition), Bloomberg Press, Princeton, NJ, 2002.

Bodie, Z. *Essentials of Investments* (5th Edition), Irwin/McGraw-Hill, New York, NY, 2003.

Case, B. "Loss Characteristics of Commercial Real Estate Loan Portfolios," Federal Reserve White Paper, June 2003.

Chen, J., and P. Hobbs, "Global Real Estate Risk Index," *The Journal of Portfolio Management–Real Estate Special Issue*, September 2003, pp. 66–75.

Clayton, J., and G. MacKinnon, "Explaining the Discount to NAV in REIT Pricing: Noise or Information?" Real Estate Research Institute Working Paper, 2002.

Conner, P., and R. Falzon, "Volatility Differences between the Public and Private Real Estate Markets," *Briefings in Real Estate Finance*, September 2004, pp. 102–117.

Esaki, H., M. de Beur, and M. Pearl, "Introduction," *Transforming Real Estate Finance: A CMBS Primer* (3rd Edition), Morgan Stanley, Spring 2003.

Fisher, J., D. Gatzlaff, D. Geltner, and D. Haurin, "Controlling for the Impact of Variable Liquidity in Commercial Real Estate Price Indices," *Real Estate Economics*, vol. 31, 2003, pp. 269–303.

Geltner, D. "IRR-Based Property-Level Performance Attribution," *The Journal of Portfolio Management*, September 2003, pp. 138–151.

Giliberto, M., and A. Mengden, "REITs and Real Estate: Two Markets Reexamined," *Real Estate Finance*, 1996, pp. 56–60.

Glascock, J., D. Michayluk, and K. Neuhauser, "The Riskiness of REITs Surrounding the October 1997 Stock Market Decline," *The Journal of Real Estate Finance and Economics*, June 2004, pp. 339–354.

Gyourko, J. "Real Estate Returns in Public and Private Markets," *Wharton Real Estate Review*, Spring 2004, pp. 34–47.

Hahn, T., D. Geltner and N. Gerardo-Leitz, "Real Estate Opportunity Funds: Past Fund Performance as an Indicator of Subsequent Fund Performance," *The Journal of Portfolio Management, Real Estate Special Issue,* Fall 2005, forthcoming.

Heckman, J. "Sample Selection Bias as a Specification Error," *Econometrica*, vol. 47, 1979, pp. 153–161.

Hess, R., and Y. Liang, "Strategies of Focus and Opportunity: Trends in Public-Market Commercial Real Estate Penetration From 1998 to 2003," Prudential Real Estate Investors, 2004.

Lee, M., and K. Chiang, "Substitutability between Equity REITs and Mortgage REITs," *Journal of Real Estate Research*, March 2004, pp. 95–113.

Pagliari, J., K. Scherer, and R. Monopoli, "Public versus Private Real Estate Equities," *The Journal of Portfolio Management*, September 2003, pp. 101–111.

Pappadopoulos, G., and C. Chen, "Commercial Real Estate Loan Default Frequency," *The Journal of Portfolio Management*, September 2002, pp. 115–119.

CHAPTER 10

TIMBERLAND: THE NATURAL ALTERNATIVE

Clark S. Binkley, Courtland Washburn, Mary Ellen Aronow
Hancock Timber Resource Group

INTRODUCTION

As we peer into the murky future of the 21st century, the investment landscape looks precarious. Despite material downward adjustments, equity markets still trade above long-term price-to-earnings ratios, and the outlook for future earnings does not appear adequate to offset this comparatively risky pricing. A rising interest-rate environment, as many expect, may produce losses in fixed-income portfolios. Real estate capitalization rates have fallen perhaps 200 bps between 2002 and 2004, and, by this measure, that asset class is more expensive than it has been for over a decade. Inflation may be heating up on the back of large and sustained increases in energy prices, a weakening US dollar, and still-loose monetary and fiscal policies. Under such circumstances, wise investors look to alternative assets as a source of stability and return. Timberland merits attention.

This chapter provides an introduction to timberland investment. The first section describes the asset class, its history and the underlying investment logic. The next section reviews the historical evidence on risk and returns, including (as befits this book) a particularly close analysis of the performance of timberland with respect to inflation. The third section describes how timberland properties produce returns for investors. Presuming that the first three sections have been compelling, the final section provides some practical advice on how one might move forward with an investment program in this area.

WHAT IS A TIMBERLAND INVESTMENT?

By a "timberland investment" we mean the ownership of forest land properties and the trees standing on them. This definition excludes most obviously, such woodproduct manufacturing facilities as sawmills, pulpmills and paper mills that are owned by integrated forest products companies. The timberland asset may be held in a special purpose investment vehicle, or may be held as a direct investment in real estate. It may be levered or not. Sometimes the land and timber are separated, where the investor might own just the trees (this situation is called a timber deed or forestry right), or just the land (a timber lease). The usual case, especially in the United States, is to own the land and trees.

The Earth's forests comprise about 3 billion hectares (FAO, 2000). Much of this land is not investable—it is too remote or too sparsely stocked with trees to have economic value; it is owned by governments who show little sign of making it available for private investors; or it is in countries that are too risky for attractive long-term investments in fixed assets. While there are no definitive figures, we think that the investable universe now amounts to about $200 billion, with about half of this total in the US and the other half widely dispersed in Canada, Australia, New Zealand, South America and Europe. We believe that Africa, Russia and Southeast Asia are currently outside the investable universe for most institutions as a result of country risk and economic factors, but this situation, of course, may change.

Forestland can be categorized in many different ways, but for investors, it is useful to distinguish hardwoods from softwoods and plantations from natural forests. The term "hardwood" refers to broadleaved trees (generally, but not always deciduous; that is, they lose their leaves in the fall). This category would include such species familiar to North Americans and Europeans as oak, cherry, birch, poplars, and maples, as well as such less familiar ones like the various eucalypts, and tropical hardwoods—*Swetinia* (the true mahoganies), *Dipterocarps* ("luan") and *Nothafagus* (southern beech). Hardwood timber is used to manufacture a myriad of products, including fine papers, golf tees, furniture, flooring, and shipping pallets. Softwoods are needle-bearing trees (usually but not always evergreen), including pines, firs, spruces, Douglas-fir, cedars and cypress. Most wood-based construction products are produced from softwood trees, as is much of the world's paper and boxes.

Plantations are, as the name suggests, forests established by planting. Such forests generally have higher input and maintenance costs, but much higher productivity and the opportunity to access gains from various kinds of tree-growing technologies (e.g., fertilization, control of competing vegetation, genetic improvement). Natural forests may be managed, and might include environmentally-controversial old-growth. Natural forests typically have lower capital and ongoing management costs, but lower levels of productivity. Both hardwoods and softwoods may be found in plantations and in natural forests.

Institutional ownership of timberland includes both hardwoods and softwoods (although mainly the latter), and focuses primarily on plantations. Such ownerships have been increasing at a rate of about 20% per year for the past two decades. Exhibit 10–1 shows the development of these trends in the United States. The chart labels private equity investments as "TIMOs" or Timberland Investment Management Organizations (the investment advisors who support institutional investments in timberland).

The growth has included both private equity vehicles and publicly traded timberland-intensive firms (this latter category excludes companies that own significant manufacturing assets). Exhibit 10–2 shows the rapid ascendancy of the Timber Real Estate Investment Trust (TREIT) as the preferred public-equity

EXHIBIT   10–1

Institutional Ownership of US Timberland, 1985 to 2004

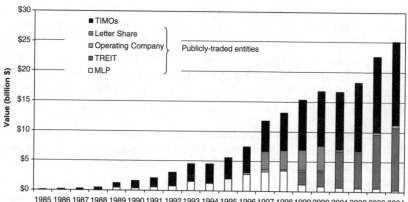

Source: HTRG Research.
Notes: MLP = master limited partnership; TREIT = timber real estate investment trust; Operating Company = 'C'corporation, Letter Share = trading stock.

investment vehicle. Similar to Master Limited Partnerships (MLPs), TREITs suffer no entity-level taxes as long as they remain qualified as REITs; but, unlike an MLP, a TREIT *per se* creates no unrelated-business taxable income, and is therefore structurally preferable for tax-exempt institutions.

Private equity owners acquire their timberland from two main sources: sales by integrated forest products companies and governmental privatizations. The reasons for governmental privatizations (such as have occurred in New Zealand and Australia) are perhaps obvious, and two are particularly common—a change in political ideology questions public ownership of an essentially private asset;

EXHIBIT   10–2

Historical Timberland Returns

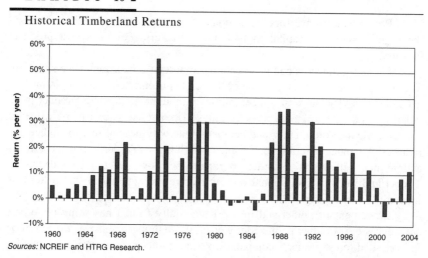

Sources: NCREIF and HTRG Research.

a government needs money to pay down public debt or to finance public infrastructure or social programs.

The reasons for integrated companies selling their timberland are perhaps a
bit more obscure—if timberland is an attractive investment, why would a company sell it? The answer to this question has both strategic and financial elements.

In the past two decades more and more firms have realized that timberland
ownership is not a prerequisite for successful wood products manufacturing or marketing. Such significant firms as Kimberly Clark, Proctor Gamble, Georgia Pacific,
Smurfit Stone, and StoraEnso have divested all, or nearly all, of their timberland. A
combination of factors has fueled disintegration of timberland from manufacturing:

> US Generally Accepted Accounting Principles (GAAP) consistently under-
> state the returns from timberland—book values cannot be written up as trees
> grow; and a noncash cost, "depletion" (similar to depreciation) is deducted
> from operating EBITDA to compute GAAP net income, despite the fact that
> the forest asset may be accreting in value (proposed International Financial
> Accounting Standards rectify the first problem, but not the second)

> The return to shareholders, whether measured by return on capital employed
> or return on equity, for integrated forests products companies has been
> comparatively low (5% to 7%), while returns from timberland have been far
> higher (as we will see below, the returns from US timberland have averaged
> 15.3% since 1987). Since integrated forest products companies are nothing
> more than a collection of timberland and manufacturing assets, the dispar-
> ity of returns highlights the comparatively poor operating performance of
> the manufacturing assets. Investors have urged companies in this position
> to sell their timberland and use the capital either to reward investors directly
> or to revitalize their manufacturing businesses.

> Undervalued timberland assets can make an integrated company a target for
> unwelcome attention from LBO specialists.

Private equity investors suffer none of these problems, and have become
the logical source of capital to fuel the restructuring of the forest products
industry.

Financial concerns comprise another important dimension of the situation.
The forest products industry is one of the least concentrated of the basic materials industries. The lack of concentration is thought to increase product-price
volatility and perhaps to depress earnings. Timberland sales can be a useful
means to finance the merger and acquisition activity needed to consolidate the
industry. A typical pattern is for a company to borrow in order to finance a transaction then sell assets in order to repair their over-levered balance sheet.
Timberland sales to institutional owners feature prominently in this pattern of
industrial restructuring.

Investment in timberland in a private equity format has some important
advantages over holding public equity positions in timber-intensive companies or
in integrated forest products companies. Private equity investors have no specific

need to cut trees to provide raw material inputs for mills, and can therefore select the best time to harvest trees and avoid doing so in poor markets.

Similarly, private equity investors have no specific need to cut trees to meet public investor expectations of a fixed yield. Furthermore, private equity investors can deploy capital investments in tree growing to maximize total return, unencumbered by such extraneous considerations as the need to supply timber to a specific mill. As a result of these advantages, private equity ownership of timberland continues to grow.

WHY INVEST IN TIMBERLAND?

The availability of investment opportunities from privatizations and forest products industry restructuring has provided the opportunity for growth in private-equity ownership, but why have investors invested?

Academic researchers started characterizing timberland returns in the late 1970s, and derived the interesting conclusion that timberland had historically generated high risk-adjusted returns. These results have been repeatedly duplicated, and the historical record now provides strong support for these early conclusions. The case for timberland investment is, in short:

Strong returns (including a significant cash component),

Low risk (as measured by volatility and correlation with the returns from other assets), and

Positive correlation with inflation, especially unanticipated inflation.

Even at comparatively modest allocations, timberland can provide meaningful improvements in the performance of a mixed-asset portfolio. This section reviews some of the evidence on each of these points.

Strong Returns

Timberland returns are comprised of two components, "income" and "capital." The income return reflects the current cash distributions from operations, and depends primarily on timber prices and harvest levels. The capital component refers to the change in asset value. This component of return responds to changes in anticipated future income levels and to changes in how timberland markets capitalize those anticipated future income levels into current asset values. Capital returns are typically measured via annual appraisals.

The main source of data on timberland returns is the National Council of Investment Fiduciaries (NCREIF) Timberland Property Index.[1] These data,

---

1. NCREIF also plans to begin publishing in 2005 a Timberland Fund Index that will report fund-level returns.

going back to 1987, reflect the actual pre-fee property-level performance of US timberland properties owned by institutional investors. As of 31 December 2004, the index included 256 properties covering about 4.7 million acres worth about $6.6 billion, or about half of the total current institutional investment. Eight managers currently contribute data to the NCREIF Timberland Property Index.

To provide a longer time series of timberland returns, the research group at the Hancock Timber Resource Group developed a second set of data, called the John Hancock Timberland Index. The John Hancock Timberland Index (JHTI) is a synthetic return series that attempts to estimate what timberland returns would have been if only someone had been prescient enough to record them.

The combined results from these two series, (NCREIF from 1987 through 2004, and JHTI from 1960 to 1986) are shown in Exhibit 10–2.

Since 1987, timberland returns have averaged 15.3% per year with an annual cash yield of 6.0% per year. Over this same period, US CPI inflation averaged 3.3%, so real timber returns were 11.6%. Note that only once during this period—in 2001—were timberland returns negative.

Such an excellent historical record of returns provides a modicum of comfort for investors, but the real question is "what returns can we expect in the future?" There is, of course, no reliable answer, but we seek to address it in two different ways:

Calculation of forward-looking returns from the NCREIF Timberland Property Index (comparable to a real estate "cap rate" analysis)[2]; and

Estimation of forward-looking returns from all the properties we manage.

These data are revealing, as seen in Exhibit 10–3 which summarizes these results, along with time series of expected real returns for core commercial properties.

There are no publicly-available estimates of expected timberland returns. While NCREIF collects and publishes extraordinarily interesting information on past returns, the shifting mix of properties in the database makes prognostication difficult. For example, if the cash yield increases, is this due to a true increase in yield, or just a shift from younger cash-poor/appreciation-rich properties to older, cash-rich ones? The core problem is to standardize the age-class structure of the NCREIF properties to provide reasonable time-series inferences.

Our methodology for doing so takes as given the NCREIF total returns. To control for the shifting mix of young and old properties in the index, we employ the common forestry assumption of a "fully-regulated forest" with an equal area of trees in each age class. Then using regional estimates of timber prices and costs

---

2. See Aronow et al. (2004) for an explanation of the methodology. These two sources for timberland returns are not wholly independent, because the NCREIF data are based on appraisals, as are the HTRG forward-looking returns.

E X H I B I T   10–3

Expected Real Returns for US Timberland Properties

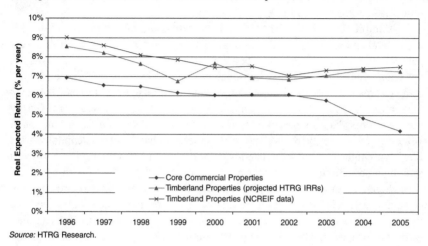

Source: HTRG Research.

we can estimate the net income that would arise from such a forest over time, and attribute the remainder of the return to changes in land values. This provides us with an estimate of the value of a standardized forest over time, and we can use this value to infer what the real discount rates are for a standardized forest as the ratio of net operating income to land value.

A second measure of timberland returns comes from our own database of properties. Every year as part of our annual hold-sell analysis we

re-forecast timber prices,

re-calculate long-term harvest levels for each property, and

re-value each property via third-party appraisals.

This collection of information permits us annually to estimate the invest-ment return available from holding each property, or, using our sample of about 75 properties together, to estimate the returns available from institutional timber-land (note that, similar to the NCREIF database, the sample of properties changes annually). Our price forecasts are proprietary and may deviate from others in the industry. To remove the impact of our price forecasts on the results, we have estimated IRRs based on timber prices remaining constant in real terms at their current levels.

Expected real timberland returns, however measured, have been roughly constant over the past 5 years. Timberland appears to be priced to generate an approximate 7.5% real return, or a 10% to 11% nominal return given current expectations for US CPI inflation. There are no discernable trends since the mid-1990s. Indeed, the spreads against real estate have actually widened significantly.

Comparatively Low Risk

Different investors consider risk in different ways. As a consequence, we provide four different measures of risk.[3]

Exhibit 10–4 shows the level and standard deviation of annual returns for timberland and a variety of other assets for the period 1975 to 2004. This 30-year period is the longest for which data are available for the majority of the assets in the chart, and also provides a reasonable approximation of mid-cycle to mid-cycle returns for timberland (although we must confess that "mid-cycle" is known only after the fact). Over this period, timberland has generated considerably higher returns than long-term corporate bonds with about the same amount of volatility. Interestingly, timberland itself appears to have its own "capital market line," with higher returns associated with higher volatility in the Pacific northwest as compared with the south or north.

Some investors are interested in Sharpe Ratios—the "excess return" per unit of volatility. Exhibit 10–5 shows the Sharpe Ratios for the same set of assets over the same period. Based on this measure of risk-adjusted returns, timberland has performed as well as any asset, and better than most. With a Sharpe ratio of 0.50, timberland's risk-adjusted return performance has been as good as that for large cap

E X H I B I T   10–4

Capital Market Line, 1975 to 2004

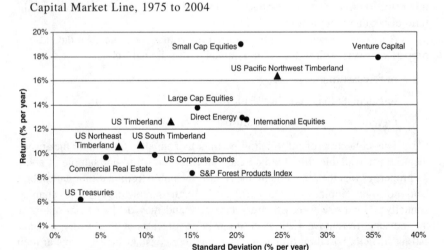

Sources: HTRG Research, Ibbotson Associates, and Venture Economics.
Note: S&P Forest Products Index 1977-2004.

---

3. All the measures of risk we consider here implicitly assume that timberland returns are symmetrically distributed. There is some evidence that timberland returns, particularly those in the US west, have been right-skewed and leptokurtic, but these deviations from normality may be due to the one-time "spotted owl" supply restriction which took place in the early 1990s.

E X H I B I T   10–5

Sharpe Ratios, 1975 to 2004

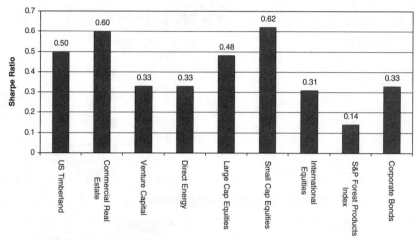

Sources: HTRG Research, Ibbotson Associates, and Venture Economics.
Note: S&P Forest Products Index 1977-2004.

equities, and far better than that of either publicly-traded forest products companies or such other alternative assets as private equity or direct energy investments.

Of course, volatility alone does not adequately measure risk for investors who hold mixed asset portfolios. The question for such investors is the amount of risk that an asset contributes, on the margin, to such a portfolio. This systematic risk depends not only on the volatility of returns, but also on the correlation of those returns with the returns of other assets. In this respect, timberland performs particularly well.

Exhibit 10–6 provides some of the relevant data. This exhibit shows the correlation between the returns from timberland and those from a variety of other assets. Note that timberland returns have had either negative or insignificantly-positive correlations with other assets, including equities and fixed income. Interestingly, timberland returns have had essentially no correlation with the returns from such other alternative assets as venture capital and direct energy investments.

Given these elements of timberland's return distribution—mean, standard deviations, and correlations—one can assess systematic risk in several ways. One way is to examine risk-efficient frontiers, and we show these results in the final part of this section. Another way to measure risk is to use an asset-pricing model, and the most common of these is the capital asset pricing model.[4] Exhibit 10–7

---

4. Several academic studies have applied the CAPM to some measure of timberland returns (Binkley et al. (1996); Hotveldt and Tedder, (1978); Redmond and Cubbage, (1988); Thomson, (1989); Washburn and Binkley, (1993)). In addition, Sun and Zhang (2001) applied the Arbitrage Pricing Model, developed by Ross (1976), to timberland. The Sun and Zhang work confirms the results of the CAPM studies.

EXHIBIT 10–6

Correlation with Timberland Returns, 1975 to 2004

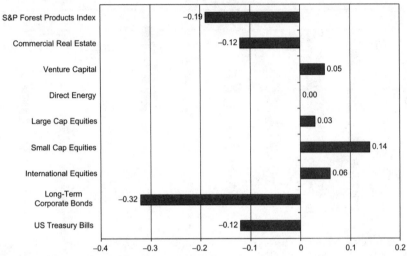

Sources: HTRG Research, Ibbotson Associates, and Venture Economics.
Note: S&P Forest Products Index 1977-2004.

EXHIBIT 10–7

Security Market Line, 1975 to 2004

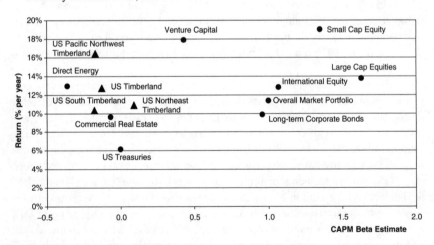

Sources: HTRG Research, Ibbotson Associates, and Venture Economics.

shows the results from estimating a standard CAPM for timberland and a collection of other assets.

As can be seen in this chart, timberland has little systematic risk (over this period, timberland's CAPM beta has not been significantly different than zero).

Indeed, like some other alternative assets, timberland has generated significant CAPM alpha—excess returns over what would be expected from the risk of the asset. The CAPM alpha has been significant, about 800 basis points.

Positive Correlations with Inflation

Exhibit 10–6 shows that timberland returns have been positively correlated with inflation, suggesting that timberland might be a good hedge against inflation. In the past, Washburn and Binkley (1993) analyzed the relationship between timberland returns and inflation in more detail, concluding that timberland has been a particularly good hedge against unexpected inflation. The data in the original paper spanned only the period 1955 to 1987, and the measures of timberland return were far less precise than those available today. As a result, we elected to update the results for this paper.

The basic model relates timberland returns to overall market returns and unanticipated inflation:

$$R_{i,t} = \gamma_{0,i} + \gamma_{1,i}R_{m,t} + \gamma_{2,i}UI_t + \varepsilon_{i,t} \qquad (10\text{–}1)$$

where

$R_{i,t}$ = return from asset i in period t,

$R_{m,t}$ = "market" return in period t (measured here by the S&P 500),

UI_t = unexpected inflation in period t (see below for a definition),

$E_{i,t}$ = an error term, assumed to be normal, and

$\gamma_{0,i}, \gamma_{1,i}, \gamma_{2,i}$ = parameters to be estimated for each asset i.

We measure unexpected inflation (UI_t) as the difference between realized US consumer price inflation (measured by the CPI-U) and a measure of expected inflation based on an ARIMA model of short-term US Treasuries, as is common in this literature.[5] The parameter $\gamma_{2,i}$ tells us how asset i responds to unexpected inflation. A value of $\gamma_{2,i}$ equal to zero means that asset i has been immune to unexpected inflation. Asset i has hedged greater-than-expected inflation if $\gamma_{2,i}$ is greater than zero, and lower-than-expected inflation if $\gamma_{2,i}$ is less than zero.

We estimated Equation (10–1) for timberland and other assets over the period 1960 to 2004 using annual data. Table 10–1 shows the results.

The results are consistent with our earlier analysis. Timberland has been a strong hedge against unexpected inflation, with the US Pacific northwest performing particularly well in this regard. Financial asset returns, on the other hand, have responded poorly to unanticipated inflation. As a result, an investor can add timberland to a portfolio of financial assets to help insulate it against unexpected inflation.

---

5. See, e.g., Hartzell et al. (1989).

Estimates of the Two-Factor Model for Real Rates of Return

Asset		γ_0	γ_1	γ_2	DW	R^2
Timberland	U.S.	0.0031	-0.0821	1.9601*	2.4178	0.1810
		0.0159	0.0761	0.8504		
	U.S. South	0.0026	-0.1170	1.1792*	2.1673	0.2458
		0.0110	0.0525	0.5864		
	U.S. Pacific Northwest	0.0033	-0.0563	3.0081*	2.4639	0.0909
		0.0319	0.1527	1.7072		
	U.S. Northeast	0.0044	-0.0117	1.4509*	2.4017	0.1799
		0.0099	0.0473	0.5287		
Financial Assets	One-month U.S. Treasury Bills	-0.0004	-0.0270*	-0.1662	1.4004	0.1529
		0.0021	0.0102	0.1139		
	Five-Year U.S. Bonds	-0.0037	-0.0181	-2.2319*	3.3571	0.2678
		0.0111	0.0531	0.5940		
	Twenty-Year U.S. Bonds	-0.0039	-0.0106	-3.5865*	3.3853	0.2176
		0.0208	0.0995	1.1119		
	Corporate Bonds	-0.0029	0.0893	-3.4180*	3.2703	0.3277
		0.0171	0.0817	0.9135		
	Small Cap Equities	0.0021	1.2005*	0.2294	2.5854	0.7060
		0.0266	0.1273	1.4225		

Notes: Standard errors of the coefficients are given below the coefficients. An asterisk (*) indicates that the coefficient is different from zero at the 0.10 level of statistical confidence.

E X H I B I T 10–8

Efficient Frontier of a Mixed Asset Portfolio with and without Timberland, 1975 to 2004

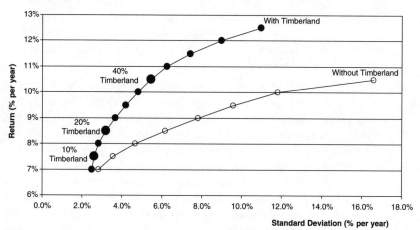

Source: HTRG Research.

Conclusions: Timberland in a mixed-asset portfolio

Timberland has generated strong risk-adjusted real terms, and we expect the asset class to continue to do so. Timberland returns have been poorly correlated with the returns of other assets, and we expect that low correlation to persist. What does this mean for the management of a mixed-asset portfolio?

Given the return parameters for timberland, the answer to this question is reasonably clear: an investor who has no constraints on liquidity should own quite a lot of timberland. Exhibit 10–8 shows the impact of adding timberland to a mixed-asset portfolio. Modest allocations to timberland can produce meaningful improvements in portfolio performance. Large allocations can produce sizable improvements. Most of our investors allocate 1% to 5% of their assets to timberland. Some investors—the Harvard University endowment is a notable example—have almost 10% of their assets in timberland.

HOW DOES TIMBERLAND GENERATE INVESTMENT RETURNS?

How has timberland generated these returns? Evaluating timberland investments does not differ conceptually from the valuation of other kinds of investments: one needs to estimate future costs and revenues and discount the resultant cashflows at the appropriate rate of interest. What differs with timberland investments is how the cashflows arise. For timberland investments, four considerations are especially important:

What is the purchase price? As with most investments, much of the return is locked in once the asset is acquired. Because of the relatively low absolute returns and long holding periods associated with timberland, over-paying can have a dramatically negative impact on investment performance. Good empirical evidence indicates that pricing is more favorable in large transactions than in smaller ones (the "wholesale discount" in timberland markets). Timberland auctions suffer the same "winner's curse" as any auction, so negotiated transactions may offer better returns.

How are the forests managed? Having acquired a property, returns can be enhanced through value-adding management activities. The choice of target products is especially important. For example, in the US south, pulpwood can be grown in 15 to 20 years with the resulting trees being worth perhaps $10/ton. In contrast, adding 5 to 7 years to the harvest age can result in larger volumes of small sawlogs worth perhaps $30/ton. The additional holding period not only results in the unit value increasing by a factor of three, but also of the volume of timber perhaps doubling. The IRR associated with patience is quite high. As another example, fertilizing the trees 5 years before they are harvested can yield exceptional returns. Such management activities, called "silviculture" by foresters, can add material value to a timberland investment.

When are the trees cut? Timber prices fluctuate. These fluctuations give rise to financial risk, but also create option value in timberland. If a manager can systematically cut trees when prices are relatively high, and refrain from cutting when they are low, he/she can add a great deal of return. Trees are relatively cheap to "store on the stump"—if a tree is not cut this year, all that happens is that the tree grows larger and more valuable. Following such a strategy of course requires knowing when prices are "low" or "high." It appears that timber markets are weak-form informationally efficient, at least in the longer term. Astute local foresters may have access to private information on local market conditions and such information can support value-adding decisions on market timing.

What is the exit mechanism? Investors crystallize timberland values in three ways. The first and most obvious is through the ongoing sales of timber. The cash component of timber returns typically amount to one- to two-thirds of the total, but examples outside these ranges frequently occur. Second, many timberland properties contain a modest amount of land that has higher value than can be supported by timber revenues alone. These "higher and better use" (HBU) lands can be sold to create additional cash-flow. Such sales need to be limited in nature or the Internal Revenue Service might deem the seller to be a "dealer" in land, declare the sales "active" income and assess higher taxes. Finally, much of the value of a timberland investment comes when the assets are sold. This is especially true in instances where investors have acquired young properties and have held them as they mature with little intervening cashflow.

The key point is to think of timberland as a financial investment and not as a source of timber supply, as some integrated forest products companies do. Focus on financial returns leads to many sensible value-adding activities. More and more managers are available to deliver these returns.

WHAT SHOULD YOU DO NEXT?

Timberland appears to be an attractive addition to many mixed asset portfolios, whether individual or institutional, public or private, taxable or tax-exempt. The asset class has historically delivered strong real returns with material cash yields. The returns have had essentially no positive correlation with mainstream equity and fixed-income assets, or with such alternatives as commercial real estate, direct energy investments and private equity. Timberland has served as a reasonably strong hedge against inflation, especially against unexpected inflation, and can therefore immunize a portfolio of financial assets against unexpected inflation. Imagining that the investment case is at least interesting, if not compelling, we will conclude with some practical considerations in investing in the asset class.

We believe that there is no substitute for an on-the-ground tour of forestry operations. If a picture is worth a thousand words, seeing an actual operation is worth a million.

Seeing a forestry operation is a particularly good way to understand the risks associated with a timberland investment. These include uncertainty related to future timber prices and harvest volumes, and the vicissitudes of selling timberland properties. They also include such physical risk factors as fires, attacks by insects or diseases, windthrow and ice damage. Our experience is that these physical risks are small, and have averaged only 4 basis points annually across our entire portfolio.

Investment structuring is likely to be important. For tax-exempt investors, avoiding unrelated business taxable income is often critical. There are several ways to do so, including utilizing specialized timber-cutting contracts so forest operations are classified as passive, or investing via structures that serve as *per se* UBTI blockers (e.g., real estate investment trusts or variable annuity contracts). For taxable investors the situation may be more complex depending on whether the objective is GAAP net income or cashflow. Timberland may be a particularly tax-attractive option for a taxable individual. Timber harvested after a 1-year holding period can create income that is taxed at favorable long-term capital-gains rates, and the basis in the timber is returned tax-free as the trees are harvested.

In conclusion, timberland has many desirable investment attributes. The asset class may require more time and effort to understand than many others, and there may be material complications in structuring your timberland investments in a tax-efficient way, but the effort put into this work may be rewarded with superior risk-adjusted returns and a reasonably good hedge against inflation.

REFERENCES

Aronow, M.E., C.L. Washburn, and C.S. Binkley, "Explaining Timberland Values in the United States," *Journal of Forestry*, vol. 102, December 2004, pp. 14–18.

Binkley, C.S., C. Raper, and C.L. Washburn, "Institutional Ownership of US Timberland: History, Rationale, and Implications for Forest Management," *Journal of Forestry*, vol. 94, September 1996, pp. 21–28.

Food and Agriculture Organization of the United Nations (FAO), "Global Forest Resources Assessment 2000," *FAO Forestry Paper 140*, Rome, 2000, 512pp.

Hartzell, D., J.S. Hekman, and M.E. Miles, "Real Estate Returns and Inflation," *AREUEA Journal*, vol. 15, 1989, pp. 617–637.

Hotvedt, J.E., and P.L. Tedder, "Systematic and Unsystematic Risk and Rates of Return Associated with Selected Forest Products Companies," *Southern Journal of Agricultural Economics*, vol. 10, 1978, pp. 135–138.

Redmond, C.H., and F.W. Cubbage, "Risk and Returns from Timber Investments," *Land Economics*, vol. 64, November 1988, pp. 325–337.

Ross, S.A. "The Arbitrage Pricing Theory of Capital Assets Pricing," *Journal of Economic Theory*, vol. 12, 1976, pp. 341–360.

Sun, C., and D. Zhang, "Assessing the Financial Performance of Foresty-Related Investment Vehicles: Capital Asset Pricing Model vs. Arbitrage Pricing Theory," *American Journal of Agricultural Economics*, vol. 83, August 2001, pp. 617–628.

Thomson, T.A. "Evaluating Some Financial Uncertainties of Tree Improvement Using the Capital Asset Pricing Model and Dominant Analysis," *Canadian Journal of Forest Research*, vol. 19, 1989, pp. 1380–1388.

Washburn, C.L., and C.S. Binkley, "Do Forest Assets Hedge Inflation?" *Land Economics*, vol. 69, August 1993, pp. 215–224.

CHAPTER 11

INVESTING IN ENERGY

Sam Oh and Dan Nash
Morgan Stanley Commodities

INTRODUCTION

The purpose of this chapter is to explore a variety of investment options for gaining exposure to energy assets and examine the returns of these options against other benchmarks, including inflation. There are increasingly more investment options available to investors seeking exposure to energy assets, directly and/or indirectly. While many of these investment options have energy as the underlying asset, the returns of some of these options can diverge materially from the returns of energy prices. As a result, finding investment options that are strongly correlated to energy prices is easier said than done.

Part of the problem in assessing an investment's true exposure and hence correlation to energy is trying to establish a proper benchmark. Commodities futures, namely the first nearby contract or "spot" is what is commonly thought of as "commodities prices." It is important to note that commodity futures do not represent direct exposure to the physical commodities themselves. Rather, futures prices are merely the financial market's expectation of energy prices for that period. Futures prices rarely trade beyond 2 to 3 years. Actual physical energy prices may deviate from the financial prices (basis differential), depending on numerous factors such as differences in quality, location, and suitability vs. the financial benchmarks. For example, the benchmark futures contract for crude oil is West Texas Intermediate ("WTI"), which is a crude oil with low sulfur content for delivery in west Texas. A higher sulfur crude for delivery in an off-market location such as California would undoubtedly be sold at a discount to WTI. In addition to the basis differential, energy assets are long-term assets associated with many years of future production. Hence the purchase price of an energy investment can also be thought of as the discounted cashflow of its future stream of income, where the future realized prices of these cashflows will drive the investments correlation, or lack thereof, to other benchmarks. Therefore, measuring an energy investment, a long-term asset, against futures prices, short-term pricing (duration mismatch), can produce misleading results.[1] While many energy investments will

---

1. For example: the annual change in WTI crude oil spot price has been 2.9% since 1983, compared with a return of 17.1% for an unlevered investment in a WTI Index (see Greer, 2000; Nash, 2001). This is particularly relevant since one cannot actually invest in the spot price.

briefly realize spot energy pricing, the realization is only on a small portion of their aggregate cashflows.

Another potential problem in measuring real assets against financial benchmarks is the fact that the financial benchmarks (e.g., futures contracts) do not take into account the logistical consideration of consuming the commodity. Buyers of commodities futures contracts have the option of taking delivery of the physical commodity when the contract expires. Many choose not to take delivery and either roll the financial position to the next contract or simply sell out of the existing position before delivery. So while futures prices may be a reflection of energy prices, futures prices do not consider the implications of actually selling and consuming the product to generate a margin or return. Therefore, futures and financial prices are a useful indicator of energy prices and subsequently energy assets, but by no means should they be considered the same as owning an energy asset.

In analyzing the energy sector, we examined the relationships between investments in different commodities (Direct Energy, commodity indices) and select financial benchmarks. In particular, we considered inflation (produced price index—"PPI"), equities (Standard & Poors 500—"S&P500"), and bond prices (World Government Bond Index—"WGBI"). We found that generally, energy investments tend to exhibit positive correlation with inflation, negative correlation to bond prices, and no correlation to the equity markets (Exhibit 11–1).

There are two ways to make a long-term investment in commodities. The first is through a commodity index which tracks the dynamics of the soon-to-be-delivered futures contracts (see Greer, 2000; Nash, 2001). The other is to invest directly in the physical commodities, sometimes referred to as "direct

E X H I B I T   11–1

Correlations Table

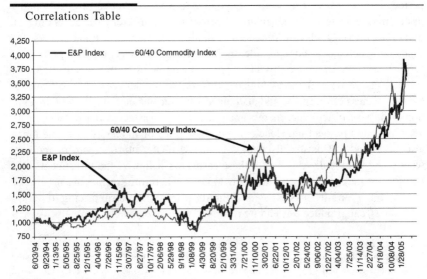

Source: Morgan Stanley Equity Research.

investing." We shall discuss a number of ways to implement the latter with emphasis on the oil and gas industry.

Energy Industry

The energy industry primarily consists of three broad categories: the upstream, midstream, and downstream categories. The upstream sector manages the exploration and production ("E&P") of crude hydrocarbons, where companies drill for new oil and gas reserves (exploration) and extract and gather existing oil and gas (production). The midstream sector manages the transportation and logistics of the oil and gas industry such as pipelines. The downstream sector is comprised of two principal segments. The primary downstream segment handles the transformation of the oil and gas into useful products (refining, chemical, or other manufacturing plants). The secondary downstream segment is the distribution to the customers or commercial end-users of the products. Integrated energy companies (e.g., BP, Chevron Texaco, Exxon Mobil, and Shell) may have all three sectors in their enterprise.

While the broader energy sector encompasses many different types of assets involved in different parts of the value chain, as we briefly described above, this chapter will primarily focus on oil and gas and oil and gas-related investments. Further, we focus on two broad categories of energy investing: (a) public instruments and securities, and (b) private investment options. For public investment options, we examine (i) public equities, (ii) master limited partnerships (MLPs), (iii) US royalty trusts, and (iv) to a lesser extent, Canadian income trusts. For private investment options, we only consider private investment funds such as private equity funds and Direct Energy funds.

Theoretical Direct Energy Portfolio

We constructed a theoretical portfolio of oil and gas investments ("Direct Energy") for two purposes: (1) to use the portfolio to examine theoretical returns and correlations of a direct investment in oil and gas and, (2) to use the portfolio as a benchmark representing physical oil and gas assets. The portfolio was constructed as the present value of a series of future cashflows derived from the production of oil and natural gas, measuring the changes in value of this stream of cashflows through time. Certain costs were ignored such as real estate costs, production costs, taxes, and other operational considerations. These costs can vary significantly and would affect the purchase price of the investment (e.g., whether the investment is cheap or dear with respect to fundamentals). Our aim was to create a simple proxy for direct investing in oil and gas that is economically replicable. To that end we used NYMEX[2] WTI crude oil and natural gas futures prices to model the forward prices for the next 15 years at every date (when futures prices did not exist we

---

2. New York Mercantile Exchange.

carried the furthest ones forward as proxy, correcting for seasonality in natural gas). We further assumed a decline curve of 30% per year, and theoretical leverage of 2:1 debt to equity. Finally we assume a mix of 60% crude oil revenue and 40% gas revenue. In this way we have constructed a very simple investment that, can in theory be realized, and can be analogous to a Direct Energy investment.

PUBLIC INVESTMENT OPTIONS
Public Equities

Still the Most Popular Investment Option

Public equities still remain the deepest and broadest investment option for investors to gain access to the oil and gas sector. Investors can invest in companies that have direct exposure to oil and gas (e.g., E&P companies) or companies that have indirect exposure such as oil services companies. There are many public oil and gas companies giving investors freedom to invest in the various segments of the energy-value chain. These choices also give investors the ability to size their exposure/positions to energy prices and assets. However, in contrast to other public/private investment options that are more directly linked to oil and gas assets and prices, public equities exhibit return characteristics and behavior that can diverge materially from the underlying energy prices. In addition, tax structures of public equities create a source of return leakage vs. other direct investment alternatives.

Valuation Disconnect?

Not surprisingly, public oil and gas equities have exhibited one of the strongest correlations to the broader equity markets relative to the other investment options we consider. The correlations in Table 11–1 suggest that E&P Equities have only a

T A B L E   11–1

Correlation Matrix

	Direct Energy	Royalty Trusts (%)	MLPs (%)	E&P Equities (%)
Direct Energy	NA	55.37	18.47	39.07
60/40 Futures[1]	82.75%	58.68	12.45	60.03
Crude Oil Index[2]	50.09%	47.72	5.75	36.59
Natural Gas Index[3]	34.14%	50.41	17.75	58.95
S&P 500	−1.76%	26.93	35.83	35.34
PPI	28.17%	−4.38	−6.23	3.02
WGBI	−24.43%	−18.92	−8.01	−16.21

[1]Composite of 60% crude oil futures and 40% natural gas futures.
[2]NYMEX WTI futures.
[3]NYMEX Henry Hub futures.

modest correlation to various energy benchmarks. Even when measured against our theoretical energy asset portfolio (Direct Energy, as defined above), E&P Equities were not materially different from its correlation to the other benchmark energy prices. While the underlying asset for these companies is oil and gas, the returns of the equity may not always correlate directly to oil and gas prices. Supply/demand for the underlying commodity will determine the price for that commodity, while supply/demand for the stock will determine the stock price. Obviously, the supply/demand for either of these do not necessarily need to be the same. As Exhibit 11–2 illustrates, over time, public equities and the corresponding oil and gas prices tend to oscillate around each other but are not perfectly correlated.

Several explanations help bridge the disconnect between what is sometimes referred to as "strip vs. street," where the "strip" is the valuation based purely on oil and gas forward prices and "street" is the valuation that the capital markets and research analysts have assigned. At the core, public equities are (first) enterprises with management teams and a growth story, and (second) an oil and gas investment. Closer examination of the various public companies suggests that each has a slightly different business plan and the execution and focus may differ dramatically from company to company. The public equities are complex organizations with an infrastructure in place that is aimed at delivering current production but with an eye towards the longterm. As such, in most cases these enterprises are simply not equipped or positioned to capitalize on every

E X H I B I T   11–2

E&P index vs. 60/40 oil to gas (12-month strip)

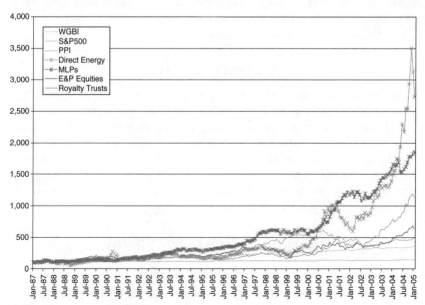

Source: Morgan Stanley Commodities Research.

commodity price move at a moment's notice. Rather, capital allocation decisions take time, are subject to existing supply/demand infrastructure constraints, and must be based on longer-term fundamental views of energy prices. In fact, many companies base their capital allocation decisions on internal price forecasts that in many cases do not even remotely resemble current prices.

Lack of precise information on the underlying oil and gas asset may contribute to a valuation disconnect. Disclosure requirements often to not provide enough visibility on a company's oil and gas assets, such that investors are unable to determine the precise sensitivity that energy prices will have on the company's assets. While lack of disclosure varies from company to company, oil and gas reserve data and/or use of price-risk management (e.g., hedging) tend to be the areas where disclosure is often the weakest.

Lastly, the dynamics of the equity market itself can have a large effect on the company's fundamentals. Note that E&P companies have a 35.34% correlation to the S&P500, which is only slightly less than their 39% correlation to our hypothetical Direct Energy investment.

Saving for a Rainy Day

Newly-lowered tax rates for dividends and capital gains have given corporations added incentives to increase dividends and buy back stock, but public equities tend to reinvest a large portion of their free cashflow in capital projects that are expected to bear fruit down the road. Unlike their pass-through cousins, as discussed below, public equities are largely viewed as growth vehicles and not yield instruments. Public equities have asset and infrastructure configurations that require ongoing development and capital investment not only to prolong, but to allow growth of their current assets. As such, the core driver of energy equities valuation tends to be their growth potential.

Summary Remarks

Energy equities are the broadest and perhaps easiest way for investors to gain exposure to energy assets. These companies have assets and infrastructure configurations that are complex, requiring continuous reinvestment. Generally, these companies are focused on long-term growth with a strong bias towards reinvesting capital based on capital market expectations. As a result the enterprise as a whole is not likely to perfectly track short-term energy prices. Further, given their lack of correlation to energy prices they are also not likely to be strongly correlated to inflation, either positively or negatively.

MASTER LIMITED PARTNERSHIPS
Defined

MLPs, sometimes referred to as publicly-traded partnerships (PTPs), are PTPs with a general partner and one or more limited partners. The general partner (GP) manages the day-to-day operations of the business, while the limited partners

(LP) are typically the investors, who do not participate in the day-to-day operations and are in almost all cases shielded from liability. Currently, the majority of energy-related MLPs are generally engaged in the midstream sector, focusing on wholesale-level transport, storage and/or processing of crude oil, refiner products, natural gas, and natural gas liquids. MLPs are by and large yield-oriented vehicles, paying out the majority of their income to investors/LPs.

Structure

Like public equities, MLPs trade on public exchanges but trade as "units" instead of shares. Instead of paying out dividends, they pay out quarterly "distributions." Similar to real estate investment trusts (REITs) and other "pass-through" vehicles, MLPs distribute all "available cash." Available cash is defined as cash from operations less operating disbursements and reserves, where disbursements include operating expenses, incidental taxes, debt service, maintenance capital expenditures and reserves. Like other pass-through entities, MLPs themselves do not pay taxes (i.e., no corporate-level tax). Rather, the individual investors pay taxes. MLPs essentially pass-through all of their income and expenses, including tax-deductible items such as depreciation and depletion to the unit holders.

Incentive Mechanisms

MLPs are generally formed with incentive structures that allow the GP share in distributions as certain payout targets are met over time as a means of encouraging the GP to increase distributions. In some cases, this incentive structure allows the GP to share in up to 50% of the distributions, even though the GP's economic interest may only be 1% or 2%. Hence, as MLPs mature they begin to creep toward their top income-sharing tier such that the GPs allocation of income asymptotically approaches the percentage of that top tier.

Tax Considerations

Since MLPs are partnerships the partnership itself does not pay taxes, rather the investor pays income taxes on his/her share of the partnership's taxable income. Despite the tax advantages, it is important to note that MLPs are not tax exempt and in most cases merely provide for tax deferral, which is clearly not the same as being tax exempt. Cash distributions to the investor can be treated as a return of basis for tax purposes, and therefore do not show up as income on the investor's income tax return. To the extent that cash distributions exceed the amount of taxable income allocated to the investor (typically the case due to accelerated depreciation for tax purposes vs. book); the difference is tax deferred. The investor will eventually pay tax on the amount of the tax deferral when the units are sold. Depending on the investor's tax situation and the use of tax items such as depreciation, the gain at the time of sale may be ordinary income, capital gain, or a combination of both.

Despite the tax benefits for tax-paying investors, tax-exempt investors face more complicated challenges. The income generated from MLPs usually gives rise to unrelated business taxable income ("UBTI") for tax exempt entities (such as pension funds and endowments). As a result, an otherwise tax-exempt entity will be required to pay tax on investment just as a tax-paying investor would, which also entails filing a tax return.

The tax returns of investors investing in MLPs are further complicated. Sponsors of an MLP will distribute a Form K-1 statement every year to investors. The K-1s provide details on the relevant tax items, enabling investors to file their taxes with the requisite partnership tax information. To the extent that a MLP is conducting business in multiple states, which is typical, depending on the state tax laws, investors may be required to file taxes in that state. It is incumbent on the individual partners to incorporate the information from their K-1s into their tax returns. As a result, two investors with identical investments in a MLP may have different tax results of the investment, based on their specific tax situation.

Hurdles for Institutional Investors

A limiting factor to MLP ownership has been the "qualifying income" test for regulated investment companies (mutual funds). Under Internal Revenue Code Section 851, regulated investment companies must derive 90% of their income from so-called "qualifying sources" which include interest and dividends. Distributions from MLPs while not explicitly excluded are not explicitly included, but recently in October 2004, H.R. 4520—the American Jobs Creation Act—was passed into law. While this did not completely remove the hurdles to institutional ownership of MLPs, it did provide some guidance for limited institutional partici- pation. Effectively the new law states that regulated investment companies cannot have more than 25% of its holdings in PTP securities, and may not own more than 10% of any one partnership. For this reason, as well as other tax considerations discussed above, many institutional investors have shied away from MLPs.

MLP Returns

As described above, MLPs offer a unique tax advantage to taxable investors relative to public equities. The absence of a corporate level tax creates a significant advan- tage that can, over time, result in material return enhancement to the investor. Investors have generally been attracted to MLPs due to the tax-advantaged nature of their recurring distributions and view MLPs largely as yield oriented investments. As Exhibit 11–3 demonstrates, since 1987 MLPs (with the exception of Direct Energy) have significantly outperformed the broader equity index and the other assets classes on a total return basis. The strong MLP performance can be attributed in large part to the absence of corporate level taxes and to the nature of their disciplined commit- ment to distributions. The compounding of distributions over time creates a very compelling return scenario. However, MLPs are largely seen as yield-oriented investment options. As a result, MLPs can be very sensitive to interest rates.

EXHIBIT 11–3

Total Returns

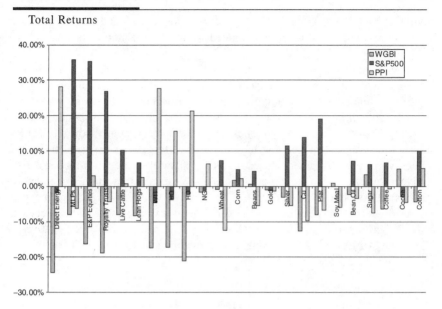

MLPs and Energy Exposure

The vast majority of MLPs are focused on the midstream and downstream sector. Structurally, MLPs are ideally suited investment vehicles for investors looking to gain access to energy. The lack of corporate-level taxes and the requirement for distributions of free cash give investors direct exposure to the underlying asset and its corresponding profitability. However, the actual amount of energy exposure may be minimal, depending on the actual assets of the MLP. Currently, many MLPs claim to be insulated from energy prices and tout themselves as yield-oriented investments. In fact for some cases this is true, where the source of earnings is largely fee-driven, irrespective of energy prices. However, to say that all MLPs are completely insulated from energy prices would be inaccurate. In certain instances, energy prices will drive throughput and volumes on a given MLP's infrastructure. High energy prices can, in some situations, lead to greater throughput on an MLP's system as producers ratchet up production to get their product to market and realize the higher prices. High prices can also influence certain economic and processing decisions for MLPs that have processing infrastructures. Table 11–1 suggests that correlation between MLPs and energy prices is relatively small. While the fundamental argument we have described above suggests it may be stronger, perhaps one explanation for the weak correlation is that the equity markets have not fully appreciated the commodity price risk. In addition, MLPs are a relatively new investment option and our historical sample may have been too short.

Summary Remarks

Not surprisingly, MLPs exhibit a strong correlation to the broader equity markets which are comparable to those exhibited by the E&P Equities in Table 11–1. While MLPs are largely viewed as yield investments, their correlation to the broader equity indexes can in part be explained by their explicit desire for growth of this yield. As a result of a favorable GP profit-sharing mechanism, GPs of MLPs are highly motivated to grow yield. The growth in yield explains why some of the MLPs have growth expectations built into their valuations. At the end of the day, the MLP units are still equity and not debt. Although currently MLPs have structural advantages that lend themselves to gaining exposure to Direct Energy, currently the assets of existing MLPs themselves are typically one derivative away from the actual oil and gas assets. That said, they are not completely insulated from energy prices and perhaps provide an indirect way to gain exposure to energy. Despite the lack of pure energy exposure, MLPs have been a strong performer against the other investment alternatives. However, relative to inflation, MLPs exhibit weak benefits in providing a hedge against inflation.

ROYALTY TRUSTS (UNITED STATES)

Defined

In the United States, investments in royalty trusts provide investors with a direct interest in specified oil and gas properties without actually operating the asset and with no personal liability. The actual interest underlying a royalty trust is technically referred to as an overriding royalty interests (ORRIs). Therefore, royalty trusts are a form of ORRIs that trade publicly, providing investors with a direct interest in specified oil and gas properties. Like an MLP that has an operating partner (general partner) and a passive partner (limited partner), oil and gas properties subject to an ORRI are also bifurcated between an operating partner (commonly referred to as the working interest owner) and passive partner (in this case the owner of the ORRI). Since royalty trusts are interests in real property, owners of the royalty trust should bear no bankruptcy risk with respect to the working interest owner (e.g., royalty trust interest will survive bankruptcy of the working interest owner and continue to burden the oil and gas property out of bankruptcy).

Basic Structure

Royalty trusts are created when the owner/sponsor of a "working interest" sells an ORRI in oil and gas properties to a trust. Units in the trust are then sold to the public in a public offering. There are many different forms of ORRIs, entitling the owner of an ORRI an interest in oil and gas properties. One of the more common forms of royalty trust ORRIs are net profit interests (NPIs), where the interest is defined as actual profits or net cashflow, thereby giving the ORRI holder net proceeds from the sale of hydrocarbon production. Other forms of ORRIs are volumetric production payments (VPPs) which entitle the acquirer of a VPP to a specified volume of hydrocarbons. However, VPPs are not commonly found in royalty trusts. ORRIs are generally considered undivided interests in real property, giving the owner direct title to the underlying asset. In comparison to MLPs, royalty trusts are somewhat simpler, with several royalty trusts currently available to the public. However, royalty trusts tend to be much smaller than MLPs, making liquidity and size an issue.

Additional Considerations

There are some factors that complicate a royalty trust. The sale of a royalty trust will generally be a taxable event to the sponsor, where taxes are to be paid on the selling/offering price less the tax basis of the asset which is likely to be lower than the selling price due to tax deductions. The sponsor is also faced with the complicated task of determining the net profits interest formula which will have a direct impact on the selling/offering price of the royalty trust. A royalty trust, because it must be a fixed-investment trust for federal income tax purposes, does not offer the flexibility of adding properties to the structure following its formation. Therefore, royalty trusts are fixed and depleting investments such that their distributions include both return on and return of capital with no hedging or leverage. With regards to UBTI, royalty trusts are treated as either royalty income or interest income, neither of which is subject to UBTI. As a result, tax-exempt entities (pension fund and endowments) can invest in royalty trusts with no adverse consequences, unlike investing in MLPs (mentioned above). One challenge that investors will face is whether they have the technical sophistication to value the underlying oil and gas properties.

Old Kid on the New Block

Royalty trusts, perhaps offer one of the purest form of Direct-Energy investment. Owners of a royalty trust receive distributions that are based solely on the profitability of the underlying oil and gas reserves. Unlike public equities, royalty trusts are not companies and therefore valuation elements such as the "equity story" and "growth story" do not typically play a part in their underlying valuation. While royalty trusts share similar pass-through benefits like MLPs (e.g., no corporate- or entity-level income tax), their similarities stop there. Royalty trusts generally do not have an ability to be leveraged, nor are they structurally equipped to handle acquisitions of other oil and gas interests. Royalty trusts are based on specific oil and gas leases or acreage. Acquiring additional interests would potentially require the formation of another royalty trust. MLPs on the other hand, are actual companies that can be levered and can acquire assets on an ongoing basis. In fact, MLPs in many cases require continuous acquisition of assets to sustain growth in distributions.

Summary Remarks

The correlations between royalty trusts and the energy benchmarks are very robust (Table 11–1), particularly its correlation with Direct Energy. This result comes as no surprise given that, structurally, royalty trusts are in essence discreet pools of assets. However, while they exhibit some negative correlation to bonds (WGBI), their correlation to inflation (PPI) is less than robust. As with the E&P Equities and MLPs, the royalty trust's ability to act as a hedge against inflation is minimal. Part of the explanation lies in the fact that all of the public investment options have meaningful correlations to the equity markets, which may minimize their ability to hedge inflation.

CANADIAN INCOME & ROYALTY TRUSTS
Defined

For one of the more interesting structures on the market, one need only look to the north—Canada. Proliferation and popularity of the Canadian income and royalty trusts—not to be confused with their American royalty trust cousin—has been remarkable. The Canadian income trust concept essentially interposes a tax-exempt/pass-through entity (the income trust) in between public investors (unithold-ers) and an operating corporation that would normally be subject to corporate level taxes. Income trusts are mutual fund trusts for Canadian tax purposes, and hence generally not subject to corporate-level taxes. Further, the income trust owns both the equity and debt of the operating corporation. Therefore, the unitholders of the income trust are indirect owners of both equity and debt at the same time. In essence, the income trust is merely a financing entity for the underlying corporation.

In the case of the Canadian royalty trust, the operating corporation owns oil and gas properties or royalties interests. The royalty trust ends up owning a roy-alty interest (typically a net profits interest) conveyed to it by the operating cor-poration and burdening the corporation's properties which is only taxable at the unitholder level.

Like their American cousins, the MLPs and the royalty trusts, Canadian income/royalty trusts are essentially tax advantaged yield products which offer unitholders regular cashflows. With regards to the Canadian income trusts, the structure gives the operating corporation access to relatively inexpensive equity capital in a tax-advantaged format. The overall tax savings are principally generated in two forms; (1) the income trust is not subject to corporate-level taxes, and (2) the underlying corporation will typically employ a significant amount of leverage which is owned by the income trust, where the interest expense is tax-deductible to the corporation. As such, the corporation enjoys certain benefits of the corporate form such as limited liability, while simultaneously enjoying the benefits of a pass-through entity by substantially deferring or eliminating tax through the use of high-yield debt. Further, to the extent that the investors in the income trust are tax-exempt entities, such as pension plans and deferred-income plans, the income distributed by the income trust is tax deferred. To the extent investors in the income trust are tax-paying persons, the income distributed is tax-deferred to the extent that the "yield" is characterized as return *of* capital rather than return *on* capital.

With regards to Canadian royalty trusts, they are merely more flexible versions of their US cousins. The operating corporation that is interposed between the trust and the assets allows the structure to be more acquisitive than the US royalty trusts. The operating corporation typically carves up the oil and gas assets into a 99% royalty (net profits) interest which it conveys to the trust, and a 1% operating (working) interest retained by the corporation. Income from the royalty interests are only taxable at the unitholder level since the trust is generally not a taxable entity. The working interest that remains at the operating company is typically small enough that corporation itself can minimize the taxes from such interest through the deduction of other expenses. Therefore, the Canadian royalty trust is in essence a hybrid of a MLP, and US royalty trust in that, like a MLP it has the ability to make ongoing acquisitions, but utilizes royalty interests as the underlying oil and gas interest. Further, it is a pass-through entity and hence taxes are paid only at the unitholder level.

Income Trust—Elegant Paradox?

Perhaps the most interesting element of the Canadian income trust structure is that fact that the unitholders of the income trust indirectly own both the equity and debt of the underlying corporate entity. In more conventional corporate structures the equity holders are different from the debt holders, at times creating divergent interests.

Debt holders are typically the collateral owners of a leveraged corporation, while the equity holders are the economic owners of the company. As a result, debt holders will typically be more focused on the preservation of their collateral, while equity holders will be more focused on the economic upside. To the extent that the equity and debt holders are the same person(s) the interests become aligned, effectively collapsing the units into one. The net effect of this is to synthetically convert a taxable corporation into a pass-through entity but results in tax risk that the debt will be treated as equity such that the payments denominated as "interest" will not be deductible and the structure loses its tax advantage.

Summary Remarks

While we have not included Canadian Income/Royalty trusts in our quantitative analysis (below), we preliminary conclude that their return and correlation profiles would be similar to those of MLPs and US royalty trusts.

PRIVATE INVESTMENT OPTIONS
Private Investment Vehicles

For most investors, owning oil and gas reserves directly, or any other energy asset for that matter, is generally too complicated or simply not feasible. Direct Energy assets requires some ability to extract the hydrocarbons and sell them. Additionally, energy assets can be extremely complicated to operate and manage. Therefore, private investment vehicles such as private equity funds and Direct Energy funds are the most popular routes for investment.

Private Equity

Fueled by investor demand and increased investment opportunities, energy-oriented private equity funds and general private equity funds with energy expertise have enjoyed a successful run. Energy investments within private equity funds share some characteristics with public equities. It is no coincidence that energy investments (portfolio companies) within a private equity fund are generally structured as corporate entities with management teams, since private equity funds often look to the public markets as an exit strategy for their investments through an initial pubic offering. As such, many of the portfolio companies will exhibit characteristics of their already-public equities and therefore tend to be valued on longer-term fundamentals, rather than near-term energy pricing. Similar to public equities where companies with compelling growth stories command higher premiums, investors in private equity funds are relying on the general partner's ability to create value (alpha generation) to augment returns. As a result, the primary driver of returns will be the manager's alpha, leaving energy prices to play a secondary role.

Direct Energy Funds/Private Partnerships

Direct Energy funds and private partnerships are growing in popularity. As a proxy for investing directly in energy, we created the theoretical portfolio described previously—Direct Energy investment. Such investment entities are in many ways the private equivalent of MLPs, where the entity aims to acquire and operate energy assets directly, without employing a management team between the investment entity and the asset. These entities generally structure investments as partnerships, thereby avoiding corporate-level tax. Of all the investment alternatives presented in this chapter, Direct Energy funds/private partnerships are the most direct way to invest in oil and gas. They are generally tax-efficient, not subject to the vagaries of the capital markets and have finite lives, which forces a more disciplined capital allocation.

Shortcomings of Private Investments

While top-tier private equity and Direct Energy funds have performed exceptionally well and often benefit from a focused strategy, there are some shortcomings. Through the use of "lock-ups," fund managers are able to secure capital over a long period of time. Lock-ups essentially mean that the funds do not provide ready liquidity for investors to move in and out of funds. Although lock-ups allow managers to remain focused on the longterm, investors must rely upon more liquid investments to reallocate their portfolios. A fund's actual deployment of capital (e.g., investing) can take years. Funds typically have an investment period during which they can invest the committed capital. It is highly unusual for a fund to be fully investing within a year. Therefore commitment to a fund does not necessarily mean that all the capital will be deployed immediately.

Summary Remarks

Since data on private investment options is limited, our theoretical oil and gas port-folio (Direct Energy) serves as our proxy for private investments. The actual per-formance of a private investment is likely to be materially different to the results of our theoretical portfolio. Some of the reasons for this discrepancy may include: free cashflow used to fund capital expenditures, funds/partnerships themselves may have limited oil and gas investments, manager alpha or lack thereof, timing of investments and ability to buy low and sell high, and actual operating and produc-tion costs. However, to the extent that private investment options do not suffer from these discrepancies or at least are minimally impacted by these factors, the private investment options deliver some very positive results. The results for Direct Energy show strong total returns compared to the other investment options, with significant positive correlation to inflation (PPI) and negative correlation to bonds (WGBI).

HEDGING AND PRICE-RISK MANAGEMENT

Hedging forward oil and gas prices can be employed by negotiating marketing agreements with fixed prices and/or through the use of financial derivatives and futures. One of the unique characteristics of energy investing is the availability of a financial market where energy prices can be risk-managed. In fact, hedging is widely used among public equities, MLPs, private equity funds, and Direct Energy funds with the only exception being royalty trusts. Therefore, to the extent an entity hedges, the impact of energy prices will be muted. Hedging may also explain the lack of correlation that some "energy investments" have to energy prices.

Nevertheless, uncovering what an entity has hedged can be challenging. Disclosure on a company's hedge position(s) may not be completely transparent. Some hedging is done at the physical level and may not show up in financial statements. For private investments, this information may be even harder to obtain. Therefore, since information is not completely transparent, investors should be cautioned about synthetically trying to create absolute return positions by buying long positions in energy instruments and selling forward energy prices.

CONCLUSION
Summary Findings

Exploring the various investment options for energy, we find that public invest-ment options have very little correlation to inflation (PPI), some modest negative correlation to bonds (WGBI) and a higher correlation to the equity markets (S&P500). WTI crude oil futures and Direct Energy exhibited the strongest cor-relations to inflation. While investors have several different options to invest in energy through a handful of private and public options, each have their pros and cons. The public investment options offer investors liquidity but must sacrifice correlations to energy. Private investment options, on the other hand, have the reverse problem, they are likely to have better correlations, but less liquidity.

Investing in Energy

Energy investing is becoming an increasingly important component of any diversified investment portfolio. Direct Energy investments can offer potentially significant diversification benefits, and should be considered when constructing a long-term asset allocation policy (Chen and Pinsky). Institutional investors have been increasing their allocations to energy but still face a few hurdles and must make key decisions to invest appropriately. Investing directly in energy and MLPs create potential tax issues for tax-exempt investors where UBTI is generated from the investment which would require the tax-exempt investor to pay taxes and file tax returns. The energy asset class is still relatively small in comparison to other asset classes such as real estate. For larger institutional investors, finding quality energy investment options in size can be challenging. Given the complexity of the energy sector, investors must decide: (i) how much energy exposure they want, (ii) how much risk they want, and (iii) what point in the energy value chain best meets their investment objectives. For example, even within the oil and gas sector there exists a wide range of investment options with varying degrees of risk. On the most risky side of the spectrum are exploration-oriented companies and on the other end are production-oriented companies. While both may offer exposure to oil and gas, the amount of risk they offer varies substantially. Once the decision is made concerning where in the value chain the investor wants to invest, the manager/management selection can be made. By concentrating on what part of the value chain and how much risk an investor wants to take, the selection of a manager/management is made much easier.

SOURCES AND CONTRIBUTORS

Chen, Peng and Pinsky, Joe—Invest in Direct Energy, February 2002
Factset
Byrne, Lloyd, Managing Director, Morgan Stanley Equity Research
Greer, Robert J. (2000), "The Nature of Commodity Index Returns," Journal of Alternative Investments 3 (1), pp. 45–52
Helios Capital Management LLC
Miller, Barry, Partner, Vinson & Elkins
Nash, Daniel J. (2001) "Long-term Investing in Commodities," Global Pensions Quarterly, Morgan Stanley Global Pensions Group 4, (1) 25–31
Shapiro, John, Managing Director, Morgan Stanley
Terreson, Doug, Managing Director, Morgan Stanley Equity Research

INDICES

Master Limited Partner Index: Alliance Resource Partners L.P., Amerigas Partners L.P., Buckeye Partners L.P., Enbridge Energy Partners L.P., Enterprise Products Partners L.P., Ferrellgas Partners L.P., Kaneb Pipe Line Partners L.P., Kinder Morgan Energy Partners L.P.

Magellan Midstream Partners L.P., Natural Resource Partners L.P., Northern Border Partners L.P., Pacific Energy Partners L.P., Plains All American Pipeline L.P., Suburban Propane Partners L.P., Sunoco Logistics Partners L.P., TC PipeLines L.P., TEPPCO Partners L.P., Valero L.P.

Public E&P Index: Apache Corp., Anadarko Petroleum Corp., Burlington Resources Inc., Devon Energy Corp., EOG Resources Inc., Kerr-McGee Corp., Unocal Corp., Noble Energy Inc., Forest Oil Corp., Pogo Producing Co., Pioneer Natural Resources Co., XTO Energy Inc., Chesapeake Energy Corp., Comstock Resources Inc., Cabot Oil & Gas Corp., Houston Exploration Co., Swift Energy Co., Ultra Petroleum Corp., Canadian Natural Resources Ltd.

EnCana Corp., Nexen Inc., Penn West Petroleum Ltd., Talisman Energy Inc., Suncor Energy Inc.

Royalty Trust Index: BP Prudhoe Bay, Hugoton, Dominion Black Warrior, Torch Energy, Burlington Coal Seam, Eastern American, Williams Coal Seam, Santa Fe Energy, Crosstimbers

CHAPTER 12

ALTERNATIVE ASSET ALLOCATION FOR REAL RETURN

Robert D. Arnott
Research Affiiliates, LLC

Robert J. Greer[1]
PIMCO

INTRODUCTION

We are all social creatures, to one extent or another. We are happy when people we respect agree with us and concerned if they do not. We remember recent successes fondly and recent failures with dismay and perhaps embarrassment—if we remember them at all. This has direct consequences for the ways in which we succeed or fail in our investments.

This chapter will discuss how recent successes in the stock and bond markets (over the last quarter-century) shape our expectations for the future. We will discuss why that view of the investment future must change if we want to achieve solid inflation-adjusted returns that will meet our liabilities. Those changes in attitude require that we lower our expectations of future returns from traditional stocks and bonds. We must also more actively consider including alternative investments in our portfolios. And, in a world of expected low returns, we must seek alpha wherever we can. This includes alpha from active management of the securities in a particular portfolio and from actively managing the mix of asset classes in our portfolios. We conclude with a hopeful suggestion that, if we think broadly, boldly, and actively, it may still be possible to achieve real rates of return that satisfy our sensible portfolio return goals.

THE PAST

During the 1980s and 1990s, with some pauses along the way, we experienced a relentless bull market, the largest in the history of US capital markets. Between 1989 and 2001, the US equity market (S&P 500) generated annualized returns of 13.6%. By comparison, the US equity market produced annualized returns of 8.2% over the 1802 to 2001 time period.[2] Bonds also posted remarkable gains

---

1. We gratefully acknowledge the considerable help of Robert Huntsman, and the suggestions of Jason Hsu, of Research Affiliates LLC. Parts of this chapter were also drawn from selected Editor's Corners, in the Financial Analysts Journal, authored by Rob Arnott during 2003 and 2004.
2. Combination of data from Shiller and Schwert.

during the bull market of the 1980s and 1990s. Between 1989 and 2001, the Lehman Aggregate Index increased 8.6% per year.

The bull market of the 1980s and 1990s allowed us to embrace the illusion that a typical portfolio can sustain 5% spending as a "conservative" choice, but the lofty real returns during these decades benefited considerably from revaluation, not from the sustainable components of return, which are income and growth. For foundations, which typically have no source of supplementary contributions, this means that the foundation ultimately might not earn the 5% real return required to maintain the real value of the corpus of the foundation portfolio. The consequence is that most foundations, while enjoying a very long lifespan, may not produce returns in perpetuity, and so may not serve the goals of the founder forever.

None of this can be comforting to those who would like to rely on lofty return assumptions to justify hefty spending or skinny contributions. It is far better to plan for the future on assumptions that are sound, rather than relying on hope as our strategy for the future. The same applies for the individual investors planning for their future retirement: working a few extra years to "contribute" more to our retirement reserves is better than running out when we can least afford it, as a consequence of foolish or unrealistic assumptions.

FORECASTING THE FUTURE BY EXTRAPOLATING THE PAST

All too often, we forecast the future through extrapolation, arguably the worst way to forecast. If bond yields fall from 8% to 4%, and the bonds thereby deliver a 15% annualized return, should we assume 15% as a future bond return? Of course not! The capital gains that push our 8% yield up to a 15% return are non-recurring. Should we "conservatively" assume continued capital gains of 7% per annum on top of our new 4% yield? Of course not! Should we be "even more conservative," assuming just the 8% yield we started with? This is still far too optimistic, as any bond investor knows full-well. Yet, much of our industry is wedded to forecasting *equity* returns in this fashion—with assistance from assorted academic luminaries.

Returns are, for the most part, a function of simple arithmetic. For almost any investment, our total return consists of yield, growth, and multiple expansion or yield change. For bonds, the growth is simple: fixed income implies zero growth of capital and income. For high-yield or emerging-markets debt, capital and income growth is negative, due to the occasional defaults. For stocks, capital and income growth tends to be around 1% above inflation, based on very long-term history.

The 7% real stock market returns for the past 78 years covered in the Ibbotson data consist of roughly 4.3% from dividend yield, plus a bit over 1% each from real dividend growth and from multiple expansion. So, why can we not expect 7% in the future? That is simple—we cannot rely on multiple expansion, since the market is not cheap by any conventional definition. Most observers would, at a minimum, subtract multiple expansion from future-return expectations. Now we are down to roughly 5.5%, but our current dividend yield is just 1.9%, not 4.3%, which takes our real return down to around 3%. And, that is without any "mean reversion" towards historical valuation levels. *Much of our industry seems fearful of this simple arithmetic, preferring to forecast the future by extrapolating the past.*

Why is a low (even negative) expected excess return considered shocking? There is no reason, outside of the illusionary world of financial theory, to believe that a temporary negative expected excess return should be impossible. Financial theory suggests that this should not be possible (*if* investors are rational, *if* there are no taxes, *if* utility functions flatten with increasing wealth, and so forth). However, financial theory would also demand that lotteries and casinos should have no customers.

Should there be a positive equity risk premium relative to bonds? Of course. Is it written into contract law for any assets we buy that at the current price levels we would receive return commensurate with investment risk? Of course not. Yet, the notion of a negative risk premium seems downright scandalous to our industry.

In the long run, the market must adjust to provide a positive risk premium. Otherwise, why buy the riskier asset for a lower return? Nevertheless, the adjustment to a positive risk premium can be painful. A 5% risk premium is often taken as fact, but it is only a hypothesis, and often an ill-reasoned one. If we take a 5% risk premium as a fact, rather than as a hypothesis, this shortcut frees us to focus on asset selection, since we have now dispensed with the risk premium and, by extension, the resulting asset mix decision.

Even the most aggressive intellectually-honest forecasts of long-term earnings or dividends growth would see GDP growth as an upper bound. GDP growth has two engines: the growth of existing enterprises and the creation of new enterprises through entrepreneurial capitalism. Our stock market investments allow us to participate in the former but not the latter. Since over half of real GDP growth comes from entrepreneurial capitalism, real earnings and dividends from existing stocks should collectively grow a little under half the rate of economic growth.

Surprisingly, consensus long-term earnings growth estimates routinely exceed sustainable GDP growth. The current consensus growth rate for earnings on the S&P 500, according to the 2005 Zacks survey, is 10%. This corresponds to 7% to 8% real growth, assuming the consensus inflation expectation of 2% to 3%. Real earnings growth of 8% is six times the real earnings growth of the past century, and three times the consensus long-term GDP growth rate. This is not possible, unless either GDP growth quadruples or stock buybacks exceed new share issuance by an unprecedented margin. Otherwise, aggregate earnings would eventually exceed our GDP.

GDP growth, less the economic dilution associated with entrepreneurial capitalism, basically defines the sustainable growth in per-share earnings and dividends. Accordingly, it is hard to imagine that, at the top of the bubble in late-1999 and early-2000, stocks offered a positive risk premium, when dividend yields were a scant 1.1%, far lower than the over-4% yield on inflation-indexed government-guaranteed bonds (TIPS).[3] The earnings and dividends for stocks

---

3. Treasury Inflation-Protected Securities, the US government's inflation-indexed bonds.

would have needed to grow 3.3% per annum above the rate of inflation (triple the real growth rate of the prior century) in order for stocks to merely *match* the total return of TIPS. Was the market priced to produce a positive risk premium for broad stock market averages, relative to TIPS, at the beginning of 2000? History since 2000 has shown otherwise.

Many market observers would agree that the "cult of equities," the reliance on a 5% risk premium, was the single most damaging error in the institutional investing community in the past quarter-century. Should not our industry, as a matter of course, question aggressive, unsustainable growth forecasts before acting on them?

Closely related, why do we accept rising return expectations in a rising market? In 1982, the average pension return assumption was barely 6%. This was at a time when stock yields were 5% and both the earnings yield for stocks (the reciprocal of the price/earnings ratio) and bond yields were in the low teens. By the year 2000, the average pension return assumption had risen to approximately 9.5%, even though stock dividend yields and bond yields were down nearly 400 basis points and 800 basis points, respectively. Since then markets have fallen, and we are seeing pension return assumptions drifting *downward* again.

If we see bond yields fall 800 basis points, fueling substantial capital gains on top of a substantial initial yield, do we assume that the future returns will be better because the bonds exceeded expectations? No, we will be grateful for the returns of the past and we will expect less, not more, in the future. Why cannot we use the same logic in equities and other asset classes?

WEALTH AND SUSTAINABLE SPENDING

What spending can our portfolios sustain? Many of the recent problems in the newly-underfunded pension, endowment and foundation world stem from: (1) return expectations that are unrealistic, and (2) a desire to spend more than market returns can support. A "need" for a particular rate of return, or a "hope" for performance that can sustain outsized spending, does not allow us to *expect* that return.

How do we define wealth? Is it the size of our portfolio? No, a century ago, a $1-million portfolio was huge; today assuredly it is not. Is wealth defined as the real (inflation-adjusted) value of our portfolio? Not really, spending needs change and the real returns that our portfolio can sustain will change over time. Even though the CPI has risen 20-fold over the past century, a $20-million portfolio will not sustain the level of real spending that a $1-million portfolio could sustain a century ago. Real yields are lower.

A better, albeit still imperfect, definition of wealth is the real spending that our portfolio can sustain, over the span that the portfolio is intended to serve. An 80-year-old with $1 million is far wealthier than a 40-year-old with $1 million. A $1-billion pension fund can sustain larger payouts than a $1-billion endowment or foundation, due to the finite life of pensioners (hence of current pension obligations).

Our industry pays scant attention to the concept of "sustainable spending," which is key to effective strategic planning for corporate pensions, public pensions, foundations, endowments and even for individuals. *Sustainable spending typically starts with sustaining the real value of the assets.* This requires realistic return assumptions. We need to know how much we can spend on a near-risk-free basis, in order to know how much of our intended spending comes from wishful thinking—from hope. This exercise sets the stage for a reasoned, risk-controlled quest for the incremental returns that we "hope" to achieve. Financial theory has paid this whole subject little heed.

"Sustainable spending" is not a fixed rate on assets. It changes as real yields change. Most foundations and endowments have used a 5% or 6% spending rule for many years. The capital markets have sometimes been priced to make this an easy goal, and sometimes (e.g., in recent years) a very difficult goal. For the same reasons, pensions cannot hope to duplicate the 1990s experience of replacing pension contributions with pension fund returns.

In recent years, many otherwise-sophisticated institutional investors have taken the view that they "need" a higher rate of return than the return that is assuredly available in the lowest-risk strategies (long, laddered treasury bonds for most pension funds, or long, laddered TIPS portfolios for endowments and foundations), and therefore "need" more in risky assets in order to earn their risk premium. It is a truism that one cannot earn a lofty return *or incur miserable losses* without above-average risk. It is very dangerous, however, to assume that higher risk will reliably lead to higher returns.

If we cannot be assured of a substantial risk premium, is not it better to commit to a spending stream that we can *reliably* earn, boosting our spending only as future happy surprises increase our sustainable spending? Of course, this option is not available for foundations which must spend 5% each year, or lose their tax exemption. Alternatively, if we choose to spend more than our sustainable, should we not at least acknowledge that we are spending future investment returns—that we may or may not earn?

For example, if we can assuredly earn a real return of 2% and want to spend 5%, then we need to find an incremental 3%. This must come from: (1) a risk premium earned on our selected departures from our risk-minimizing portfolio, (2) an alpha from our superior choice of investment managers and strategies, or (3) additional contributions to our asset base.

Today, the average corporate pension fund is using a *pension return assumption* of roughly 8.5% in their earnings statement, and the average public fund is using a discount rate of 7.5% to 8%. With the bond markets currently yielding about 4%, and with most funds having about 30% to 40% in mainstream bonds, this means that most sponsors are expecting to earn at least 10% on their nonbond assets—a 6% increment over bonds—either from the equity risk premium or from alpha.

It is the conventional view that there is a large risk premium for equities and other risky assets. So, many sponsors expect to make up some of the difference with riskier assets, but the current risk premium *cannot* be assessed by looking at past excess returns. This would lead us to boost our expectations at market tops and lower them at market bottoms. Instead, we should examine the building blocks of return. As we have already demonstrated, from current market levels, we do not find a large risk premium in most of the markets that we typically rely upon for this extra return.

THE ROLE OF INFLATION

At the same time that current market levels are not priced to produce large risk premiums, rising inflation threatens to reduce the real returns actually available. During the bull market of the 1980s and 1990s, inflation declined, while equity and fixed income returns increased. From 1929 to 1989, 43% of the total US equity market return was a result of inflation. From 1989 to 2001, only 20% of the annualized return of the US equity market was attributable to inflation. With nominal yields far lower today than in recent decades, real returns will decline if inflation rises, which may well happen in the years ahead.

For the long-term investor, return expectations of 8% and 9% cannot be achieved in a world of stock yields below 2% and bond yields of 4%. If the intended spending rises with inflation, as it often does, then sustainable spending falls well short of 5%, if there are no contributions to the portfolio. In this environment, we must think creatively to meet our investment needs. We must look beyond traditional stocks and bonds to alternative asset classes that can be priced to offer better returns. We must actively manage our asset mix, including alternative assets in our decisions. Finally, and within each asset class, we must actively manage individual securities to seek those that are out of favor and priced for better returns. Pursuing these steps in parallel can improve our outlook for real inflation-adjusted returns.

THE OUTLOOK FOR STOCKS AND BONDS

The current outlook for bond and equity markets reveals why investors must look beyond traditional stocks and bonds for real returns. Returns are generated by three components: income (dividends), growth in income (dividend growth) and valuation expansion (P/E increases), or the price that the market is willing to pay for the income generated by an asset. Examination of these three components of returns for the US equity market reveals that the market is in the midst of a "perfect storm" as shown in Exhibit 12–1. A combination of high valuations (i.e., P/E ratios), low quality earnings, and a low risk premium create the possibility of lower equity returns going forward.

The first element of our "perfect storm" is earnings quality. In 2000, the S&P 500 reported a then-all-time-peak of $54 in earnings. While that peak was exceeded in 2004, it remains the all-time-high in real, inflation-adjusted terms. How real was the $54 in reported earnings? Hypothetically, if corporate pension-return assumptions had been set at 6%—a yield that was then available in the bond market to defease the long-term pension liabilities—instead of the

E X H I B I T   12–1

Quality of Equity Earnings

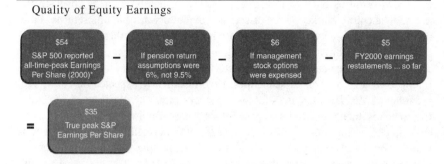

9.6% reported, the earnings figure would have been reduced by $8. Reported earnings would have dropped by another $6 if, hypothetically, management stock options had been expensed. In addition, as of early 2005, earnings restatements for FY 2000 have resulted in a $5 reduction to reported earnings. In other words, the true peak earnings for FY 2000 were closer to $35, rather than the $54 actually reported to Wall Street by Standard and Poor.

Not only are earnings overstated but the price assigned to overstated earnings numbers is well above historical levels and so may well decline. Exhibit 12–2 shows that, as P/E ratios return to within one standard deviation of their historical level after a boom, several or more years of compression in price/earnings ratios have typically followed.

Past is not prologue. Three previous secular bear markets, following a secular bull market peak, does not mean that we must assuredly repeat this pattern, but it is dangerously naïve to suggest that this cannot happen. And, it is equally

E X H I B I T   12–2

Historical P/E Ratios

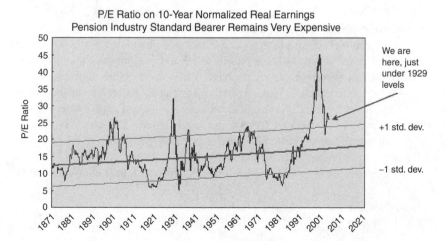

dangerous and equally naïve to suggest that one nasty bear market, which served merely to bring us back to historical *peak* levels, has brought us "back to the races." The equity markets seem priced to provide forward-looking returns below historical norms—even if current valuation levels hold and there is no reversion back towards historical "normal" valuation levels.

The third element of the "perfect storm" is the decline of the equity risk premium. Investors, as well as academics, have historically expected an equity risk premium of 5%. The logic is as follows: *If* stocks offer a 5% "risk premium" relative to bonds, then it makes little sense for any long-term investor to diversify away from stocks. The arithmetic is compelling. *If* stocks normally deliver better returns than bonds, by 5% per year, compounded over time, the long-term investor has almost a 95% chance of winning with stocks by the end of a 20-year span. The "cult of equities," the notion of "stocks for the long run," is predicated on that lofty risk premium. If the risk premium is smaller, then the arithmetic quickly becomes less interesting: If the risk premium falls by half, the time required to have high confidence of winning with stocks quadruples. It is simple, but powerful, arithmetic.[4]

Many in academia like the simplicity of a fixed risk premium, matching the historical excess return of stocks relative to bonds or cash. Simplicity is often a good thing. Although, as Albert Einstein was fond of saying, we should seek the simplest idea that matches reality—*but no simpler!* A fixed risk premium is a hypothesis, not a fact; indeed, it is one of the least defensible hypotheses in the finance world today.

What is the equity risk premium today? It is the difference between the current yield on equity, plus reasonable real-growth expectations, and the current real yield on bonds. The long-term real return to stocks can be calculated using the building blocks of return—income (dividends), plus the likely future real growth in income. The latter can be approximated by GDP growth, less growth in income attributable to the creation of new enterprises, in which today's equities cannot participate. (The new enterprises have yet to be created. Therefore, you cannot today purchase equities for these entities.) The magnitude of this growth from new enterprises has been estimated to be as much as 1.6% per year.[5] The real bond return is simply the current TIPS yield. As shown in the hypothetical illustration of Exhibit 12–3, subtracting the two real returns produces an equity risk premium of approximately 1%, far smaller than the "fixed" risk premium of 5% built into the models of far too many academics and investment professionals.

Given conservative real stock returns of 3% and an equity risk premium of a little over 1%, investors might be tempted to turn to the other traditional asset class—bonds. Like equities, bonds experienced a rampant bull market in the 1980s and 1990s, driven by falling yields and historically low interest rates (Exhibit 12–4).

However, if the Federal Reserve no longer allows interest rates to drift lower, but either keeps them stable or raises rates (which might happen in a reflationary environment), then bond yields should continue to rise, and there is no guarantee that bonds will outperform stocks. The result: the outlook for bonds

---

4. Thanks to Andre Perold for pointing this out.
5. Arnott, Rob and Bernstein, Peter. Financial Analysts Journal, Mar/April 2002.

E X H I B I T   12–3

Low Equity Risk Premium

Real Stock Returns

1.9%
Dividend Yield
+
2.7%
Long-Term Real
GDP Growth
–
1.6%
Growth from New
Enterprise Creation
=
3.0%
Long-Term Real
Return from Stocks

Real Bond Returns

1.8%
Yield Long TIPS
May 2005

E X H I B I T   12–4

Bond Yields vs. Bond Returns

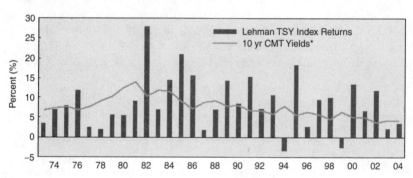

Source: PIMCO.

is modest. The best estimate of future returns on bonds is probably the yield on the day that you buy one. In early 2005 the notional long-bond yield is between 4% and 5%. As previously demonstrated, TIPS represent the expected real long-term bond yield because TIPS are adjusted for inflation. With a TIPS yield of around 1.8%, the best estimate of future real bond returns is around 1.8%.

THE CASE FOR ALTERNATIVE ASSETS

The modest real return available with stocks and bonds creates a compelling case for the use of alternative asset classes. The power of alternative asset classes is that they are uncorrelated or negatively correlated, providing the opportunity for an effective asset allocation in almost any market environment.

Table 12–1 demonstrates the performance potential of alternative asset classes. In an era in which most investors remained wedded to stocks and bonds or a traditional 60/40 portfolio, commodities outperformed all other asset classes and US equities finished second from the bottom on the list of asset classes as measured by annualized returns during the period. Depending on the market environment (falling rates, rising rates, inflation, deflation, growth, stagnation), there is an optimal mix of asset classes that may produce superior returns relative to any other mix of asset classes. Asset classes do not necessarily move together, which is why it makes sense to allocate assets among different asset classes depending on the current or expected market environment and the degree of correlation among asset classes. Table 12–2 demonstrates the correlation of asset classes from the inception date listed on the chart for each through December 31, 2004. Clearly, as some asset classes do better than their long term average, others do worse.

ALTERNATIVE ASSET ALLOCATION

The fact that asset classes do not move together creates the opportunity for active asset allocation, or the choice of how much to invest in various asset classes at various points in time based on current and predicted market conditions (opportunities). Active asset allocation has evolved from its first incarnation as tactical asset allocation (TAA) to its more complete form, known as alternative asset allocation (AAA). AAA involves the periodic reallocation of portfolio assets among different asset classes based on near-term market conditions or forecasts. AAA enables

T A B L E   12–1

Asset Class Returns (1997 to 2004)

Asset Class	Return (Cumulative)	Risk* (Ann. Std Dev)	Correlation with 60/40*
Commodities	+ 113%	15%	8%
Real Estate (REIT)	+ 107%	15%	31%
Emerging Mkt Debt	+ 89%	16%	58%
TIPS Composite	+ 66%	5%	– 6%
Long Govts	+ 61%	9%	– 3%
Salomon World Bonds	+ 53%	7%	4%
**Lehman Agg	+ 44%	4%	4%
GNMAs	+ 40%	3%	9%
High Yield Bonds	+ 36%	7%	52%
Short-Term Bonds	+ 27%	2%	– 13%
Convertibles	+ 14%	14%	77%
**60/40 Passive Mix	+ 10%	11%	100%
**S&P 500	– 11%	17%	99%
EAFE Intl Stocks	– 38%	16%	74%

*Risk and Correlation from 1/97 to 12/04
Source: PIMCO.

TABLE 12–2

Asset Class Correlations

Product Characteristics	Global Real: US Tips Indexas of 1/31/97	Dow Jones AIG Total Return as of 12/31/90	3 Month T-Bill Index as of 12/31/90	Lehman Long-Term Treasury as of 12/31/90	Lehman Aggregate as of 12/31/90	JPM Govt Bnd Non-US HED G0 as of 12/31/90	ML US High Yield, BB-B Rated as of 12/31/92	JP Morgan Emerging Markets + as of 12/31/93	S&P 500 as of 12/31/90	MSCIEAFE Index as of 12/31/90	Wils hire REIT as of 12/31/90	LBAG(40%) S&P 500(60%) as of 12/31/90
Global Real: US Tips index	1.0											
Dow Jones AIG Total Return	0.2	1.0										
3 Month T-Bill index	(0.0)	(0.1)	1.0									
Lehman Long-Term Treasury	0.8	0.0	0.1	1.0								
Lehman Aggregate	0.8	0.0	0.1	1.0	1.0							
JPM Govt Bnd Non-US HED G0	0.6	(0.0)	0.3	0.6	0.6	1.0						
ML US High Yield, BB-B Rated	0.1	0.1	(0.0)	0.2	0.3	0.2	1.0					
JP Morgan Emerging Markets +	0.2	0.2	(0.0)	0.1	0.2	0.2	0.5	1.0				
S&P 500	(0.2)	0.1	0.1	0.0	0.1	0.1	0.5	0.5	1.0			
MSCIEAFE Index	(0.2)	0.2	(0.1)	(0.0)	0.0	(0.0)	0.4	0.5	0.7	1.0		
Wils hire REIT	0.2	0.1	(0.1)	0.1	0.1	0.1	0.3	0.3	0.3	0.3	1.0	
LBAG(40%) S&P 500(60%)	(0.1)	0.1	0.1	0.2	0.3	0.2	0.5	0.5	1.0	0.7	0.3	1.0
Annualized Standard Deviations	5.25%	11.99%	0.47%	8.58%	3.91%	3.02%	6.50%	16.25%	14.48%	15.14%	13.22%	8.96%
Annualized Period Returns	8.40%	7.27%	3.93%	8.96%	7.25%	7.67%	7.30%	13.55%	11.17%	11.7%	14.13%	9.86%

Source: PIMCO.

portfolio weights to deviate temporarily from their long-term targets to optimize returns, preserve capital, or exploit investment opportunities as they arise. For example, between January 1998 and December 1999, US equities produced annualized returns of 25%. During this same time period, the Lehman Aggregate generated annualized returns of approximately 4%. Traditional 60/40 asset allocation would have resulted in total annualized returns of 16% when an investor could have utilized AAA to allocate more heavily towards equities based on current market opportunities and, therefore, enhanced returns.

In the past, TAA involved tactical allocation among three asset classes: stocks, bonds, and cash. However, TAA has evolved to encompass a broad array of asset classes, including real estate, emerging market equity, and commodities, among others. As it has developed, this broadened form of TAA (AAA) has become more sophisticated and more widely adopted in the marketplace.

Why might AAA be expected to generate positive real returns? There are two reasons. First, there is the use of alternative assets. Consider a portfolio composed of the asset classes in Table 12–2. The portfolio would have at its discretion long US government bonds, US Treasuries, European and Asian equities, high-yield bonds, international bonds, commodities, US real estate and US equities. Assume that over a long time period valuation levels do not change. Anything riskier than a risk-free asset should earn a premium. TIPS can be considered the risk-free asset, as we explain later. With the exception of treasuries and bonds, all other asset classes have low TIPS correlations and all have correlations (in absolute terms) less than 1. As the TIPS yield (risk-free rate) moves, all other asset classes move less than TIPS. Given a risk premium associated with each asset class, the risk premium would also move with TIPS but to a lesser degree (or in the opposite direction, depending on correlation). If the risk-free rate decreases by 1%, the Lehman Long-term Treasury yield might decrease by 80 bps while the yield on the S&P 500 might actually increase by 20 bps. In this example, the portfolio's real return could increase by 100 bps overall, or 1%, due to the low correlations among these asset classes, despite the 1% decrease in the risk-free rate.

The second reason that AAA might be expected to generate positive real returns is its ability to allocate portfolio weights among different asset classes based on a shifting pattern of market and economic opportunities. For example, in a rising interest rate environment in which total bond returns decline, AAA could allocate portfolio assets to noncorrelated or negatively-correlated asset classes to avoid the negative return-drag inherent to fixed income in that environment, and to capitalize on the positive returns available with asset classes whose returns respond positively to rising interest rates.

TIPS

What real return could one expect with AAA? To answer this question, we need a reliable risk-free rate. As stated previously, TIPS can proxy for the risk-free rate.

   Simplistically stated, stocks give us: (1) a real yield, (2) a default premium for the risk of bankruptcy, and (3) a real growth expectation. For a broad market index, the latter two factors converge on a real growth rate of about 1%, so that the real cost of corporate capital is approximately the dividend yield plus 1%. In other words the average *real* cost of capital for the broad market averages, when funded through the equity markets, lies about 1% above the average dividend yield. Surprisingly, corporate bonds are a weaker measure of the real cost of corporate capital, due to the unknowable future rate of inflation.

   TIPS clearly define the *real* cost of capital to the government. Before the launch of TIPS, we needed to infer that cost. Finance literature suggests that the real cost of capital should reflect expected real productivity growth, plus some premium for default risk and/or illiquidity. Since productivity growth closely tracks real per-capita GDP growth, this would point to a real cost of capital for the government (assuming zero default risk, which is not quite true) approximately matching real per-capita GDP growth, which has averaged 1.4% since World War II. Equities should have a risk premium, reflecting both the volatility of equities and the uncertain rate of real earnings or dividend growth.

   Exhibit 12–5 shows that this has been an inaccurate picture, with the government cost of capital sharply exceeding these levels (particularly in the 1980s, as investors factored in a large premium for expected inflation, which failed to materialize). The corporate cost of capital, as measured by stock dividend yields plus growth, swung sharply *below* the government's cost of capital at the peak of the 1998 to 2000 bubble. The cost of capital for the government and for the corporate arena (defined in this fashion) have also seen sharply negative correlations since late-1996, just before the launch of the TIPS market.

E X H I B I T   12–5

Corporate and Government Cost of Capital (1960 to 2005)

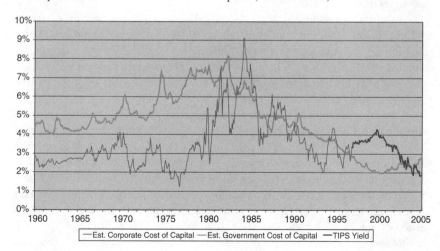

Source: Research Affiliates, LLC.

TIPS yields and stock market yields (plus a 1% growth premium) are the best measures of the cost of capital for the government and for the corporate world, respectively. The relative comparison of the two is, in our view, the best measure of the relative attractiveness of stocks and bonds, given the remarkable (and largely unnoticed) parallels in the ways that the two assets deliver returns to their investors.

Given the TIPS yield as the real "risk-free" cost of capital, the risk-free rate has ranged from 3.3% in January 1997 to a high of 4.3% in January 2000 and a low of 1.8% in April 2005. The best estimate of the risk-free rate going forward is the current TIPS yield, or about 1.8% in spring 2005. ("Risk-free" traditionally referred to T-Bills, which have no credit risk and no interest rate risk. However T-Bills have inflation risk, which TIPS, if held to maturity, do not have.)

RISK PREMIA FOR ALTERNATIVE ASSETS

Given our choice of TIPS as the risk-free rate, what are the potential risk premia associated with the asset classes in a highly diversified portfolio? Starting from the top of the correlation matrix in Table 12–2 (but leaving commodities for later), the risk premium of low-duration Treasuries would be small and primarily reflect inflation and credit risk. The risk premium associated with long-term government bonds would reflect inflation risk, since holders of this asset class bear the risk that the real value of future coupon payments will decline with rising inflation. The risk premium associated with intermediate-duration government and corporate bonds (the Lehman Aggregate) would primarily reflect credit risk with a small component for inflation risk since the largest risk that holders of this asset class bear is the risk that issuers of corporate debt will default on promised payments or declare bankruptcy. Inflation risk represents a much smaller component of the risk premium associated with government and corporate debt given its low to intermediate duration.

The risk premium associated with global government bonds primarily reflects currency risk, since inflation risk and credit risk are not significant, given monitoring by international monetary authorities and the low to intermediate duration of this asset class. The high-yield debt premium primarily reflects credit risk, given its low duration, and the premium associated with US equities (the S&P 500) solely reflects equity risk.

The risk premia associated with emerging market debt and equity are more complicated. Emerging market equity bears significant risk from the potential lack of corporate governance due either to lack of resources or lack of experience in establishing and enforcing corporate-governance standards. However, holders of emerging market equity are often unaware of the extent of the risk they bear and, therefore, pay a higher risk premium than they realize. Emerging market debt entails less risk than does emerging market equity due to controls by international monetary authorities and experience by the banks and financial institutions that issue emerging market debt in doing so historically. There is a higher penalty imposed on foreign debt issuers who "game" foreign investors than there is on foreign equity issuers who exhibit the same behavior but who are not monitored by international monetary authorities or similar governing bodies.

The risk premium associated with REITs is composed of both an equity component, since REITs are traded as equities, as well as a duration component, since the underlying assets in which REITs invest behave like fixed income assets.

The risk premium associated with commodities is difficult to measure, since investors typically invest in long-only, fully-collateralized, futures indexes rather than actually owning commodities. For reasons that have been explained in various academic papers,[6] this form of investment might be expected to provide a "risk premium" over the collateral return. That premium has averaged 5% to 6% over collateral since 1960, but may not be as great in the future, as more institutions make allocations to this asset class. Nevertheless, it seems reasonable to expect some level of premium in addition to the return from the collateral chosen to support the long-only futures.

Averaging the potential long-term risk premia associated with each asset class in the matrix might generate a total estimated long-term risk premium of 2% over TIPS, depending on an investor's assumptions. TIPS themselves might offer a real return of 1.5% to 2%, based on current yields in the first half of 2005. The strength of AAA is the incremental alpha that results from each part of the asset allocation process. On top of the 2% risk premium that might hypothetically be earned through including alternative asset classes, additional alpha can be earned through the choice of which alternative asset classes to use and the choice of manager(s) within each asset class. This additional AAA step, of activity-managing each asset class, might hypothetically produce an extra 100 to 150 bps of alpha if the right portfolio managers are chosen and an efficient set of asset classes as designated.

Finally, actively rebalancing the asset mix among the selected asset classes and managers might produce additional alpha on top of that already generated. Consider for instance, that a simple rule of rebalancing the asset classes of Table 12–2 back to an equal weight every month would have provided a return from 1997 to 2004 that was about 80 bp greater than an equally-weighted "buy and hold" of those asset classes. Is it unreasonable to think that intelligent and timely rebalancing might achieve even better returns?

In short, it is reasonable to assume that AAA can potentially produce incremental returns on top of TIPS, which themselves might produce an incremental return on top of inflation of 1% to 2%. If so, AAA might generate incremental returns significantly above inflation. AAA can be an important real return strategy.

A WORD ON DEMOGRAPHICS

The demographic patterns that have been evolving over the past 60 years have implications for retirement plans and for financial markets, not only for today but

---

6. See, for instance, Greer, Robert J., "The Nature of Commodity Index Returns," Journal of Alternative Investments, Summer 2000. Also see Gorton, Gary and Rouwenhorst, Geert, "Facts and Fantasies about Commodity Futures," Yale ICF Working Paper (2005).

for the decades ahead. The first element of the demographic problem is the increase in the percentage of the population that is over 65. The proportion of the US population over 65 will increase from 13% today to 20% in 2030. This is a result of the aging of the "baby boom," born in the 15-odd years after World War II, coupled with the fact that life expectancy is much higher than 60 years ago, as shown in Exhibit 12–6. Because the birth rate since the early 1960s has been far lower than it was during the "baby boom," the proportion of the population between ages 20 and 65 will steadily decrease over this same time period. The ratio of people aged 20 to 65 to people over the age of 65 will decrease from 4.9:1 in 2005 to 2.7:1 by 2035. The result will be a significant increase in the ratio of dependants to workers (who typically comprise about 60% to 65% of the population aged 20 to 65), beginning before 2010.

An adjusted dependency ratio should take into account not only older dependants but also children, further adjusted for the relatively higher proportion of resources consumed by the elderly relative to the young. This adjusted dependency ratio rises from 0.36 dependents per worker in 2008 to over 0.5 dependents per worker by 2030, an increase of over 38%.

There are several implications that stem from this looming increase in the adjusted dependency ratio. First, the value of goods and services demanded by retirees (health care, leisure) may increase as they are provided by a shrinking supply (relative) of workers. Wages for those providing goods and services demanded by retirees should rise. Second, as retirees liquidate assets to purchase goods and services the value of these assets will decline. Retirees will likely favor

E X H I B I T 12–6

Life Expectancy, 1940 to 2050

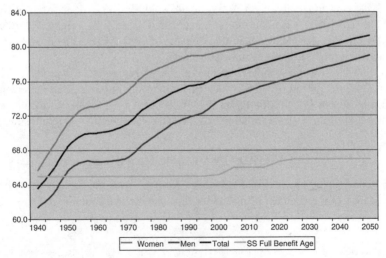

Source: US Census Bureau.

fixed-income investments, especially TIPS, which provide inflation-adjusted income. Growth stocks will decline in value as retirees attempt to unload them to a relatively smaller population of workers. The supply and demand imbalance may very drive down the real value of paper assets (especially the riskier assets, like stocks) and increase the value of goods and services demanded by retirees (as well as the wages of workers in favored industries).

In short, investors will likely be willing to sell paper assets to buy real assets, which can be a driver of inflation. An asset allocation program must recognize the consequences of this demographic shift and incorporate it into its investment process and choice of asset classes.

One other complication, associated with an aging population, has garnered little attention. While there are many exceptions to the rule, as people age, their productivity, their risk tolerance, their creativity and their entrepreneurialism typically decline (sad to say, as both authors of this chapter are past 50!). This means that the real per-capita GDP growth may slow as a falling fraction of the population works, and as we see a modest decline in productivity, creativity and entrepreneurialism. This should ripple through to a decline in the real growth in earnings and dividends, and also in the natural level of risk-free yields. Also, as the average risk tolerance in the investment community falls, the appetite for inflation-linked assets and lower-volatility assets may rise as the appetite for volatile assets, and assets that are vulnerable to inflation, falls.

CONCLUSION

Traditional asset classes are not positioned to deliver the returns that they have produced historically. Any asset class has three sources of return: income, growth in income, and increasing valuations. The combination of current equity dividends, expected dividend growth and constant valuation levels (that are far above historical levels) would produce future real US equity returns of 3% without considering mean reversion. Expected real fixed-income returns are also modest with a current TIPS yield of 1.8%. Despite low forward-looking real stock and bond returns, and an erosion of the expected equity risk premium to approximately 1%, many investors continue to incorporate return forecasts of 8% or 9% in their actuarial and personal investment assumptions and in their financial planning.

We cannot forecast the future by extrapolating the past. Doing so leads to assumptions that are not only inaccurate, but that prevent us from making choices that will enable us to reach our investment objectives. As the value of liabilities increases with inflation while real returns possible with traditional asset classes (i.e., stocks and bonds) diminish, investors must turn to alternative assets to fund their liabilities, and they must actively manage their asset mix.

AAA is a powerful tool for producing real returns that can be utilized to provide the real returns necessary to meet (or exceed) liability requirements. AAA tactically allocates across numerous asset classes to exploit intermediate-term opportunities. AAA has three sources of alpha that may enable it to produce real returns above inflation: the risk premium inherent to each asset class, the alpha generated by asset class and manager selection, and the changing choice of portfolio weights within each asset class throughout time.

Demographics will play a powerful role in the future of any asset allocation program. The retirement of the baby boomer generation will produce an increase in the ratio of dependents to workers that will drive down the value of paper assets, particularly relative to the value of goods and services demanded by retirees. Any asset allocation program must incorporate this fact into its investment process and asset selection.

Our ability to deviate from the crowd and to invest our resources in the highest potential assets is essential to our ability to meet our retirement objectives and to succeed in our investments.

CHAPTER 13

THE ROLE OF REAL RETURN ASSETS IN A PORTFOLIO

Robert J. Greer and Don Yocham
PIMCO

This handbook has presented several choices for adding inflation hedging investments to a portfolio. Many of the discussions of specific investments also noted that, besides inflation hedging, these assets often offer diversification benefits. Some of the asset categories, if purchased at the right time, might also provide attractive levels of absolute return on a tactical basis—if an investor chooses to use them for that purpose.

However, the inflation-hedging investor still is left with many decisions:

How important is inflation hedging for the portfolio?

Which Inflation Hedges Are Best?

How much should be allocated to real return in total, and to each specific investment?

What is the best means for implementation?

The chapters on each of the individual inflation hedges addressed to varying degrees this fourth question of implementation, which is specific to each strategy. This concluding chapter provides a framework and some analytical approaches for considering the first three issues.

HOW IMPORTANT ARE REAL RETURN ASSETS?

To answer this first question on a strategic basis, an investor needs to consider the sensitivity of his liabilities to inflation. Let us revisit these sensitivities as laid out in Chapter 1.

Defined benefit plans certainly have sensitivity to inflation. Put simply, the higher inflation runs in the long term, the higher will be the total benefits paid out to beneficiaries. Some defined-benefit investment officers argue that inflation does not matter that much, since higher inflation leads to higher interest rates, which gives them a higher discount rate with which to calculate the present value of their liabilities. That thinking is valid only in the rare case where a defined benefit plan actually locks in predetermined benefits upon hire that do not adjust with rising wages. This is because they will ultimately be paying fixed dollars at some future date while in the interim they are investing at interest rates that rise as inflation rises. However, most plans have benefits that rise with inflation and hold a mix of assets that, for the most part, neither provide protection against inflation nor rise or fall in value in a way that is related to the present value of liabilities. Finally, if the pension plan also has COLA provisions, their liabilities are even more closely tied to inflation.

Endowments also have liabilities tied to inflation. Universities look to their endowments to help pay for a variety of operations, plant maintenance, salaries, etc. All of these costs rise with inflation. Endowments also can benefit, especially from the diversification aspects of real return assets. Because they do not control the flow of new contributions to the fund, they must be cautious about maintaining a steady value for the fund, since they typically pay out a set percentage of assets. Any diversifying asset will help a portfolio achieve lower volatility for the same level of return.

Foundations are similar to endowments, though they do have more flexibility in their funding commitments. Foundations typically have little new money coming in, so their need for steady portfolio values is similar to endowments. Additionally foundations would like to maintain the same level of grant-giving every year in real terms, in order to provide a constant level of societal benefit, but as one CIO of a foundation put it, "Most of our grants are fairly short-term in nature. Though we wouldn't like to, we could reduce the number of grants we give in a year where investment returns are poor."

Insurance companies have varying levels of need for inflation assets. Life companies typically have little need, since their liabilities, as determined by their actuaries, are usually in nominal terms. Property and casualty companies, on the other hand, have a little more exposure to inflation, since some of their liabilities are impacted by price increases. Unlike the institutions mentioned above, though, P&C liabilities are generally fairly short-term, as they can adjust somewhat to higher expected costs by adjusting their premium charges when policies renew.

Individual investors have perhaps the greatest need for inflation hedges, as they save for retirement, whether in an IRA or as part of their employer's defined contribution plan. These investors are not looking for absolute funds when they retire; they are looking for purchasing power. They cannot consume dollars. They will, however, need to consume groceries, healthcare, gasoline, and a host of other living expenses and those expenses surely will go up as inflation goes up. The individual is not like a corporate pension plan that can look to its sponsor for additional funding if needed. The individual is not like a college that does have other resources (including a drive for alumni contributions) if the endowment falters. The individual is not like a foundation which can cut back on its funding of grants. That individual investor—and those who are responsible for the investments of that individual—has the greatest exposure to inflation and hence the greatest need for real return assets.

WHICH INFLATION HEDGES ARE BEST?

There is no single answer to this question. An investor has to consider questions such as:

> What is my risk tolerance? (Including a consideration of how is "risk" being defined?)

What resources do I have for managing specialized assets?

Can I consider using outside managers? If so, do I have the ability to evaluate them and to monitor their performance?

What are my liquidity requirements?

Am I going to try to actively manage my asset mix vs. my policy portfolio?

Table 13–1 lists the various real-return assets considered in this handbook and categorizes them on several dimensions.

These characteristics have already been discussed in detail, but a few comments are worth noting:

Some real estate is more like private equity. Also some is liquid, but not all.

Satellite commodity strategies (active futures, direct energy, gold, timber) should be evaluated in conjunction with a core allocation to the asset class as measured by an index.

Inflation futures are best considered as an active tool in conjunction with (but not as part of) an allocation to inflation-linked bonds, since the futures, for now, are not liquid enough to be used on a stand-alone basis.

Inflation linked bond allocations should be evaluated in conjunction with the investor's nominal bond allocation, since there is fundamental correlation between the two.

DUAL DURATION BOND ANALYSIS[1]

As an example of the last point above, consider that bond returns (nominal or inflation-linked) respond to inflation as well as to changes in real yields. This means that there is no single "best" mix of nominal and inflation-linked bonds in a portfolio.

Most readers are familiar with the standard duration measure. This tells us how much the price of a bond or the present value of liabilities will change as nominal yields change. However, nominal yields can be decomposed into real yields and inflation *expectations*. To serve as a reminder, real yields plus inflation expectations equal nominal yields. Since real yields and inflation *expectations* can change independently, considering the impact of changes of either on bond and liability values *independently* can provide a more accurate measure of risk.

First, we decompose the traditional duration measure into real duration and inflation duration. Second, we will illustrate the price sensitivities of nominal and

---

1. This framework was originally laid out in "TIPS, the Dual Duration, and the Pension Plan," (Siegel/Waring), Financial Analyst Journal, September/October 2004. The author's borrow liberally from this published work and expand on the framework by applying the results in an efficient frontier.

Characteristics of Inflation Hedging Investments

	Inflation Linked Bonds	Commodities	Timber	Gold	Direct Energy	Real Estate	Active Asset Allocation
Correlation to inflation	High	High	Medium	High	Medium	Medium	Medium
Correlation to inflation expectations	High	High	Low	High	Medium	Low	Low
Diversification from stocks and bonds	Good	Excellent	Good	Good	Good	Good	Medium
Historical level of returns	Good from 1997–2004. Expect moderate thereafter	Comparable to equity returns for 1970–2005	Good	Only kept up with inflation	Good	Comparable to equities	Better in volatile markets
Volatility	Low	High	Medium	Medium	High	Medium	Medium
Liquidity	High	High	Low	High	Low	Depends on vehicle	High if use liquid alternatives
Ease of Implementation	Easy for passive. Requires specialized management for active	Requires a manager and/or use of derivatives to get index exposure	Requires a specialized manager—directly or through a fund	Relatively easy for passive exposure	Requires a specialized manager—directly or through a fund	Easy for REITS; More challenging for other vehicles	Requires specialized expertise

Source: Bob Greer.

inflation-linked bonds to changes in inflation expectations and changes in real yields. We will then do the same to liabilities and, finally, review a framework that can help investment professionals align their assets to their objectives.

Let us first consider traditional duration as illustrated below on the left portion of Exhibit 13–1, with the price of the bond represented by the vertical axis and the level of nominal yields represented by the horizontal axis. If we plot the expected change in the price of a bond per change in level of nominal yields, we get a line, the slope of which determines the duration of a bond. In this example, you can see we are looking at a long duration bond because the slope is quite steep. Since nominal yields have two components, we can consider the impact on price from the two factors separately. This same bond can be viewed as having a real duration and inflation duration (sensitivity to changing inflation expectations)—or "dual" durations.

Now look specifically at nominal and inflation-linked bonds. As illustrated below in the top two graphs of Exhibit 13–2, the real duration of a nominal bond is the same as its inflation duration, (e.g., the slope of the two lines are the same). Why is this? If nominal yields rise by 100 basis points, the impact on the price of the nominal bond is the same whether nominal yields rose due to rising inflation expectations or rising real yields. However, the price of an inflation-linked bond, represented by the two bottom graphs, only responds to changes in real yields. Thus, the line in the graph at the bottom right of the page is flat, as the price of the inflation-linked bond will not change as inflation expectations change.

E X H I B I T   13–1

Decomposing Traditional Duration

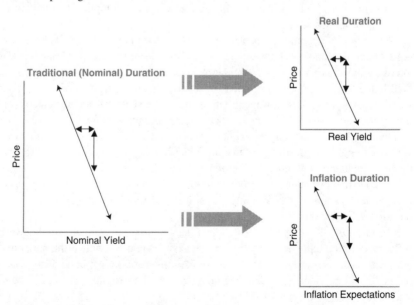

E X H I B I T   13–2

Real and Inflation Durations for Nominal and Inflation-Linked Bonds

Nominal bonds have roughly equal real and inflation durations

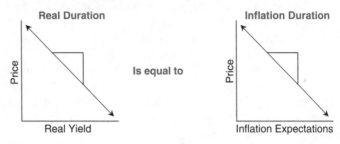

Inflation-linked bonds respond only to changes in real yields

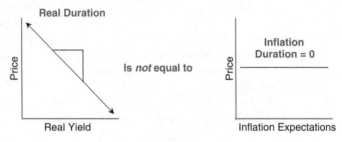

Now that we have decomposed asset-price sensitivity, look at the various investment objectives and apply the above, certainly simplified, analysis to liabilities of an investor.

Consider a hypothetical pension plan where the total final benefits are determined upon hire and fixed thereafter. This hypothetical plan, as represented by the top two graphs in Exhibit 13–3, would look much like a traditional nominal bond, as final benefits would not be impacted by actual inflation. Second, consider a plan where benefits increase with wage inflation until retirement, with an explicit cost-of-living allowance (COLA) thereafter. This plan, as indicated by the two bottom graphs, may have significant real requirements but have very little inflation duration. While these graphs illustrate the extremes, the liability of pension plans, endowments, foundations and individual retirement plans fall somewhere in between.

Now that we have an understanding for how assets and liabilities look independently, consider combining the assets and liabilities by examining real duration vs. inflation duration.

On Graph 13–1, we have plotted inflation duration vs. real duration with inflation duration represented by the vertical axis and real duration as the horizontal axis. Since real and inflation durations are the same for nominal bonds, any nominal bond will lie along a 45° line beginning at zero. For example, a nominal bond with a 15-year duration will fall at the point represented by 15 years inflation

EXHIBIT   13–3

Real and Inflation Durations of Liabilities[1]

Assuming fixed benefits that do not adjust with rising wages

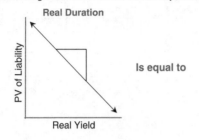
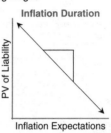

Is equal to

Assuming benefits move lockstep with inflation

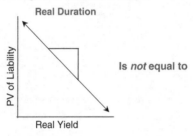

Is *not* equal to

[1]The vertical axes of these graphs represent the present value (PV) of liabilities,
which are analogous to the price of a bond

duration and 15 years real duration (point B). Since an inflation-linked bond has no inflation duration, any inflation-linked bond will lie along the horizontal axis. For example, an inflation-linked bond with 20 years real duration falls at the point represented by 20 years real duration and zero inflation duration (point E).

Now consider a hypothetical pension plan whose actuaries have determined that it has 7.6 years of inflation duration and 17.5 years of real duration. We can indicate the liability on the graph, represented by the diamond. The appropriate combination of nominal bonds and inflation-linked bonds needed to defease this particular liability can be solved for by drawing a line through the liability, beginning at a particular nominal bond duration, and solving for the length of the two segments that bisect the liability. Let us assume that we will make "some" allocation to a nominal bond with a 15-year duration. What should be the duration of the inflation-linked bond allocation and how much should we allocate to each? In this example, the duration of the inflation-linked bond should be 20 years. The allocations can be calculated by utilizing the Pythagorean Theorem as the line can be broken down into three right triangles, with the allocations determined by the length of the two segments as a percentage of the overall length of the line (see Graph 13–6 in the appendix). In the example below, the top segment of the line is 49% of the total length of the line. Therefore, 49% should be allocated to a 20-year duration inflation-linked

G R A P H   13–1

Portfolios of Nominal and Inflation-Linked Bonds to Defease Hypothetical
Pension Liability (without COLA provisions)

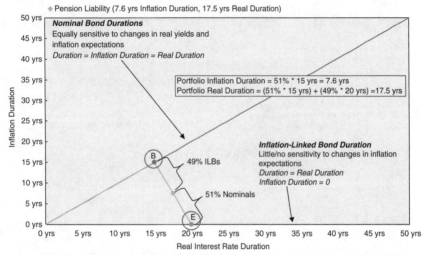

Reference: Laurence B. Siegel and M. Barton Waring 2004. "TIPS, the Dual Duration, and the Pension Plan." Financial Analyst
Journal (September/October)

bond. The intuition for this is as follows: If the hypothetical pension plan had zero
years of inflation duration and 20 years of real duration, then the diamond would lie
along the horizontal axis at 20 years and the length of the top segment would be 100%
of the length of the line. Thus, the allocation for a pension plan with no inflation duration and 20 years real duration would be 100% in a 20-year duration inflation-linked
bond. Back to our original example, the remainder, or 51%, should be allocated to a
nominal bond with a 15-year duration. However, this is not the only solution.

There are a multitude of combinations of inflation-linked bonds and nominal bonds that can defease this particular hypothetical liability as is suggested in
Graph 13–2. The combinations are only constrained by the available nominal and
inflation-linked bonds and the investors appetite for leverage. For example, a
combination of nominal bonds with 25 years duration (remember, nominal and
inflation duration are equal for nominal bonds) and inflation-linked bonds with
just over 14 years real duration may be equally, if not more, appropriate than the
previous example. The allocations in this example would be 70% inflation-linked
bonds and 30% nominal bonds—certainly an appealing and liquid benchmark for
those plans looking to defease their pension liabilities.

HOW MUCH TO ALLOCATE

Besides determining the range of choices for real return investments, an investor
must determine how much of each choice. This again depends on some of the
same issues listed earlier (risk appetite, liquidity, etc.). It also depends on the

GRAPH 13–2

Portfolios of Nominal and Inflation-Linked Bonds to Defease Hypothetical Pension Liability

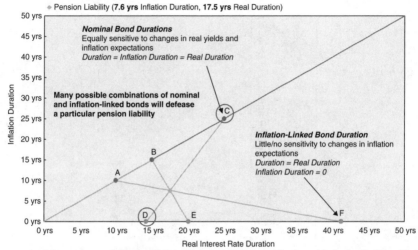

Reference: Laurence B. Siegel and M. Barton Waring 2004. "TIPS, the Dual Duration, and the Pension Plan." Financial Analyst Journal (September/October)

investor's ability to withstand the results of an asset mix that might be different from his peers, and it will depend on how sensitive his liabilities are to inflation. One way to assess the attractiveness of different asset mixes (nominal assets plus inflation hedges) is to modify the traditional mean-variance optimization approach. For example, pension plans can evaluate their liabilities as a "negative-return asset" with its own unique volatility and correlations alongside the asset choices. This results in an optimized allocation relative to the unique character-istics of the liabilities of the pension plan. Also, inflation can be modeled as the liability. Therefore the optimization can be conducted in purely real terms. This second approach may be more appropriate for those investors with long investment horizons but little need to report the present value of their liabilities/ obligations over shorter time horizons. This approach captures a more complete spectrum of the total risks since correlations and volatilities may change once assets are viewed either relative to liabilities or in inflation adjusted terms.

For instance, consider a portfolio that has four assets—stocks, nominal bonds, inflation linked bonds, and commodities. Assume that these are the only assets of a defined benefit plan that has a COLA provision, which means that liabilities are heavily influenced by inflation. Assume, for hypothetical purposes, that Table 13–2 represents capital market assumptions in nominal terms for these four assets, for inflation and for the pension liability. Table 13–2, based on annual returns, shows the correlations, standard deviation and hypothetical return assumptions for US equities, nominal bonds, inflation-linked bonds, and commo-dities. It also shows those same statistics for inflation and the liabilities of a

TABLE 13-2

Correlation Matrix

Based on Annual Returns, 1900–2003 (with Exception of Commodities)	US Equity	10-Year US Bonds	10-Year US ILBs	Commodities (1970–2003)	US Inflation	Hypothetical Pension Liability (15 Years Real Duration, 5 Years Inflation Duration)
US equity	1.00					
10-Year US Bonds	0.12	1.00				
US ILBs	0.01	0.51	1.00			
Commodities	-0.27	-0.18	0.10	1.00		
US inflation	-0.05	-0.13	0.71	0.28	1.00	
Hypothetical pension liability (15 years real duration, 5 years inflation duration)	0.05	0.75	0.95	-0.01	0.50	1.00
Standard deviation	**20.2%**	**7.6%**	**5.6%**	**24.5%**	**4.9%**	**10.3%**
Hypothetical return assumptions	**7.0%**	**4.3%**	**4.6%**	**4.9%**	**3%**	**4.7%**

Source: PIMCO, Global Financial Data Inc. Return assumptions are purely hypothetical for illustrative purposes only. Please see appendix for index descriptions.

hypothetical pension plan with 15 years of real duration and 5 years of inflation duration. The inflation-linked bond and hypothetical liability data are based on simulations, with the methodology for modeling long-term inflation-linked bond returns detailed in Table 13–3 of the appendix. In modeling the pension plan liability, we take into account the 15-year inflation duration and 5-year real duration, solve for a mix of nominal and inflation-linked bonds using the methodology described above, and model the liability as if it were the resulting mix of nominal and real return bonds. Based on the above assumptions, we can run a mean-variance optimization with the risk and returns relative to the liability shown in Graph 13–3. To run an asset allocation analysis relative to the hypothetical pension liability, the liability is set at minus 100%, to offset the positive 100% allocation to the assets. In other words, the model assumes you are long a basket of the assets and short the pension liability.

Now, consider the same optimization in real terms, i.e., relative to inflation. In Graph 13–4, notice that the allocations across assets are similar, with one glaring difference—no allocation to nominal bonds. Of course, the results will change depending on your assumptions, but the important realization is the impact of inflation on the allocation decision. To illustrate the difference between real and nominal allocations, we offer one more optimization, but in nominal terms, (i.e., ignoring the impact of inflation). You will notice in Graph 13–5, that nominal bonds come back into the picture because their risk relative to inflation is ignored. For example, Portfolio 1 (the minimum variance portfolio) has no allocation to nominal bonds when run vs. inflation and a 22% allocation to nominal bonds when the impact of inflation is ignored.

T A B L E   13–3

US Equity: S&P 500® Total Return Index (w/Global Financial Data extension).

10-year US Bonds: SA 10-year Government Bond Total Return Index.

US ILBs: For years ended 1900 through 1997, TIPS Total Returns were calculated by estimating price returns and real coupons along with inflation data. Price returns were estimated from the monthly change in 10 year constant maturity treasury yield and an assumed yield beta of 0.6. Real coupons were based on average nominal yield less trailing 3-year inflation, from 1900 to 2003, which averaged 1.25%. Monthly inflation accruals were based on monthly changes in the CPI index. From February 1997 through 2003, TIPS Total Returns are represented by the Lehman TIPS Index.

Commodities: Goldman Sachs Commodity Index Total Return, 1970–2003.

US Inflation: USA BLS Consumer Price Index.

G R A P H   13–3

Efficient Frontier vs. Hypothetical Pension Liability

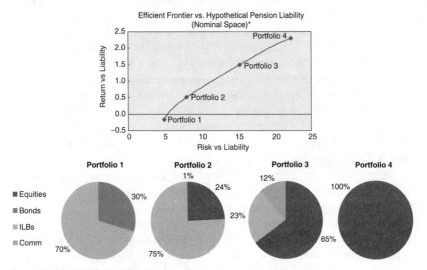

Source: PIMCO, Global Financial Data Inc.
*This is a hypothetical example of an efficient frontier model shown for illustrative purposes only. See appendix for index descriptions

G R A P H   13–4

Inflation as Liability

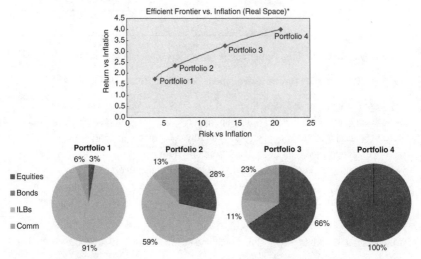

Source: PIMCO, Global Financial Data Inc.
*This is a hypothetical example of an efficient frontier model shown for illustrative purposes only. See appendix for index descriptions

G R A P H   13–5

Nominal Efficient Frontier

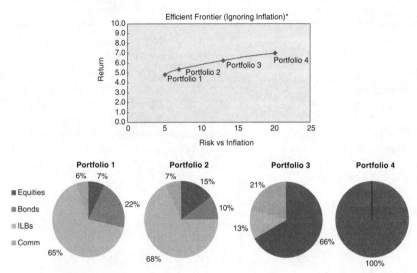

Source: PIMCO, Global Financial Data Inc.

*This is a hypothetical example of an efficient frontier model shown for illustrative purposes only. See appendix for index descriptions

CONCLUSION

There have been periods of rising inflation in the past, and there will no doubt be periods of rising inflation in the future. Furthermore, inflation cannot be predicted with certainty. What we can predict with certainty, however, is that liabilities of many investors will rise as inflation increases. Therefore investors need to consider the role of various inflation hedging strategies in their portfolios. We have called these strategies "inflation hedges" and also "real return" strategies. That is because they offer two benefits. First, they in fact can offer varying degrees of hedging from inflation, thus providing a return that is adjusted for inflation, or a "real return." However real return implies something broader than just hedging inflation-related liabilities. It implies a search for positive return and it also connotes that these returns might have other benefits as well, such as diversification.

We have seen that there are many real return strategies to choose from, some offering more inflation hedging or more diversification than others. Because these strategies do not all react the same way to different economic scenarios or different stages of the business cycle, they offer the opportunity for active management of the asset mix while still providing a hedge from the uncertainty of changes in inflation.

When used intelligently, real return strategies can be viewed as opportunities to expand the efficient frontier of a portfolio—higher return for the same level of risk, especially when "risk" includes the impact of inflation on liabilities. Used in this manner, these strategies cannot be ignored.

APPENDIX

G R A P H   13–6

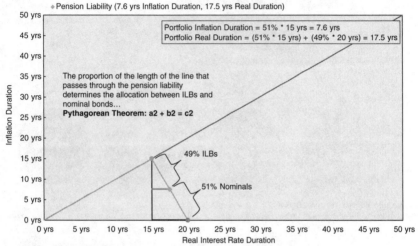

Portfolios of Nominal and Inflation-Linked Bonds to Defease Hypothetical Pension Liability
(without COLA provisions)

Reference: Laurence B. Siegel and M. Barton Waring 2004. "TIPS, the Dual Duration, and the Pension Plan." Financial
Analyst Journal (September/October)

INDEX